THE TREATISE OF THE POOL

Al-Maqāla al-Ḥawḍiyya

THE TREATISE OF THE POOL

Al-Maqāla al-Ḥawḍiyya

by

ʻObadyāh b. Abraham b. Moses Maimonides

Edited for the first time from a
Manuscript in the Bodleian Library, Oxford
and Genizah fragments with
Translation and Notes
by

PAUL FENTON
Docteur-ès-Lettres Orientales (Paris)

With a Preface by
Professor Georges Vajda

THE OCTAGON PRESS
LONDON

ISBN 0 900860 87 1

Published for The Sufi Trust by
The Octagon Press

First impression in this Edition 1981
Second impression 1995

Photoset, printed and bound
in Great Britain

In loving memory of
   my father Hayyim
   who taught me that

'Above all that thou guardest,
   keep thy heart;
For out of it
   are the issues of life (ḥayyim).'

Proverbs IV:23

CONTENTS

FOREWORD

The remarkable spiritual document, which is here edited and translated for the very first time, has several claims to our attention. Its publication by the Sufi Trust, whose serious involvement with and contribution to the furtherance of Sufi studies is well known, rescues from oblivion the name of a little known Sufi-philosopher, ‘Obadyāh Maimonides (1228–1265), grandson of the greatest figure in Mediaeval Jewish thought, Moses Maimonides (1135–1204). Due perhaps to the persistence of family tradition, ‘Obadyāh's doctrine exhibits many analogies with, and may perhaps elucidate obscurities in, the system of his illustrious forbear. At the same time it is certainly not without intrinsic value in itself, since ‘Obadyāh's philosophical precoccupations differed markedly from those of his grandfather. To be sure, his system, couched in a peculiar Judaeo-Arabic idiom, is permeated with a philosophical mysticism that owes much to the influence of Sufism.

As such, in addition to its linguistic significance, the present edition throws much light on the insufficiently known mystical movements that arose in the Islamic East in the wake of Maimonidism, which were to alter the flow of intellectual activity and prepare the way for the later spread of the Qabbālāh.

However it is above all as a testimony to the intimacy with which Israel of the past has dwelt in the tents of Ishmael that this book still holds a message for the present. For if, as it has been said, each of the three great monotheistic traditions reflects at some point an aspect of its sister faiths, then ‘Obadyāh's treatise clearly represents the most intimate symbiosis of Judaism and Islam. It would however be inaccurate to qualify as mere syncretism the extensive familiarity with Sufi doctrine which our author displays in the present work. For his vision of Sufism, like that of his father Abraham, as the ‘pride of Israel bestowed upon the Nations' is but another expression of the *Sophia Perennis*, in whose quest the triple light of Love communes.

It is my pleasure to express at the threshold of this book, my debt of gratitude toward my teacher, Professor Georges Vajda, for his invaluable guidance and encouragement throughout my labours. My thanks are also extended to Dr Stefan C. Reif of the University of Cambridge for his useful suggestions concerning the redaction and to the Curators of the Bodleian Library, Oxford and the Syndics of the University Library, Cambridge, for having kindly granted permission to publish manuscript material in their custody.

Paul Fenton
Cambridge, 1980

ABBREVIATIONS

Chapter on Beatitude	*De Beatitudine Capita Duo R.Mosi ben Maimon abscripta,* ed. and trans. H.S. Dawidowitz and D.H. Baneth, Jerusalem, 1939.
Comm.	Abrāhām b.Mōšeh ben Maymūn, *Pērūš 'al bĕrēšīt ūšĕmōt,* ed. and trans. E.J. Wiesenberg, London, 1959.
Guide	Mōšeh ben Maymūn, *Mōreh ha-nĕbūḵīm, Dalālat al-ḥā'irīn,* ed. and trans. Y. Qāfiḥ, Jerusalem, 1972, 3 vols.
Ḥawḍiyya	'Obadyāh Maimonides, *al-Maqāla al-Ḥawḍiyya*, MS. Or.661, folios 3–27, Bodleian Library, Oxford.
Hidāya	Baḥya Ibn Paqūda, *al-Hidāya ilä farā'iḍ al-qulūb*, ed. A.S. Yahuda, Leiden, 1912.
Iḥyā'	Abū Ḥāmid Muḥammad al-Ġazzālī, *Iḥyā' 'ulūm ad-dīn,* edn. Beirut, n.d., 5 vols.
Juda ben Nissim	G.Vajda, *Juda ben Nissim Ibn Malka, philosophe juif marocain,* Paris, 1954.
Kifāya	Abraham Maimonides, *Kifāyat al-'abidīn,* ed. and trans. S. Rosenblatt, *The High Ways to Perfection*, vol.I, New York, 1927, vol.II, Baltimore, 1938.
Kuzarī	Judah ha-Levi, *Kitāb al-Radd wa'l-Dalīl fi l-dīn al-ḍalīl (Kitāb al-*

	Khazari), ed. Ď.H. Baneth, Jerusalem, 1977.
Luma‘	Abu Nasr ‘Abdallah as-Sarrāǧ, *Kitāb al-Luma‘ fi at-Taṣawwuf*, ed. R.A. Nicholson, London, 1914.
Ma‘āni an-nafs	*Kitāb Ma‘ānī an-Nafs,* ed. I. Goldziher, Berlin, 1907.
Midraš Rabbi David	*Midraš David ha-Nagīd,* trans. A. Katsh, vol.I, Jerusalem, 1964, vol.II, Jerusalem, 1968.
Qāfiḥ	*Vide supra Guide*
Risāla	Abū l-Qāsim ‘Abd al-Karīm al-Qušayri, *ar-Risāla al-Qušayriyya,* ed. A. Maḥmūd and M. aš-Šarif, Cairo, 1966, 2 vols.
Tamāniya fuṣūl	Mōšeh ben Maymūn, *Ţamāniya fuṣūl,* 2nd ed., M. Wolff, Leiden, 1903.
Théologie	G.Vajda, *La théologie ascétique de Bahya ibn Paquda*, Cahiers de la Société Asiatique, VII, Paris, 1947.
Wieder	N.Wieder, *Islamic Influences on the Jewish Worship*, Oxford, 1947.

PERIODICALS

Arabica		Leiden, 1954–
AHDLMA	=	*Archives d'Histoire Doctrinale et Littéraire du Moyen Age,* Paris 1926–
HUCA	=	*Hebrew Union College Annual,* Cincinnati, 1924–
IOS	=	*Israel Oriental Studies,* Jerusalem, 1971–
JAOS	=	*Journal of the American Oriental Society,* New York, 1843–
JJS	=	*Journal of Jewish Studies,* London, 1948–
JSS	=	*Journal of Semitic Studies,* Manchester, 1956–
KS	=	*Qiryat Sefer,* Jerusalem, 1924–
MGWJ	=	*Monatschrift für Geschichte und Wissenschaft des Judenthums,* Dresden, etc., 1851–1939.
PAAJR	=	*Proceedings of the American Academy for Jewish Research,* Philadelphia, 1928–
REJ	=	*Revue des Etudes Juives,* Paris, 1880–
Sinai		Jerusalem, 1937–
Tarbiẓ		Jerusalem, 1929–
ZDMG	=	*Zeitschrift der Deutschen morgenländischen Gesellschaft,* Leipzig, 1845–

BM	=	British Library, London
BNU	=	Bibliothèque Nationale et Universitaire, Strasbourg
Bodl.	=	Bodleian Library, Oxford
BT	=	Babylonian Talmud
CUL	=	Cambridge University Library Collection
EI^1	=	*Encyclopedia Islamica,* Leiden-London, 1913–29.
EI^2	=	*Encyclopedia Islamica,* Leiden-London, 1960–
EJ^2	=	*Encyclopedia Judaica,* Jerusalem, 1970–
ENA	=	Elkan Adler Collection, Jewish Theological Seminary of America, New York
T–S	=	Taylor-Schechter Genizah Collection, Cambridge University Library.

PREFACE

L'ouvrage de M. Paul Fenton que nous avons le plaisir de préfacer est une contribution fort importante, l'une des meilleures, croyons-nous, du genre, à la connaissance d'un aspect des plus significatifs de la symbiose—que l'on se gardera de qualifier d'idyllique—islamo-judaïque. Sans anticiper sur l'exposé bien à jour et abondamment documenté de l'éditeur, traducteur et annotateur de la *Maqāla al-Ḥawḍiyya,* exhortation à l'ascèse et itinéraire vers Dieu puisés aux sources de la tradition scripturaire et rabbinique imprégnée dans une large mesure d'ascétique et de mystique musulmanes, qui a pour auteur, c'est presque une certitude, R. Obadyah, fils de R. Abraham, donc petit-fils de R. Moïse Maïmonide, relevons seulement ici un trait commun à l'ensemble de la pensée et de la spiritualité juives postérieures au 'Guide des Egarés' et au 'Livre de la Connaissance' placé en tête du 'Code des Lois': l'impact de l'idéologie maïmonidienne adoptée ou remaniée, approuvée ou contestée, voire durement critiquée, au point d'être frappée d'anathème, et aussi mise au service, fût-ce au prix de déplacements d'accent et de distorsions volontaires, de conceptions du monde que le grand Docteur avait regardées comme philosophiquement débiles, scientifiquement infondées ou théologiquement discutables (c'est le cas du néoplatonisme encore en faveur auprès d'Avicenne et son école), phénomènes religieux authentiquement juifs, ceux-là, qu'il avait traités par pretérition et même ouvertement avec mépris: la contemplation extatique et la théosophie naissante, composantes de la Kabbale éclose dès la fin du XIIe siécle. C'est ce dernier courant qui s'infiltrera peu à peu dans la pensée juive médiévale en attendant d'y régner en maître, malgré quelques contre-attaques, peu efficaces, environ trois siècles plus tard. Nous n'en sommes pas encore là dans l'Egypte juive rabbanite du XIIIe siècle régentée par les descendants directs de Moïse Maïmonide. Les forces en présence—et en conflit—dans ce milieu sont, d'une part, le légalisme prudent et précautionneux plein de méfiance tant à l'égard de l'intellectualisme philosophique que des déviations piétistes qui prétendent amender la routinière pratique rituelle, d'autre part cette *devotio moderna* non sans racines en spiritualité juive, mais non moins suspecte pour autant aux yeux de ses adversaires par sa sympathie trop marquée pour le soufisme musulman, doctrine et comportements. Telle est la situation qui apparaît au travers du texte (et il n'est pas le seul) incomplet à l'heure actuelle, mais à tout prendre peu lacunaire, présenté par M. Fenton. Nous devons à ce jeune savant, également compétent *in hebraicis* et *in arabicis*, une meilleure intelligence d'un secteur de l'histoire religieuse du judaïsme qui requiert encore beaucoup de labeur tant d'exploration de sources que d'essais successifs et progressivement améliorés de synthèse doctrinale.

Georges VAJDA
Paris, 1980

INTRODUCTION

JUDAISM AND SUFISM

Early Influences

The Jewish pietist movement that arose in XIIth century Egypt in the wake of the prodigious expansion of Sufism, is of great interest for the history of Jewish spirituality and constitutes an extraordinary testimony to what was probably the most intimate influence of Islam on Judaism.

Although the fascination of Jews for Islamic mysticism had been longstanding, its impact had hitherto been sporadic and limited and had never developed into the widespread movement whose doctrines and practices are epitomized in 'Obadyāh Maimonides' *Treatise of the Pool*. Before discussing the content of the latter and indeed for a better understanding of its significance it might not be unwarranted to give a brief survey of the earlier influences of Sufism on Jewish thought and worship.

Historically, it was Judaism, through the edifying legends of the Rabbis that circulated in the Islamic world under the name of *Isrā'īliyyāt*, that first influenced the ascetic trends in Sufism in its formative years. (1) Very soon, however, Jews were to be found attending the lectures of early masters of Bagdad and the X1th century historiographers of Sufism have conserved stories about the miraculous conversion of Jews to Islam through contact with Islamic mystics. (2) Traces of Muslim ideas on the vanity of the nether-world and the felicity of the hereafter, gained through ascetic devotions, are to be found in the works of the Xth century Jewish authors of the East who display an appreciable degree of familiarity with the Sufi way of life. More pronounced evidence of Sufi influence on Jewish literature is to be found in Muslim Spain, where there had been a widespread flowering of Sufism in the Xth century, which was later to be quelled by Malikite intolerance. However in the analysis of the ascetic and mystical elements found in works of the Spanish Jewish authors, such as Solomon Ibn Gabirol (*ob. c.* 1057), Isaac Ibn Gayyāt (*c.* 1038–1089) and Yĕhūdāh ha-Lēvī (1075–1141), it is sometimes difficult to distinguish authentic Sufi themes from those common to general Islamic Neoplatonism. (3)

There is no such dilemma in the case of Baḥya Ibn Paqūda (*c.* 1080), the first important author whose mark on subsequent Jewish spirituality was to be profound, in whose Arabic work, the *Duties of the Hearts*, the teachings of Sufism play a preponderant part. In an effort to remedy the religious formalism and spiritual dessication of his fellow Jews, Baḥya composed an individualistic spiritual theology based almost entirely on Sufi pietistic manuals. (4) The details of his spiritual itinerary, which guides the soul through contemplation and love to the union with the 'supernal Light', are all culled from Sufi sources, even where Jewish literature could have furnished equivalent materials. Despite his obvious attachment to Sufi doctrine, Baḥya's adaptation of the latter is not altogether indiscriminate, for he notably rejects the extreme asceticism and the self-annihilation of certain contemplative mystics and adopts a reserved line on the question of union with God.

Despite the pain he takes to disguise all material which is too specifically Islamic, replacing the Quranic quotations of his sources by Biblical ones, Baḥya's long preamble betrays his apprehension at introducing a novel kind of devotion into the Jewish fold.

Baḥya's claims to having been the first to innovate a 'science of the hearts' cannot be verified, but it is most significant that this internal aspect of worship should have been inspired by an Islamic model. He could not, however, have concealed his use of Sufi sources from cultivated Jewish readers whose disapproval he anticipates, justifying himself with the Talmudical adage (*BT Mĕgillāh*, 16a) 'he who pronounces a word of Wisdom, even of the Gentiles, is called a wise man.' (5)

Although the *Duties of the Hearts* was to gain extensive popularity, infusing generations of Jewish readers with Sufi notions, there is no evidence that it gave rise to a following of an Islamic brand of Jewish pietists. Moreover the Islamic character of the book was greatly obliterated when it was later translated and mostly read in the Hebrew version.

The works of later Spanish authors likewise betray familiarity with Sufi writings. The allegorical commentary on the *Song of Songs* composed in Arabic by Yōsef Ibn 'Aqnīn (XII-XIIIth century), reads very much like a Sufi treatise on the love of God. Indeed the definitions that he gives of love are culled from al-Qušayrī's *Risāla*, a basic Sufi text-book. (6) Furthermore, in his *Therapy of the Souls (Ṭibb an-Nufūs)* (f° 41a), Ibn 'Aqnīn freely quotes the sayings of early mystics such as al-Ǧunayd (*ob.* 910) and Ibn Adham whom he calls respectively the 'Elder of the Community' (*Šayḫ aṭ-ṭā 'ifa*) and 'the Perfect Saint' (*ar-rūḥant al-akmal*). (7) These instances, of interest also for historians of Spanish Sufism, were nonetheless isolated and remained without literary successors on Spanish soil, where the history of Sufism was one of intolerance and persecution, scarred by the public burning before the Great Mosque of Cordova of the books both of Ibn Masarra in 961 and then of al-Ġazzālī in 1106.

Indeed, for many centuries, Islamic mysticism was looked upon with suspicion in orthodox circles throughout the Islamic world and was thus confined to a limited following.

However in the XIIth century it was elevated beyond suspicion by no less a theologian than al-Ġazzālī (*ob.* 1111) and in the wake of new circumstances, the following century was to witness its spread and growth into a powerful movement. Dissatisfied with the fruits of rational philosophy, the minds of many responded to a deeper yearning of the soul, by turning toward esotericism which was to win numerous adepts especially in the land of Egypt.

The Jewish Pietist Movement in Egypt

i. Doctrine

Egypt had long been a fertile terrain of mysticism. Earlier she had produced some outstanding Sufi masters, such as Ḏū-Nūn al-Miṣrî (796–861) and the greatest of mystical poets ʻOmar Ibn al-Fāriḍ (*ob.* 1235). It was upon her soil that institutionalised Sufism had taken root and the main brotherhoods had grown and flourished. The immense spiritual energy that the latter galvanised in the XIIIth century was not without its repercussions on the Jewish populations of Egypt, especially those of old Cairo, which constituted in that period the Jewish people's centre of activity. Jewish refugees had poured into the city as a result of the Crusader assault in the East and Al-Mohad persecution in the West.

These social upheavals together with mounting intolerance both from without and within the Jewish fold, encouraged mystical aspirations amongst Egyptian Jewry. Indeed there arose a spiritual élite, who, though hardly qualifiable as anti-intellectual, were dissatisfied with the ratiocination of Peripatetic philosophy, which they denied as a source of gnosis. Drawing their inspiration from a form of Sufism which owed much to al-Ġazzālī, they introduced a creative change in the flow of intellectual life and paved the way for the rapprochement of philosophy and mysticism which was to characterize subsequent Jewish thought for generations to come.

The exact time and personalities involved in the emergence of this tendency remain shrouded in mystery but it seems that at the time of the great scholar and leader Moses Maimonides (1135–1204), and perhaps even in preceding generations, a number of Jews had begun to adopt Sufi practices. (8)

Nurtured by Baḥya's programme of asceticism and the appeal of Maimonides' doctrine of a spiritual élite, the movement gathered momentum in the following decades and evolved a doctrine and practice of remarkable spiritual intent. The adepts of this movement called themselves *Ḥasidim*, 'Pietists', and it is interesting to note that their emergence in the East coincided with the revelation in the West of the Qabbālāh, the earlier masters of which also called themselves *Ḥasidim*. (9)

Recent discoveries in the field of Genizah research have greatly contributed to our knowledge of the Jewish Sufi movement, the extent of its activities and the sources of its doctrines. Many Islamic mystical writings have come to light, copied into Hebrew characters for the convenience of Jewish readers, which testify to the interest they displayed in this literature. These include esoterical poems by the Sufi martyr al-Ḥallāǧ (10), the concluding chapters of Ibn Sina's *Išārāt* (11), the writings of Yaḥya Abū Ḥafs as-Suhrawardī (12), treatises on divine love (13), and above all the writings of al-Ġazzālī, including his spiritual autobiography, *al Munqiḏ min aḍ-Ḍalāl*. (14) In addition to the foregoing the Genizah has also brought to light Islamic and Sufi material in Arabic characters which presumably once belonged to Jews. (15)

On the other hand specifically Jewish writings emanating from the pietist circle have also been discovered. These comprise private letters (16), mystical prayers (17), ethical manuals (18), definitions of spiritual states (19), treatises in defence of the movement (20), fragments of theological works of which the most outstanding are those of Maimonides' own son, Abraham (1186–1237), whose sympathies for Sufism are well known. Moreover, it is now possible to relate to this group certain known mystical writings that have come down to us as apocryphal works ascribed to Maimonides, as we shall later see.

While it is difficult to date with exactitude the foregoing literary documents, paleographical evidence suggests that they all belong to the so-called classical period of the Genizah (essentially XIIIth century), indicating that at that time the Jewish Sufis deployed an extensive and varied activity.

The Ḥasidim called their discipline *dereḵ ha-ḥasidūt*, 'the way of piety' (21), *maslōl la-šem*, the 'Path to God' (22), *dereḵ-ha-meleḵ*, 'the King's highway' (22), which expressions remind us of the Sufi appellations *ṭarīq* and *sulūk*, which are applied to the 'spiritual path'.

The term *ḥasid* itself was in no way new and had been employed by the ascetics of the Rabbinic period. (24) Indeed the Jewish Sufis considered their pietist ideal as a restoration of practices that had been prevalent in Israel in former times. (25)

The anonymous author of the ethical treatise, *Maqālat dereḵ ha-ḥasidūt*, which is thoroughly imbued with Sufi phraseology, suggests three etymologies for the name of the devotees of the new movement. *Ḥasīd* derives from *ḥesed we-emet*, 'piety and truth', and designates the upright who aspire after virtue. Secondly it is to be connected with the secondary meaning of the word *ḥesed*, 'contempt' and denotes those that disdain worldly ambition and seek spiritual enlightenment. Thirdly the term is to be associated with *ḥasīdāh*, the 'stork', and alludes to those who shun the corruption of mankind and, like the stork, seek the solitude of the wilderness in the sole company of their Master. (26) Abraham Maimonides in his ethical and theological treatise the *Kifāya*, supplies another explanation for the term *ḥasīd*:

> 'He who follows the special discipline (*sulūk*) is to be called *qadōš* (holy), *ḥasīd* (pious) and *'anaw* (humble) (24) and the like. The most appropriate name however is *ḥasīd*, for it is derived from the term *ḥesed*, "virtue", because the devotee exceeds that which is required of him according to the exoteric letter of the Law'. (28)

The epithet *he-ḥasid*, 'the pious', appears in a great number of Genizah documents and, in a remarkable memorial list published by S.D. Goitein (29), several generations of Maimonides' ancestors are referred to with this title, which seems to connote something more than just 'piety'.

However the first important personality who bore this epithet with its specific connotation, and about whom anything substantial is known, is Rabbi Abraham *he-Ḥasīd* (*ob*. 1223). (30) Indeed the latter, to whom Abraham Maimonides refers as 'our master in the Path of the Lord' (31) seems to have been a leading figure in the Jewish Sufi movement. (32) Some of his writings, which have recently come to light in the Genizah, include a mystical commentary on the *Song of Songs*, seen as an esoteric guide for the 'Lover' through the spiritual stations to God, and a theological treatise in which some of his ideas concerning prophetical gnosis are set forth. While both these works are thoroughly permeated with the Sufi terminology and tenets which typify the Pietist writings, they voice an original and specifically Jewish doctrine whose underlying inspiration was Yĕhūdāh ha-Lēvi's *Kuzarī* and Moses Maimonides' *Guide for the Perplexed*, tempered by Sufi ideology.

The Pietist movement undoubtedly asserted itself upon gaining the adherence, perhaps through the influence of Rabbi Abraham he-Ḥasid, of the greatest political and religious figure of the time, Abraham Maimonides (1186–1237), who became an ardent member and defender of the movement. Much more information concerning the latter is to be found in his *magnum opus*, the *Kifāyat al-'Ābidīn* 'The Compendium for the Servants of God' (33) which was intended to be a comprehensive Pietist manual.

Although apart from the influence of the *Guide*, the latter differed little from a doctrinal point of view from Baḥya's system, it was meant not as a guide for the individual but as a collective code destined to enact a spiritual reform—or, in the view of its author, a restoration—based on a synthesis of Rabbinical and Sufi pietism.

Moreover, unlike Baḥya, who had endeavoured to conceal his debt to Sufi sources, Abraham Maimonides had no misgivings about his admiration for Sufism which he overtly expresses in this work. On one occasion, after having equated the discipline of the Islamic mystics with that of the old prophets of Israel, he makes the statement:

> 'Do not regard as unseemly our comparison of that to the behaviour of the Sufis, for the latter imitate the prophets (of Israel) and walk in their footsteps, not the prophets in theirs.' (34)

Elsewhere he declares 'Thou art aware of the ways of the ancient saints of Israel, which are not or but little practised among our contemporaries, that have now become the practice of the Sufis of Islam, on account of the iniquities of Israel . . .' (35) 'Observe then these wonderful traditions and sigh with regret over how they have been transferred from us and appeared amongst a nation other than ours whereas they have disappeared in our midst. My soul shall weep . . . because of the pride of Israel that was taken from them and bestowed upon the nations of the world.'(36)

Notwithstanding this open acclaim, it is significant that Abraham Maimonides, unlike Baḥya, rarely incorporates into his work examples borrowed from Sufi literature. Instead he invariably illustrates his ethical teachings with *exempla* from Biblical and Rabbinical sources in an attempt to portray his Pietist innovations as a restoration of practices that were formerly those of the prophets of ancient Israel and which had now fallen to the lot of the Islamic mystics. This procedure is similar to that used by the Sufi reformers in depicting Muḥammed and his companions as Sufi archetypes. (37) It is noteworthy in this respect that the Jewish Pietists often referred to themselves as the 'disciples of the Prophets'. (38) In addition to the apologetic note implying the restoration of an authentically Jewish doctrine that had fallen into abeyance, this expression also held for the Pietist another more profound meaning, the clarification of which is essential for the understanding of the whole significance of their movement.

This deeper meaning of the discipleship of the Prophets is clearly implied by Abraham Maimonides when he says that the special line of conduct that he advocates is 'the way of the pious of Israel and the disciples of the prophets' and that there are some 'of the pious of Israel who are extremely pious and close to the degree of the Prophets'. (39)

It seems that the Pietists not only sincerely believed that they were reviving an extinct Jewish doctrine but that this doctrine was that revealed to Adam and inherited by the Patriarchs. After a hiatus of several generations during which it had been lost, it was again restored to Moses, who in turn imparted it to Israel. This esoterical doctrine, whose tenets were conducive to prophecy, had eventually fallen into oblivion as a result of the tribulations of Exile, but the time had now come for it to be revived. This theory of the 'Prophetic light', which was first expressed within the Jewish fold by Yĕhūdāh ha-Lēvi (40), is clearly alluded to by 'Obadyāh Maimonides in the present treatise (f° 25a):

> 'After the patriarchs the bond was severed and the intercessor passed away until the sublimest of creatures, our Master Moses, came and restored it through the Will of God'.

This restoration took place at Sinai and Abraham Maimonides maintains that during the days that preceded the Revelation, Moses imparted to Israel a doctrine whereby they could attain to the prophetic state, which indeed they did at the giving of the Law. Through the continued observance of this spiritual discipline, by which is obviously meant the Jewish Sufi doctrine, this supernal state could be attained and maintained throughout the successive generations. (41) According to Pietist doctrine all Israel were in principle to become prophets, but in view of the diversity of perception prevalent amongst the devotees, only a select few were capable of attaining this privilege through contemplation of the esoteric system, whereas the mass could nonetheless draw near to this state through the observance of the exoteric law, or as two anonymous Pietist writers put it:

> 'The Torah was revealed through the Chosen Apostle who was the élite (*ṣafwa*) of the descendants of Abraham, His beloved, and the result of the purest lineage: Abraham, Isaac, Jacob, Levi, Qehat, 'Amram and then Moses, all of whom had been instruments of the Divine Word (*ḥuṣṣil bihim al-amr al-ilāhī*).

So that through the Torah which was revealed to him, they may become prophets, and he that does not attain to prophecy shall draw nigh to its state through commendable deeds' (42). 'In Moses' days all Israel were set aside for the Path of proximity to God . . . indeed it was intended that they all become prophets as Scripture states "And ye shall be unto me (a Kingdom of priests and a holy nation)". (Ex. XIX:6) Likewise we were promised (for the future) "Ye shall be named the priests of the Lord". (Is. LXI:6) They should have received all the precepts in the same way as they received the Ten Commandments at Sinai, were it not for their feebleness and incapacity to continue to receive in this manner, as Moses said "Would that all the Lord's people were prophets".' (Num. XI:29) (43)

However, Scripture had foretold that at the end of days prophecy would again be restored to Israel (44) and it is not unlikely that Abraham Maimonides' circle believed that the promised hour had now come. Indeed Moses Maimonides in his *Iggeret Tēmān*, clearly states that according to a family tradition, prophecy was shortly to be renewed, and further evidence indicates that this belief was quite widespread. (45)

Thus it seems that the goal of the special Path, which Abraham Maimonides set forth in his works, was the attainment of the prophetic state. However, as in former times, the gift of prophecy was not to be a phenomenon shared by all, but a state that could be attained solely by the select few. 'The special Path is something which not every one of the adepts of the Law arrives at' (46) but it was intended for those only that could endure the stringent moral discipline and penetrate the hidden mysteries of the Torah.

In the distinction Abraham Maimonides establishes between the common mass who consider only the external letter of the Law and the élite who grasp its esoteric significance, one can recognize the influence of his father's *Guide for the Perplexed*. It is, however, to be noted that a very subtle but significant shift in meaning has taken place in his thought. Whereas Moses Maimonides saw the chosen few as prophet-philosophers of sound intellect, Abraham emphasizes in his system most insistently the importance of great moral as well as intellectual achievement.

The *Kifāya* and less systematically 'Obadyah's *Ḥawḍiyya* 'Treatise of the Pool', both discuss the various virtues which the Pietist must cultivate and the moral stations which the wayfarer must traverse on his path to the final goal, a spiritual itinerary which owes much to the ethical manuals current among the Sufis: sincerity, mercy, generosity, gentleness, humility, faith, contentedness, abstinence, striving, solitude. Passing through 'fear' 'love' and 'cleaving to God' (47) he will be uplifted to true sanctity and will comprehend the nobleness of the bond between himself and God.

Another speculative aspect of Abraham Maimonides' thought which received significantly less attention in the *Guide*, but not of course in the *Code*, is his repeated insistence on the scrupulous observance of the revealed Law. Whereas his father displayed something of an ambivalence in his respective attitudes toward philosophy and religious observance (48), Abraham repeatedly underlines the necessity of conforming strictly to the dictates of the religious Law. 'We say that the correct opinion and the proper order when pursuing this Path, is to begin by observing the exoteric Law. For it is a gross error that a person consider himself or others consider him a *ḥasīd* because he observes abstinence or fasts continually or eats little or wears wool, while he is remiss in certain precepts or transgresses certain prohibitions. Of this the Rabbis have said "Nor can an ignorant man be pious".' (Abōt 11.5) (49) Similarly in his *Treatise in Defence of the Pietists*, Abraham Maimonides stresses that the true Pietists are those that properly observe the religious Law. (50)

The selfsame attitude is moreover echoed by 'Obadyāh in the *Ḥawḍiyya* (f° 5a) 'If thou art to attain anything of this science . . . it need be after mastering the exoteric Law. For the latter is the axis upon which moral discipline pivoteth, it is the ladder whereby thou mightest ascend to the Most High.' (f° 23a) 'Thou knowest full well that the observance of the religious precepts is a preparation for man and a moral training in order that he may be worthy of the true Law (*at-Tōrāh al-ḥaqīqiyya*) which is really intended for us.'

Such allusions were not fortuitous and were no doubt intended to place the Pietist ideals beyond suspicion and counter the accusations that had been levelled against them. This attitude affords yet another parallel to the literary activities of the Sufi reformer al-Ġazzālī who set out his *Iḥyā* along strictly orthodox lines in order to allay the suspicions of antinomianism which had been imputed to Sufism in conservative circles.

It is apparent from the aforementioned *Treatise in Defence* that the Pietists had likewise come under severe attack from the Jewish intellectual leaders and congregational dignitaries of their time. The latter accused them of being remiss in the observance of ritual, careless in their language about religious matters and above all guilty of spreading false and dissident views amongst their Jewish brethren. The controversy was far reaching and Abraham Maimonides who was an important political figure, was even denounced before the Muslim authorities as an innovator of tenets forbidden by the Jewish faith. The orthodox Sunni Sultan, al-Mālik al-'Ādil, the brother and successor of Saladin, took the accusation of *bida'* (unlawful innovation) very seriously, even in the case of the non-Islamic faiths under his protection. Abraham retorted however with a memorandum signed by two hundred of his followers, in which he stated that the Pietist practices alluded to were conducted in complete liberty and confined to his own private synagogue. (51)

In addition to being politically motivated, the vehement opposition which the Jewish Sufis encountered was aroused not so much by their novel doctrines but by those ascetic practices which they endeavoured to introduce. Although the Pietists insisted that these were restorations of ancient Jewish custom, they were nonetheless manifestly inspired by Islamic models. The various sources at our disposal allow us to draw up a picture of what some of these practices actually entailed (52) and demonstrate quite strikingly the extent to which the Pietists had been influenced by Islamic models.

ii. Practices

The Pietists felt that the prevailing methods of worship were not sufficiently conducive to the elevated and intense spiritual concentration to which they aspired. Consequently they sought further means of satisfying their otherworldliness, either by restoring modes of worship that had previously existed or by introducing new principles borrowed from their Islamic environment. One is reminded here of the similar reforms that were later enacted by the Qabbalists. The innovations are of two sorts, those that concern the internal worship of the heart and those, the external worship of the body.

Among the first category the following are to be reckoned:

1. *Ablution*: In imitation of Muslim custom the Pietists instituted stringent laws of ablution before prayer, including the washing of the feet (53), which Jewish law did not strictly require.
2. *Prostration*: Prostrations in various parts of the liturgy, which had formerly been abolished in Jewish custom, were now restored. In one chapter of the *Kifāya*, Abraham advocates the furnishing of the synagogues with cushions in Muslim fashion and he contrasts the admirable decorum of the mosque with the lack of respect and order in the synagogues of his day. (54)
3. *Kneeling*: In other parts of the daily liturgy the worshippers would remain kneeling as in Muslim practice. (55)
4. *The Spreading of the hand*: At certain supplications the worshipper would stretch forth his hands with upturned palms. (56)
5. *Weeping*: Many of the first Sufis were known as the 'weepers' because of the profusion of their tears during prayer. Abraham Maimonides also advocates weeping as a necessary expedient to prayer. (57)
6. *Orientation*: To enhance the decorum of the Synagogue, worshippers would stand in rows, in Muslim fashion, and face the Holy Ark at all times. (58)
7. *Vigils and fasting*: Prayer occupied a central position in the Pietist doctrine and in addition to the canonical prayers they

would practise supererogatory supplication, which most often took the form of nocturnal vigils.

In this connection it is interesting to note that amongst the letters of the Pietists that have come down to us, one is addressed to Rabbi Abraham he-Ḥasîd and his brother Joseph, the heads of the Pietists that 'spend their nights in vigils and their days in fasting as on the Day of Atonement purging their souls and purifying their bodies . . . and many are their followers.' (59) This is furthermore an allusion to the common Sufi practice known as *al-qiyām waṣ-ṣiyām* 'standing and fasting', which the Pietists had adopted, although similar spiritual exercises were known in Jewish worship from ancient and mediaeval times, especially in connection with the midnight lamentation. (60) Abraham Maimonides himself advocates nightly vigils:

> 'It is commendable to spend the end of the night in prayer and to awaken in the middle thereof . . . as David hath said "At midnight do I rise up to give thanks unto thee". (Ps. CXIX:62) Moreover he that pursueth this Path might not slumber at all during certain nights of his solitary retreats as it is said, "Neither shall I give sleep unto mine eyes."' (Ps. CXXXII:4) (61)

Similarly 'Obadyāh considers nightly vigils as an essential expedient in one's spiritual devotion (*Ḥawḍiyya*, f° 10b):

> 'I recommend thee to seek the face of the Lord in moments of respite from the burden of our matter. When Satan is slumbering, rise up in the dead of night and turn to the Most High in prayer and supplication, as it is said "Arise and cry out in the night in the beginning of the watches . . . pour out thine heart like water before the face of the the Lord" (Lam. II:19) and ever face the door in the direction of the sanctuary'.

8. *Solitude*: Control of sleep and diet as well as supererogatory prayers and meditation were especially practised during periods of voluntary seclusion, *ḫalwa*. The custom of entering into solitary retreats in order to give oneself over to prayer and meditation is already mentioned by Baḥya. (62) An inkling into how this was practised by the Pietists is afforded by a letter written by one of their number, in which the writer comforts the addressee on the departure of his father, the *dayyān*, into solitary meditation, which was to last for a period of forty days:

> 'May God guide him on his journey as He did the Prophets and Saints in ther journeys and retreats (*ḫalwātihim*) in that they beheld the Majesty, Beauty, Splendour and Perfection of the Divine Presence (*al-ḥaḍraal-ilāhiyya*). Through their great longing, He poured upon them Divine Science (*'ilm*[an] *laduniyy*[an]) (63) and revealed to them the mysteries of His holy books and instructed them in its theory and practice which are the way and guide which lead to the perception of the Divine within the limits of human possibility . . . though he be aloof from the company of men during his journey we will be in the intimacy of Him who hath created man, the angels and the prophetṣ . . . So fear not for him in his solitude, for God shall recompense him as He does all that long for Him . . . even as He hath rewarded him in his previous journeys. The latter were long whereas this journey is short and the period of this retreat (*ḫalwa*) is to be compared to that of our Master Moses, forty days and forty nights . . .' (64).

Amongst Sufis this period was known as the '*Arba'īn* and as-Suhrawardī devotes a whole chapter to it in his '*Awārif*, wherein he invokes an Islamic Tradition as well as the example of Moses' sojourn on the mountain of God as proof of its validity.(65)

This form of retreat is still practised by Sufis to this very day and a modern visitor to Egypt has recently described the ceremony which takes place before the Sufis enter into confinement. (66) It is not impossible that Jews also retired at the time to solitary synagogues such as that of Dammuh, which was indeed associated in local tradition with Moses. (67) In other Islamic countries, such as Morocco and Tunisia, even in recent times Jews would retire to pray and meditate in particularly revered synagogues, some of which had hostels attached to them for the use of worshippers. (68)

Abraham Maimonides devotes a whole chapter of his *Kifāya* to the virtues of *ḫalwa*, which he considers the highest of the mystical paths. (69) He further distinguishes between external seclusion of varying lengths, which is mainly carried out in the solitude of the mountains and the desert, and internal seclusion (*ḫalwa bāṭina*) which is the most noble of spiritual states and approaches prophetic communion (*wuṣūl nabawī*). (70)

Likewise ʿObadyāh mentions the purification of one's thoughts (f° 12a) and the necessity to be on one's guard against false notions (f° 20b) during *ḫalwa*. He also recognizes the superiority of internal seclusion (f° 14a):

> Withdraw from that which distracts thee from Him while still amongst thy family and kinsfolk. Do not believe like the poor in spirit that seclusion is meant for the mountains and caves and that by merely withdrawing thereunto they will accomplish something, for it is not so.

The withdrawal to the mountains and caves is no doubt a reference to the Muqaṭṭam mountains that overlook Cairo, which were a favourite haunt for Sufi hermits.

Ḫalwa was to be practised in dark places in order to encourage an internal illumination (*nūr bāṭin*) in accordance with Rabbi Abraham he-Ḥasīd's interpretation of Isaiah L:10: 'Who among you feareth the Lord, he who walketh in darkness and hath no light.' (71)

9. *Incubation*: Assuming that the Pietists read into Scriptures

their own rites and theories, it would seem also that during *ḫalwa* they would practise incubation. In reply to a question concerning the interpretation of I. Samuel III:3 'And Samuel slept in the sanctuary of the Lord', Abraham Maimonides replied that this practice was a form of prophecy and a mystery about which he could divulge no more. However in the *Kifāya* he expands on this allusion saying that Samuel practised *ḫalwa* in the tabernacle until he attained communion with the Divine through prophetic sleep. (72)

10. *D̮ikr*: It is most surprising that no description is found in the texts at our disposal of a Jewish ceremony comparable to the most characteristic of Sufi devotions, the *d̮ikr*. (73) Although the Genizah has preserved examples of non-canonical mystical prayers and individual meditations, no evidence can be adduced that the Jewish Sufis practised communal *d̮ikr*'s. One can only assume that such a ceremony would have met with severe disapproval from more conservative circles in view of its strictly Islamic character. (74) Perhaps, however, a fleeting reference in Abraham he-Ḥasīd's commentary on the *Song of Songs* alludes to this practice:

> 'One can attain to the spiritual world through the practice of outward and inward holiness, excessive love of God and the delight in His recollection (*d̮ikr*) and Holy names'. (75)

On the other hand the continuous 'rememberance of God' is a common theme in the earlier Spanish-Hebrew poetry and may be associated with the notion of '*d̮ikr* of the heart.' Furthermore, although Rabbinical tradition had expressed opposition to the multiplication of Divine attributes (76), several devotional aids in the form of lists of *asmā al-ḥusnä* and praises to God, have come to light in the Genizah.

In the domain of the duties of the limbs the Jewish Sufis adhered to strict ascetic principles, shunning all superfluities:

'Cover thy head, let thy tears fall, and be of good conduct,

> fasting throughout the day. Do not delight in the joys of the vulgar and be not sad with that which grieves them. In a word be not sad with their sadness and rejoice not with their merriment.
>
> 'Despise frivolity and laughter, rather observe silence and speak not except out of necessity. Do not eat except out of compulsion and do not sleep unless overcome, and all the while thy heart should contemplate this pursuit and thy thoughts be engaged therein.' (77)

In keeping with their ascetic ideal but quite exceptionally in relation to mediaeval Jewish ethics, the Jewish Pietists considered marriage and offspring an impediment to religious fulfilment; consequently the taking of a wife was to be delayed if possible until the age of 40 years. Both Abraham and his son 'Obadyāh in this respect do violence to the Scriptural text in an endeavour to find support for the delaying of marriage:

> Know that the true mystics of this path strived to perfect their souls before marriage knowing full well that after begetting spouse and offspring there would be little opportunity for spiritual achievement and, if they were to achieve anything, it would be small and after much hardship. Thus Abraham sought a wife for his son Isaac only after he had attained spiritual perfection—at the age of 40 years which is a marriageable age'. (78)

Such an attitude can only be explained in the light of Sufi teaching, since the traditional Jewish stand and indeed even that of Baḥya is to encourage the early observance of the divine precept of procreation. (79)

Another obvious imitation of Sufi custom was the wearing of modest raiment and woollen garments as a sign of austerity. In a passage of the *Kifāya*, Abraham Maimonides intimates that the Jewish Sufis and even he himself wore the sleeveless garments (80) typical of Sufi attire.

On two occasions 'Obadyāh recommends that one should be careful not to disclose one's spiritual state to those who are not worthy. Indiscretion could lead to misfortune in this respect and while in the company of the vulgar, one should conduct oneself in an ordinary fashion and exercise *kitmān* (discretion). The latter practice was well known amongst Sufis who, either through humility or, more often, through persecution, were obliged to conceal their religious convictions. (81)

Here we have a further hint of the opposition and hostility of the communal leaders to the Pietist movement which has been mentioned earlier. This hostility probably did much to impede the growth and development of the movement. Indeed it remains to consider what became of Abraham Maimonides' great reform and to estimate the influence the movement was to exercise on later currents of Jewish thought and spirituality.

Later Influences

Although Abraham Maimonides' religious ideas did not provoke the extensive response he had anticipated, as the greatest political and spiritual Jewish figure of his day, his adherence to the Pietist movement must have had far-reaching repercussions on the destiny of Jewish Sufism. Nor too were his writings to supersede those of his father, whose ideology in its various shades of interpretations was to assert its supremacy in subsequent generations, possibly because Abraham himself saw his own works as a corollary exposition of his father's doctrines, of which they may indeed have been considered by others as the authentic exponent. Assuredly, his compositions may in several ways be construed as the mystical development of some of the more devotional themes in the *Guide* and the *Code*. On the other hand, Pietist compositions by other authors, such as Rabbi Abraham he-Ḥasīd, readily espouse Sufi doctrines as the practical application of the *Guide* and it is then no wonder that certain Pietist writings such as the *Chapter on Beatitude* and the *Treatise on Unity* (82) have even come to be ascribed to Moses Maimonides himself. The association of the movement with the Maimonides family was still more strengthened by the support that ‘Obadyāh, Abraham Maimonides’ son, lent to it in the following generation. His *Treatise of the Pool*, as we shall see, seems to have been composed for a following of Jewish Sufis. There is also some indication that his brother David, who succeeded their father as leader of Egyptian Jewry, likewise shared this sympathy. As a result of the support of such a renowned dynasty, Jewish Sufism rapidly expanded within Egypt and abroad. Even in the time of Abraham Maimonides, the latter would receive enquiries from the Pietist community in Alexandria (83) and he himself testifies that his *Kifāya* had already been diffused in his day to distant lands. (84)

Within Egypt, Sufism continued to hold a fascination for Jews well into the XIVth century, as we learn from a Genizah letter addressed to David b. Joshua b. Abraham II b. David b. Abraham Maimonides (XIVth–XVth century), by a Jewish woman complaining that her husband's frequentation of a Sufi convent in the Muqaṭṭam mountains was distracting him from his paternal duties. (85) At more or less the same time Jewish Sufis are known to have existed in localities outside of Egypt, such as Jerusalem (86) and Baghdad (87). Information concerning Damascus is furnished by the Arab biographer al-Kutubī, who relates that Jews would assemble in the house of the Sufi al-Ḥasan Ibn Hūd (XIIIth century) in order to study under his guidance Maimonides' *Guide for the Perplexed*. (88) Although it is unlikely that these individuals were connected with the Egyptian movement they were in a sense the latter's literary and spiritual heirs. Indeed for a period of more than two hundred years, Judaeo-Arabic writings, thoroughly imbued with Maimonidean ideology, were to endeavour to synthesize Rabbinical—and later Qabbalistic—spirituality with Islamic mysticism, either in the form of pure Sufism or that of philosophical mysticism. Such an attitude is typified in the remarkable Jewish

Sufi treatise which dates from this period, *al-Maqāla fi dereḵ ha-ḥasidūt*, which, steeped in Sufi terminology, outlines the spiritual stations along the Pietist path (89). In this and other works, the anonymous author quotes from Sufi sources alongside Moses, Abraham and ʻObadyāh Maimonides together with, more significantly, the works of the early Qabbālāh. (90)

Similar interests prevail in the works of certain XVth century Yemenite authors, who, impregnated with a blend of Maimonidean philosophy and Arabic Neoplatonism, especially that of the *Iḫwān aṣ-ṣafā'* and other Isma'īlī inspired sources, freely assimilate Sufi concepts and quote in their compositions verses from the *Dīwān* of al-Ḥallāǧ. (91).

A quite different type of mysticism which, although unrelated to the Jewish Sufi movement, nonetheless betrays an unmistakable use of Sufi elements, is to be found in the works of Abraham Abū l-ʻĀfiya (*ob. c.* 1295) and his school. Born in Spain, Abūl ʻĀfiya wandered for many years in the East, where he no doubt came into contact with Sufis, for the techniques for mystical meditation which he advocates in his works, and in particular his *Maftēaḥ ha-šēmōt,* include control of the breath and the repetition of sacred formulae (92), and are no doubt inspired by similar Sufi practices. Indeed, one of his disciples has left us a most remarkable description of the *ḏikr* ceremony in one of his works:

"'There are three types of ecstasy, the common, the philosophic and the qabbalistic. The common type is, so I have heard, that practised by the mystics of Islam. It consists in their divesting their souls of all natural forms by various procedures to such a degree, so they claim, that if any spiritual form were to enter their soul, it is singled out in their imagination and this enables them to foretell coming events prior to their occurrence. Some are not sufficiently capable of such a degree of revelation and are uplifted by a spiritual revelation commensurate with their essence. I enquired as to how they achieve this and was informed that they do so by repeating the Divine name, which in the

Arabic tongue is Allah... After having repeated the letters thereof and entirely divested their thoughts of all other natural forms, the letters of the name Allah take effect on them, each in accordance with his nature and the intensity of his devotions. They eventually enter into ecstasy but they know not wherefore, since they do not possess the esoteric tradition (*Qabbālāh*) They call this removal of natural forms "effacement".'(93)

Definite traces of Sufism are to be found in the works of other contemplative Qabbalists, who lived at some time in Spain and the East, such as Isaac of Acco (XIIIth-XIVth century) and Yĕhūdāh al-Buṭinī (*ob.* 1519). (94) Another XIVth century Spanish Qabbalist, Yōsef b. Šalōm Aškĕnazī, provides us with an astonishing testimony of the intimacy and syncretism of Jewish-Muslim relations in his time, albeit not in a Sufi sense:

'Consider attentively the foolishness of those of our fellow Jews who not only praise the Muslim faith ... but when the Muslims profess their creed at prayer times in their mosques, these dim-witted Jews join them and recite "Hear O Israel". Furthermore they highly commend the nation of Muḥammad and consequently they and their children have become attached to the Muslims and they denigrate the holy faith of Israel... I am astonished that even the dignitaries of our community praise the Muslims and testify to the latter's faith in one God.' (95)

An illustration of such Jewish admiration for Muslims can be still found in the works of Abraham Gavison of Tlemçen (*ob.* 1605), who concludes his Hebrew translation of one of al-Ġazzali's mystical poems with the words '(I have translated) the poetry of this sage, for even though he be not of the Children of Israel, it is accepted that the pious of the Gentiles have a share in the World to Come and surely Heaven will not withhold from him the reward for his faith.' (96)

Sufi influences can be discerned too in the writings and ritual of the later Qabbalists, especially in the domain of their poetical and musical compositions. (97) The possible contribution of Sufism towards the development of the Luryanic Qabbālāh is an interesting question which remains to be evaluated in all its facets by modern scholars. The last significant contact between Jewish and Islamic mysticism stems from this movement and its Messianic frenzy which culminated in the saga of Šabbatai Ṣĕbī. Evidently, his apostate sectarians, later known as the *Doenme*, had close contacts with the Dervish brotherhoods in Turkey, from whom they adopted several aspects of their cult and liturgy. (98)

However these manifestations of Sufi influence on later Jewish thought and culture are marginal and unrelated to the Jewish Pietists of Egypt. The radical religious reform initiated by the latter seems indeed to have had little abiding effect. Abraham he-Ḥasīd's writings submerged into oblivion and only the specifically Jewish portions of Abraham's works, such as the chapter in the *Kifāya* on the Aggādāh, were copied for posterity.

It is highly symptomatic that this latter chapter was simultaneously translated in the XVIth century in the East by Abraham Ibn Migaš of Constantinople and Aleppo and in the West by Vidal ha-Ṣārfatī of Fez. (99)

Herein partly lies the clue to the relatively modest impact that the Pietist movement had on Jewish literature and philosophy. The waning of Muslim tolerance and the decline in the knowledge of Classical Arabic as a literary medium contributed to the social and cultural decadence of Oriental Jewry in ensuing centuries. Faced with considerable suspicion and opposition from within, the Pietist ideology with its complicated system of metaphysics, became confined to a small circle of intellectual and spiritual élite, especially as the appeal of their Sufi-orientated writings, composed in Judaeo-Arabic, could not hope to be diffused beyond the borders of the Orient. (100)

Nevertheless the elements of Sufi piety and practice which the followers of Abraham and 'Obadyāh Maimonides infused into Jewish theology, greatly enriched the spirituality of Israel, by contributing to form a particular type of pre-Qabbalistic mysticism.

The metaphysical aspirations that the latter had sought to fulfil were soon to be engulfed by the rapidly spreading doctrine of the Qabbālāh, for which the Pietists had indubitably paved the way in the East. (101)

‘Obadyāh Maimonides and The Treatise of the Pool

‘Obadyāh Maimonides

Although history has preserved several documents concerning David Maimonides (1222–1300), Abraham's eldest son, who succeeded him as Nagīd at the tender age of 16, very little has been recorded in surviving chronicles or documents concerning David's younger brother ‘Obadyāh (1228–1265). (1) No doubt the latter's premature demise and the shadow of his elder brother's political prestige accounts for this eclipse. Another possible reason is that his only known literary composition, the *Treatise of the Pool*, sank into oblivion with the disappearance of the circle of Jewish Sufis, for whom its contents were primarily intended. Notwithstanding the foregoing it is, strangely enough, ‘Obadyāh's and not David's name that figures on a number of memorial lists that have been preserved. (2) The latter perpetuated the names of those renowned for their piety and were read on the eve of Atonement; these afford however few personal details. The only substantial account concerning ‘Obadyāh recorded by a chronicler is that of Yōsef Sambari (1640–1703), who lived in Egypt and, in spite of his lateness, no doubt had access to reliable archival material that is no longer extant (3):

> ‘Rabbi ‘Obadyāh, brother of the Nagīd's son, David the Nagīd, son of Abraham the Nagīd, son of Moses Maimonides, of blessed memory, was born on the 8th of Nisan in the year 4988

> of the Creation, and passed away on the eve of Sabbath, the 12th of Šebat, in the year 1576 Sel., that is the year 5025 of the Creation. He passed away in the Synagogue of Dammūh.' (4)

It is not known whether 'Obadyāh had any offspring, although Freimann and Ashtor, following Steinschneider, state that he had a son Abraham. There is nothing however to support this assumption and it is no doubt an error based on a misreading in our treatise of the sentence (f° 13b) *yā ibnī ukrim* 'O my son honour' as *ya ibnī Abram* 'O my son Abraham', since the Hebrew spellings are quite similar. Moreover, in view of 'Obadyāh's attitude toward marriage, it is possible that he never wed at all. (5) A few further details are furnished by a letter, discovered in the Genizah, which emanated from the Pietist Circle. Therein 'Obadyāh together with his brother David are styled:

> 'The uterine brothers, the masters, the two great luminaries, the two tablets of the Law, the two Princes of the host of Israel, the two eminent dignitaries, the two Cherubim, may their position be magnified'.

A further testimony to the high esteem in which 'Obadyāh was held is again afforded by the same letter:

> 'As for our glorious teacher and Master 'Obadyāh the eminent Sage to whom mysteries are revealed, in whom "light, understanding and wisdom like the wisdom of the angels are to be found" (Dan. V:11) "no secret mystifieth him, he lieth down and all is revealed to him."' (ibid. IV:6) (6)

This allusion to 'Obadyāh's renown as a master of the esoteric method is most certainly borne out by the contents of our treatise as will be demonstrated. (7) There is some evidence that his brother David also had Pietist sympathies, although little that can be specifically qualified as Sufi is to be found in his works. However it must be borne in mind that the latter, contrary to the esoterical *Treatise of the Pool*, were of a more popular character. (8)

The Treatise of the Pool

i. Authorship

The Judaeo-Arabic *al-Maqāla al-Ḥawḍiyya, Treatise of the Pool*, was first briefly brought to the attention of the scholarly world by A. Geiger in 1846 (9) and later in somewhat more detail by M. Steinschneider who, judging by the cursory description he gave of the work, did little more than skim the surface of the Bodleian manuscript. (10)

In recent years, Professor Georges Vajda devoted an important article to the content of the *Ḥawḍiyya* (11), pointing out that there was nothing to confirm its attribution to 'Obadyāh apart from the manuscript's colophon which reads: 'Here ends the Treatise of the Pool, ascribed to Rabbi 'Obadyāh the son of Abraham the Pious the son of our Master Moses son of Maymūn, of blessed memory'. However, peremptory proof of 'Obadyāh's authorship can be adduced from further sources at our disposal.

The Jewish Sufi author of the vast philosophic-mystical compilation contained in MS. Hunt. 489, most probably written in XIV-XVth century Egypt (12), twice mentions our 'Obadyāh in his eleventh chapter:

> 'In the present chapter I have summarized the words of our Master (Moses Maimonides) . . . as well as those of his grandson Rabbi 'Obadyāh.' (13)

Unfortunately the manuscript abruptly ends a few pages later, but not before quoting one of 'Obadyāh's works (f° 150); 'As Rabbi 'Obadyāh, the grandson of our Master, has said "As for him who accepteth belief passively (*taqlīd*), it is as if he were never born", as the Sage hath said "An ultimely birth is better than he". (Eccl. VI: 13). And he went on to say "He that heareth let him hear and he that forbeareth let him forbear".' (Ezek. III: 27) These words are indeed to be found in the *Ḥawḍiyya* on f° 5a, confirming its attribution to 'Obadyāh and indicating, in addition, that the treatise continued to be read by later generations.

A further support in favour of 'Obadyāh's authorship may be gleaned from Sambari, who lists among the works of Abraham Maimonides a certain *Kitāb al-ḥawḍ,* or *Book of the Pool.* (14) Since however no such title is known to have been written by Abraham, it is reasonable to suppose that Sambari mistook the son for the father and that this work is really none other than 'Obadyāh's *Maqāla al-ḥawḍiyya.* (15)

Lastly, the overwhelming influence of the works of Moses and Abraham Maimonides, that can be discerned in the *Ḥawḍiyya*, may constitute a further indication of 'Obadyāh's authorship. Indeed, although he never mentions either of them, or for that matter any other author, by name he does in true filial tribute quote extensively from the works of his two illustrious forbears.

ii. Content

The *Treatise of the Pool* may be described as a mystical *vademecum*, a manual for the spiritual wayfarer along the Path to Godliness. Instructions as to how to obtain and safeguard one's bond with the intelligible world are set forth in plain language illustrated here and there with simple examples and less simple accounts of the mystical experience. 'Obadyāh's style has little to compare with Baḥya's rational and methodical exposé contained in the *Hidāya*. Indeed the *Ḥawḍiyya*, perhaps composed for a disciple, has all the signs of an improvised discourse which, shunning philosophical casuistry, follows its mystical lyricism from imprecision into the intentional obscurity characteristic of numerous Neoplatonic compositions. Although often repetitious, 'Obadyāh's sentences are economical, obscured by hints and allusions, to be comprehended only by the initiated. He greatly relies on his father's and grandfather's works, whole sentences of which he incorporates into the texture of his own composition. Indeed the latter can be considered an enlargement of the concluding chapters of the *Guide for the Perplexed*, albeit with a markedly more mystical bent. 'Obadyāh deals only allusively with philosophical issues, and shows much more concern about how to obtain the constant 'being-with-Reason' that Moses Maimonides had briefly outlined.

Besides the *Guide*, 'Obadyāh quotes from the *Mišneh Tōrah, Commentary on Abōt*, and the *Kifāya* as well as from general Rabbinic and Sufi sources. However, as previously stated, he never mentions any author by name. It is noteworthy that he uses midrašic passages to illustrate mystical concepts but these are usually second-hand, borrowed from the *Guide*. Another interesting aspect is the picture that may be drawn from his brief criticism of the intellectual interests of his contemporaries (Chapter XVII) and the caution he counsels in the presence of one's spiritual mentors (Exhortation).

The treatise is divided into twenty chapters, each of which begins with the word 'Know'. Although Vajda has masterfully summarised the most salient ideas of the treatise it will not be unwarranted in view of the incoherency of the chapter order, to set forth briefly the content of the successive chapters.

The Introduction has been partly lost.

The author advocates perseverance in the face of adversity, the latter being the result of one's own sins. Having thus mastered his passions, the individual will be relieved of earthly exigencies, which 'Obadyāh equates with 'other gods'.

Chapter I

Scripture and philosophy both exhort man to abandon corporeal pleasures in the interest of Reason, in the manner of Jacob who subdued his lower instincts and attained to spiritual perfection.

By being attached to Reason the individual will be protected from misfortune.

Chapter II

If the individual were to obtain Reason's favour, he should deem it a grace and persevere in its pursuit. However there is here a dilemma: man being a coarse being can never hope to be fully attached to luminous and subtle matter. One must be aware of this shortcoming but nevertheless not despair in this pursuit, for this is the true purpose of man, to strive for the truth and eschew passive acceptance (*taqlīd*).

Chapter III

This science is indeed the régime of the élite and differs from that of the vulgar. However it is attained only after a sound grounding in the exoteric Law which is conducive to higher positions. The true desire for this pursuit brings relief from earthly preoccupations. First the adept must purify himself from bodily impurities and pleasures for only then will he be apt to follow the Path. The adept must proceed gradually and not prove impetuous, for the Children of Israel brought punishment on themselves through their impatience and precocity.

Chapter IV

'Obadyāh explains his method of exposition and the part to be played by intuition in its understanding.

Chapter V

Efforts must be deployed to retain Reason's transient providence; for if the individual is deserted by it, he will remain without protection. He should thus devote to it all that he cherishes.

Chapter VI

Corporeal matter is the only obstacle to perfection, therefore it must be purified. When this has been achieved, visions will be revealed to the mystic and he will be guided with the light of Reason. Therefore he must safeguard Reason's form. Thereupon the heavens will be open to him and he will receive celestial instruction, as did the Israelites in the wilderness through the mediation of Moses.

Chapter VII

The external and internal organs of man are interdependent and when the external senses slumber the internal ones awaken. Just as bad food disturbs the function of the external senses so the internal senses require the appropriate intellectual and moral nourishment. These are furnished by the Divine precepts which safeguard body and mind and cultivate the virtues.

God beholds all man's deeds and He, together with the Soul and Reason, witness all man's acts. Consequently the individual should exercise modesty when gratifying his bodily needs.

Chapter VIII

Moreover, each time man indulges in worldly needs, the bond between him and Reason is severed and the mirror of the soul is tarnished. Therefore the most propitious moment to supplicate the Lord is at a time of respite from the body's preoccupations. 'Obadyāh compares the attitude of the ancients and moderns in their dealings with matter. Man should be filled with shame for not having hearkened to God's apostles, i.e. Reason and Soul.

Chapter IX

'Obadyāh names this Chapter the axis of his treatise and calls for it to be paid special attention. Man is the choicest creature of this world by virtue of his rational soul, the most superior of all faculties. If it is treasured then it will perform wonders and reveal mysteries. Man must be wary of enemies that bring harm through inadvertence. As soon as a good deed presents itself it must be accomplished with great love. The intensity of vision will be in accordance with the degree of one's spiritual preparation as illustrated by an example from the Midraš. The Sages have indicated the necessary preparations.

Chapter X

'Obadyāh compares the cleansing of the heart to that of a pool. The heart must be emptied of all but God or else its grasp will be distorted and that which seems truthful will really be false. He gives the Talmudic example of Eliša' who mistook the marble stone for water.

[Chapter]

One must strive to retain Reason's favour for if neglected it will disappear. To achieve this one must suffer mortification and be enraptured with the desire for Reason. The ignorant do not realize the preciousness of its favour but the wise cherish it and abandon all else for it. One must not think that withdrawal for such purposes is to be practised exclusively in the wilderness, for the discipline is to be applied even in one's domestic conduct.

Chapter XI

'Obadyāh recounts the Mystics' sayings relating to the Path. Perfection is difficult to achieve after marriage and one must therefore follow the example of the Patriarchs who delayed it until the age of 40 years. 'Obadyāh relates the allegory of the city which, only when rid of its enemies, can prosper. The body must likewise be mastered and requires proper preparation in the exoteric Law before entering 'Paradise'. Misfortune befell the companions of

Rabbi 'Aqība who entered Paradise, on account of their insufficient peparation. One cannot pursue this path and simultaneously desire this world for all one's efforts are required in this lifelong task.

Chapter XII

These notions are very subtle and cannot be comprehended by all. Preliminary training is required in the understanding of the secrets concealed in the Scriptures. The latter are revealed in accordance with the measure of one's desire. The body is like a besieged city. If even Abraham was plagued by Satan how much more care should we then take. We must therefore plead with God and chase away our enemy.

Chapter XIII

Were man conscious of the danger, who would not relent in subjugating his faculties to the rule of Reason? He must show himself merciless towards evil; only then can the 'city' prosper. One must proceed with moderation, shun superfluities and content oneself with sheer necessities alone. One must not consider those that indulge in earthly passion but rather imitate Abraham and David whose sole pursuit was the Knowledge of God.

Chapter XIV

Matter is not in itself evil but must be treated with caution.

Exhortation

Firstly one should reduce intercourse with the vulgar, seeking only the company of the virtuous. One should inure oneself to speak little, to diminish one's zest for food, reduce sleep, think continuously of God and practise purity and devotion in prayer.

Chapter XV

'Obadyāh compares the body's aversion to things spiritual with a child who does not appreciate the value of discipline. One must proceed gently in the education of matter, lest, on account of the latter's obstinacy, the task be rendered impossible. It is unnecessary to strive after material needs for they come of themselves as the Talmudic Sages, whose desire was to aid us in our path, have already indicated. One must be wary of matter's reluctance and forever be in search of water (spiritual knowledge) after the manner of the Patriarchs.

Chapter XVI

Reason is the bond between man and the intelligible world and it is strengthened by true knowledge. It is therefore important to acquire a proper understanding of the Law for the latter fortifies Reason and also regulates one's moral conduct. Sound Reason is in fact synonymous with the Divine Law. 'Obadyāh enumerates the characteristics of the adepts of this path to whom, once principles have been imparted, the secrets of the Law become clear.

Exhortation

Upon achieving a particular state one must not pay oneself credit, but remain modest. One should conceal this achievement from those who are not worthy of it, lest evil be brought upon oneself. One should not abandon the company of men but shun their coarseness and exercise dissimulation (*kitmān*) in their presence.

Chapter XVII

In days of yore the Talmudic Sages, 'disciples of the Prophets', would dispense their teachings in Academies. These teachings have since been lost on account of the Exile. Learning has declined and religious practice has become a mere habit, instead of being a preliminary to the receiving of the 'true Law'.

Observation

The vulgar think that the purpose of Scripture is in its being read or grammatically explained. One should utilise the doctrines referred to in this treatise to deepen one's understanding of Scripture. Similarly in every science one must first learn the basic principles before grasping the ultimate truths. It is also well to have recourse to the opinion of a Sage for the elucidation of one's problems.

Chapter XVIII

Preoccupation with Reason makes one oblivious to material needs. Those engaged in this pursuit thus make light of suffering, although at the beginning of the path there is always hardship. A true lover will however devote all to this endeavour and will often withdraw from the burden of society to the wilderness. Thus the Children of Israel and the Patriarchs dwelt for many years in the desert. The number of those that attain spiritual achievement in each generation is sparse. After the Patriarchs the bond was severed to be restored again only at the time of Moses. One should strive to obtain an intercessor (Reason), and this bond will vouchsafe everlasting life.

Exhortation

Notwithstanding His transcendence, God dwells amongst the humble. Since man cannot indefinitely remain in an elevated state he should remain humble and shameful of his having need of matter.

[Final] Exhortation

True service to God, which constitutes the purpose of the Law, stems from the heart. Few, however, are capable of the required wholeheartedness and their devotion is of little avail since it is performed as a matter of rote. Their example is to be avoided while that of the élite is to be emulated. However, care should be taken not to offend the latter, for their anger is merciless. One must exercise humility in their presence and constantly be aware of one's goal and the immense effort required to attain it. Nevertheless the great recompense which lies in store for the devotee will help alleviate the difficulty of his task.

iii. Exegesis

One of the most singular aspects of the *Ḥawḍiyya*, which well deserves our attention, is the method of scriptural interpretation employed therein. It is all the more important since, besides the works of Abraham Maimonides, 'Obadyāh's *Ḥawḍiyya* is the only substantial example of Pietist exegesis that we possess. As a general rule 'Obadyāh followed the allegorical-philosophical approach established by his grandfather, except that his own exegesis is characterised by a marked tendency toward mystical interpretation, based largely on Pietist doctrine, as well as by the use of technical vocabulary, borrowed from Sufi sources. Like his grandfather, 'Obadyāh does not hesitate to utilise the Midraš in order to elucidate his doctrines, subjecting it to the same exegetical methods.

'Obadyāh's interpretations are couched in a very allusive and cursory language, and he rarely enlarges on his insinuations. Their obscurity is increased by the fact that they are very often based on some underlying doctrine, which relies heavily on a highly developed system of symbolism similar to, but apparently quite independent of, the symbolism of the Qabbālāh. Moreover it seems that 'Obadyāh intentionally conceals what he regards as the deeper meaning of the verses evoked. Indeed, he explicitly states at one point (f° 6a):

> 'Know thou that meditatest this treatise that the matter to which we have alluded here cannot be more openly expounded. Thus

upon happening on a verse that can be interpreted in several manners, my goal is merely to open the gate and rely upon the disciple's comprehension. If he be endowed with insight and intuition (*ḏawq*) (16) then he will arrive at the true significance through his own resources'.

'Obadyāh mentions that Scripture contains allegories (f°s 12a, 16a) and wonderful things (f° 8a) and often draws attention to a particular point by saying (f° 12a) 'understand this allegory', (f° 23a) 'so grasp this', (f° 24a) 'turn thy mind to this'. However in the first instance, 'Obadyāh's work is intended for the initiated as he says (f° 16a):

> 'Ḳnow that it is impossible to expound and discuss the subject to which I have hinted and alluded throughout this treatise on account of its extreme abstruseness, the intricacy of its meaning and the remoteness of its essence. Consequently not all men are suited to it nor initially capable of receiving it, except after having acquired certain preliminaries. Hast thou not observed how the Pentateuch and the Prophets have expressed these notions in the form of parables in order that they may be comprehended ... for these questioṇs are at first manifest and then hidden inasmuch as man's grasp of them dependeth on the measure of his labour and passion'.

Similarly he states later: (f° 23a) 'that one must read the Scriptures as a "lover" and a "seeker"' and not as the vulgar who are interested only in the grammatical aspects of the text or a novel interpretation. The proper method of scriptural interpretation 'is to retain the verses by heart, until thy mind is crossed by one of the doctrines to which I have drawn thine attention. Thou wilt happen on a verse which correspondeth to that doctrine and thou shalt extract therefrom another doctrine, ascending from one doctrine to another, until thou be united with the object of thy quest'.

'Obadyāh rarely evokes the literal meaning of a verse and if he does so, it is often out of its context. Indeed in some instances it is difficult to decide whether a verse is intended to have a hidden meaning or whether it is simply being cited as a literary device in order to embellish his Judaeo-Arabic prose with Biblical quotations, as for example when he says of man's vices (f° 11b) that 'they hated him and could not speak peacefully unto him' (Gen. XXXVII:4) or when speaking of the evil inclination (f° 18a) he says 'Thou shalt surely slay him' (Deut. XIII:10). As far as the figurative interpretations are concerned, three types can be distinguished: (1) the doctrinal, whereby Pietist attitudes and practices are read into the Biblical text, (2) the philosophical and (3) the mystical, whereby an allegorical or symbolic dimension is lent to the text in consonance with Jewish Sufi doctrine. A few examples will be cited in illustration of these three categories.

(1) *Doctrinal*

'Obadyāh repeatedly emphasizes the necessity of careful preparation before embarking upon the spiritual path. The following verses, metaphorically interpreted, are adduced in support of this preparation (f° 5b) 'The priests also that draw near to the Lord shall purify themselves lest the Lord break forth upon them.' (Ex. XIX:22) 'Guard thy foot when thou goest to the house of the Lord.' (Eccl. IV:17) (17) As an illustration of the consequences of insufficient preparation 'Obadyāh relates that at the time of the Sinaitic Revelation, the Israelites had shown themselves impetuous and had thus incurred Divine punishment. (18)

One of the basic tenets of the spiritual path is to shun the superfluities of this world and to content oneself with the bare necessities. Thus, says 'Obadyāh (f° 20b), Jacob required of God only 'bread to eat and raiment to don'. (Gen. XXVIII:22) (19) Jacob exemplified other spiritual virtues (f° 14b) for the expression 'he was a perfect man, dwelling in tents' (Gen. XXV:27) signifies that while in his father's abode, he devoted himself to spiritual perfection. It is instructive to quote in this connection Abraham Maimonides who connects the term 'perfect' with the commandment given to Abraham 'walk before me and be perfect' (Gen. XVII:1) and concludes that Jacob followed in his forefather's footsteps with regard to the practice of solitary meditation (*ḫalwa*). (20) Moreover in the *Kifāya* (II, p.392), he states that Jacob was in fact the first devotee to practise meditation in domestic seclusion, as well as in the wilderness.

Similarly, 'Obadyāh (f° 25a) is of the opinion that the Patriarchs spent their lives in the wilderness far removed from worldly ambitions in order to meditate. This is how both he and his father (21) interpret 'and Isaac went out to meditate in the field' (Gen. XXIX:63)—he withdrew to the desert in order to practise *ḫalwa*.

It was likewise for meditational purposes that the Israelites dwelt in the wilderness for forty years. This practice was later to be found among the prophets of Israel such as Jeremiah who prayed 'Oh that I had in the wilderness a lodging place.' (Jer. IX:2) (22)

A further illustration of how the prophets are credited with Sufi virtues is afforded most strikingly by Abraham Maimonides' exegesis of II Kings I:8 where Elijah's hairy mantle is said to refer to the garb of the Sufis. (23) Elsewhere he states that the Prophets and Patriarchs were wont to marry very late, or even not at all. This opinion is echoed by 'Obadyāh who considers family life an impediment to spiritual development (24), and, in support of the deferment of marriage, he quotes the fact that Isaac did not marry until he was forty years old (Gen. XXV:20) by which time he had achieved spiritual perfection. (25)

Unfortunately there is little in the *Ḥawḍiyya* that throws light on 'Obadyāh's attitude towards the religious precepts which seem to have been interpreted by some Pietists in consonance with their Sufi teachings.

On f°s 9a–9b, his account of the significance of certain precepts owes much to the third part of the *Guide*. However, on one occasion (f° 14b) he supplies a metaphorical explanation of one particular commandment 'What man is there that hath built a new house and hath not dedicated it?' (Deut. XX:5) According to 'Obadyāh's interpretation the word 'house' represents the body or the soul—it is not clear which—and its 'dedication' is taken in the fundamental meaning of the Hebrew root 'initiation'. Wanting in perfection, the individual is exhorted to turn aside and devote himself to the initiation of his 'soul'. (26)

(2) *Philosophical*

The majority of 'Obadyāh's philosophical interpretations concern the conflict between intellect and matter, body and soul. Thus (f° 5b) he interprets Pr. XXIV:30 as an allegory referring to the neglected field which is the soul of the individual who indulges in corporeal delights. The conflict of body and soul is also portrayed (f° 16b) in Eccl. IX where the 'little city' besieged by enemies represents the soul, plagued by bodily passions and saved by the 'wise man', or Reason. (27) Likewise (f° 20b) the rebellion of Balaam's ass is understood as the revolt of matter (28) which Balaam was unable to dominate. 'Obadyāh (f° 3b) proposes a metaphorical interpretation of I Kings XIV:9 'Thou hast cast Me behind thy body', which signifies according to him 'he that hath forsaken the soul in order indulge in material (pleasures)'.

On the other hand he who entirely devotes himself to intellectual pursuits becomes completely oblivious of bodily exigencies. Thus (f° 24a) Adam was so absorbed with the dictates of Reason that he was not aware of his nakedness. (29) It is on account of the body's coarse substance (f° 7a), known as 'darkness', that man's full communion with the Divine is impeded. This 'darkness' is referred to in the verse 'He hath made darkness his hiding place' (Ps. XVIII:12) i.e. matter acts as a veil to the Divinity. (30)

Indeed, the individual who devotes himself entirely to the dictates of Reason is afforded providential protection as 'Obadyāh understands (f° 4a) from the verse 'because he hath set his love upon Me, therefore will I deliver him'. (Ps. XCI:14) (31) At one point 'Obadyāh draws an interesting parallel between Moses and the Active Intellect indicating that both liberally bestowed their instruction in accordance with the capacity of their receivers, as it is said 'And did mete out the Omer, he that gathereth much had nothing to lack, they gathered each according to his eating.' (Ex. XVI:18) (32) It is obvious from the foregoing examples that 'Obadyāh's interpretations are greatly indebted to the exegetical methods of his forbears. In the case of his mystical interpretations he seems to owe little to their influence and it would appear that they are predominantly his own, albeit based on a complex system of symbolism apparently in current use among the Pietists.

(3) *Mystical*

The elucidation of some of the symbols upon which 'Obadyāh's mystical exegesis is based can present difficulties and in their solution the context is the only aid that can be summoned. One of the most interesting symbols is the *Tree of Life*, which no doubt represents the ultimate felicity promised to the soul which, through knowledge and spiritual discipline, may return to its celestial source. Referring to the narrative in Gen. III, 'Obabyāh states (f° 3b) that it is the obsession with the Cherubim that obstructs the passage to the Tree of Life as it is said 'And the eyes of the fool are in the ends of Earth.' (Prov. XVII:24) It would seem that the Cherubim placed at the entrance to the Garden of Eden, whom the Midraš describes as 'angels of destruction' (33), are equated with the lure of matter, here called 'Earth'. This equation is borne out by 'Obadyāh's later reference (f° 5b) to 'the vanities of this nether world that guard the Tree of Life'. Moreover 'Obadyāh says of Elišaʿ ben 'Abūyāh (f° 15a) that during the latter's spiritual ascent into Paradise, 'he was troubled and turned toward the Cherubim', which could signify that he desired some material object, and that it subsequently caused his downfall. Similarly (f° 14b) in connection with Jacob's spiritual striving he allegorically interprets 'and the stone was big over the well' (Gen. XXIX:2) as a reference to 'the considerable obstacles that impede man's quest for the Tree of Life'.

A second interesting symbol that frequently recurs in the *Treat-*

ise is that of the Manna. While both Moses and Abraham Maimonides discussed the chapter concerning Manna in a literal tone, 'Obadyāh construes the whole episode as an allegory. Perhaps taking his cue from the Midraš which interprets 'the bread of the mighty' (Ps. LXXVIII: 25) as the 'bread of the Angels', (34) 'Obadyāh (f° 7b) intimates that the Manna was a spiritual food, symbolising knowledge, which was intended to bring the generation of the wilderness to spiritual perfection (*kamāl*). Indeed as we have mentioned earlier he compares Moses' distribution of the Manna, which is not in fact stated in the Biblical text, with the action of the Active Intellect which gives according to the receiver's capacity. The celestial origin of the Manna is referred to (f°s 11b, 12a) in the verse 'And the Heavens were opened' (Ezek. I:1), which is in fact, according to 'Obadyāh, a metaphor alluding to the revelation of spiritual knowledge that took place. (35)

Another theme which permeates the whole treatise is the use of water as a metaphor for spiritual knowledge. The first allusion to this theme (f° 7b) is to be found in the description of the wilderness through which the Israelites were led 'a land devoid of water, fraught with serpents'. (Deut. VIII:15) The explanation of this episode is not clear. Over the ages the mystics have oscillated between a literal interpretation of the desert as the *midbar*, i.e. 'place of the word', to which the ascetic retires from the temptations of society, and as a reference to the tribulations of the internal wilderness which the mystic must traverse while plying the spiritual path. Whatever the case, the serpents, which no doubt represent the evil instinct, perish when the Israelites obtain water, i.e. spiritual enlightenment, through the mediation of Moses. In a similar vein, 'Obadyāh refers to the images of flowing water in Joel IV:18 and Zech. XIV:18, as alluding to the revelation of spiritual knowledge and the attainment of spiritual perfection in the Messianic era. (36)

In the wilderness of the spiritual path one should take care to have a sufficient provision of water; indeed the Patriarchs busied themselves with the digging of wells (f° 21a) (e.g. Gen. IV:17 *et passim*). (37) Hagar did not find water for her son, and would have perished, had the Lord 'not opened her eyes'. (38) Thus it is incumbent on the individual to dig a well for himself, i.e. to undertake the search for spiritual knowledge.

Because Jacob dwelt with Laban, who perhaps symbolises the snare of matter, he realized the great effort which is required before being able to reach the water of the Tree of Life 'The stone was great on the mouth of the well.' (Gen. XXX:30)

The symbolism of water is also bound up with the central chapter of the *Ḥawḍiyya* which in fact provided the title of the whole work. Indeed in Chapter X, 'Obadyāh compares man's heart to a cistern or pool (*ḥawḍ*) that is to be filled with pure water. Great care is to be exercised that no impurity seep into the heart for this could be the cause of fatal errors on the spiritual path, such as that of Eliša' who mistook the marble for water. Once the heart is completely cleansed of all but God then the living water will pour into it and wonders will be revealed.

One should ever strive toward the perfect waters and avoid 'the broken cisterns'. (Jer. II:13) (39)

The well or pool as a life-giving symbol so natural in the parched lands of the East, plays a great role in both Islamic and Jewish esotericism. The famous Sufi theologian al-Ġazzālī devotes a whole chapter of his *Iḥyā' 'ulūm ad-dīn* to the symbolism of the Prophet's pool (*ḥawḍ ar-rasūl*). (40) Al-Ġazzālī was fascinated too by the symbolism of the heart, which is a central theme in Sufi gnosis, and in several of his works he devotes many pages to the various meanings of the word heart, which Sufism considers to be the seat of spiritual knowledge and 'internal vision' (*baṣīra*). (41)

In a chapter of his *Iḥyā'* a curious passage is to be found that bears a striking resemblance to 'Obadyāh's symbolism and might well have served as his model:

> 'Let us imagine a well (*ḥawḍ*) hewn out of the ground, into which water could flow from above through channels which had been dug for that purpose. Likewise the bottom of the well could be

> dug and the soil removed, so that when the level of pure water is reached, the latter would run into the well from beneath; indeed this water could well be purer and more abundant than (that of above). The heart can be likened to this well, spiritual knowledge (*'ilm*) compared to the waters thereof and the five senses to the channels. Science can enter the heart by way of the sensual channels through reflection and observation. Alternatively these channels could be obstructed through seclusion (*ḫalwa*), solitude and introspection and recourse to deepening the heart through cleansing it and lifting the veils that envelop it so that the fountain of knowledge may spring forth from within'. (42)

Al-Ġazzālī goes on to compare the heart's action to that of the *Well-Guarded Tablet (al-lawḥ al-maḥfūẓ)* (43) as indeed 'Obadyāh does in his chapter. Water as a symbol of spiritual knowledge seems to have been commonplace amongst the Pietist authors. In a fragment of a treatise which is believed to have come from the pen of Rabbi Abraham he-Ḥasid we read 'There is no bond between them and Him except through water, as it is said "Ho everyone that thirsteth come ye for water" (Is. IV:1) which alludes to His book and His Word and the guidance that is contained therein'. (44)

Similarly in the composition *Chapter on Beatitude*, the intellect's flow is compared to water from a spring (Pr. V:16) and the following explanation is given of 'my heart overfloweth with a goodly matter' (Ps. XIV:2) 'like water that has been sought after through digging, since the quest for knowledge and prophecy is comparable to him that digs for an object'. (45)

The similarity of this last reference to the doctrines expressed in the *Treatise of the Pool* is of special significance for it is one of several parallels that exist between the *Ḥawḍiyya* and this apocryphal work ascribed to Moses Maimonides. It seems in fact that a close relationship exists between the two and by way of conclusion to our short survey of 'Obadyāh's exegesis we shall briefly discuss the connection between the two works in the following section.

iv. The Treatise of the Pool and the Chapter on Beatitude

Modern scholars who have studied the curious Judaeo-Arabic treatise *Chapter on Beatitude*, have regarded its attribution to Moses Maimonides as spurious. (46) As we have already pointed out, this attribution is in itself significant in that the Pietist doctrine, to which the book in fact subscribes, doubtless represented in the eyes of its devotees the authentic interpretation of Maimonides' teachings. Basing himself on certain characteristic forms of worship, portrayed in the book, Wieder was the first to recognize the Pietist provenance of the work, suggesting its ascription to Abraham Maimonides. (47) While a writer may employ different styles for different types of composition, it is conspicuous that the language and style of the *Chapter on Beatitude* share little in common with Abraham's other known writings, where much discretion is exercised in the use of Sufi terms. Indeed the work in question abounds in Sufi terminology, of which the following are a few examples:

'awliyā'	saints, p.1, 33
kamāl (*aṣ-ṣūra*)	perfection, p.l, 10
malakūtī	appertaining to the intelligible world, p.3, 14
istiġrāq	total preoccupation, p.7
ittiṣāl	mystical union, p.9, 35, 37
qaṭ'al-'aqabāt	surmounting of obstacles, p.11
waḥī	inspiration, p.11, 13
inqiṭā'	withdrawal, p.17
ḫalwa	solitary meditation, p.17
qurb	proximity, p.18
ğamāl	divine beauty, p.18
išrāq	illumination, p.24
inqiṭa' al-huğūb	rending of veils, p.24
ḏāq	spiritual intuition, p.37

Furthermore the distinctly mystical propension and vocabulary bear a striking resemblance to those of the *Ḥawḍiyya*, not to mention the instances of specific vocabulary that ‘Obadyāh particularly employs; for example:

p.7	*qawā'im*=feet, cf. *Ḥawḍiyya* f° 25b
p.7	*lahaǧ*=to meditate, cf. *Ḥawḍiyya* f° 27b
p.28	*fi ǧiwār rabb al-‘ālamīn*=under the protection of the Master of the Universe, cf. *Ḥawḍiyya* f° 25b

In addition, the elliptic style, the constant form of address ‘Know my brother’, ‘O thou that meditatest’, together with the casual quoting of Biblical verses without interpretation and the conclusion of chapters with Biblical verses, are all typical of ‘Obadyāh's style.

There is concordance too between some of the ideas expressed in both treatises, as the following selection will show:

Chapter on Beatitude	*Ḥawḍiyya*
p.1 the freedom to attain self-perfection or perversion	cf. f° 7a
p.2 *rūḥ* (spirit) is an ambiguous term	cf. f° 12a
p.5–6 ‘other Gods’ are interpreted as referring to corporeal pleasures	cf. f° 3a
p.7–8 the description of the ecstatic state	cf. f° 7b, 12a, 15b
p.15 Man is a microcosm	cf. f° 11a
p.19 warning against disclosing esoterical doctrines to the unworthy	cf. f° 22a
p.33 Moses equated with the Active Intellect	cf. f° 7b
p.37 matter constitutes a veil between man and God	cf. f° 7a

Consequently there is strong evidence in favour of attributing to ‘Obadyāh the *Chapter on Beatitude*. Moreover the author of the latter refers to his work (p.14) as a conclusion to his *Maqāla*, which the translator took as a reference to the *Guide*, but which could well allude to the *Maqāla al-Ḥawḍiyya*. The possibility that, with the passing of time, 'Obadyāh's authorship was forgotten and the treatise attributed to his grandfather, is not at all remote.

v. The Manuscripts

Until recently only a unicum of the *Ḥawḍiyya* was known, the MS. Or. 661 (Neubauer 2389) in the Bodleian Library at Oxford. However while engaged in the cataloguing of manuscripts in the Taylor-Schechter Genizah Collection of the Cambridge University Library, the writer was able to identify a further two fragments of the treatise which together cover about half the text of the Bodleian manuscript. As the latter, designated as MS. A, is the more complete we have used it as the basis of our edition of the text with emendations based on the Cambridge manuscripts, designated as B and C respectively. The extent of eclectic text thus available is illustrated in the following table.

A	B	C
F° 1–10	—	—
F° 10a 1.1 – 1.16	F° 1a – 1b	—
F° 10b	—	—
F° 11a 1.9 – 13a 1.7	F° 2a – 6b	—
F° 13a – 15a	—	—
F° 15a 1.10 – 22b 1.1	—	F° 1a – 6b
F° 22b – 27b	—	—

A. MS. Bodleian, Or. 661

This MS. which bears the *Ex libris* of Alexander Matrix of Leghorn, was at one time in the library of Nachman Krochmal whence it entered the possession of Leopold Zunz. (48) The latter sold it to the Bodleian for the sum of £8 while on a visit to Oxford in

1856. The 219 folio manuscript is a *mağmū'* containing various mystical compositions, one of which is the *Commentary on the Sefer Yĕṣīrāh* by Yĕhūdāh Ibn Malka (49), all written on paper in the same neat Oriental cursive hand. The watermark (Briquet No. 2445) suggests the years 1450–1530 as the date of redaction. 'Obadyāh's treatise, which is unfortunately acephalous, occupies folios 3a to 27b. Extensive repair at the beginning of the MS. has modified the original quire composition but later quires are made up of four leaves. The latter measure 19.5 cms × 15 cms and contain 19 lines per page in black ink.

In its present state the treatise is divided into 18 unnumbered chapters into which are incorporated 2 observations (*tanbīh*), f° 15a, 23a, 26b and two exhortations (*waṣiyya*), 19a, 21b. The chapter divisions are not identical to those found in the other manuscripts. On the whole the text seems to have been well understood by the copyist who has however in one place at least erred in the page order. (50)

Other errors and omissions have crept into this late redaction and the text is corrupt in more than one place. When revising the text, the scribe, or a later hand, has scored certain words and written their correct form above the line or in the margin.

B.Cambridge University Library, *T–S* Arabic 43.208 and *T–S* Arabic 25.97

These two Genizah fragments, containing 6 leaves in all, belong to the same manuscript and are indeed consecutive and together originally formed a gathering, although two intermediate leaves are lacking. The leaves, some of which are damaged, measure 13.5 cms × 11 cms, contain 12 lines of black ink to the page and cover folios 10a, l. 2–16 and then folios 11a, l. 9–13a, l. 7 of MS. A. They are written in an inexpert Egyptian cursive hand and the paper and palaeography indicate the XIVth century as a likely date of redaction. Indeed the hand is very similar to that of Joshua, great-great-grandson of Moses Maimonides (1310–1355) (cf. *T–S* 12.608). The chapters are unnumbered. The small format of this manuscript suggests that it may have been used as a portative manual, to be carried, as was customary, in the sleeve.

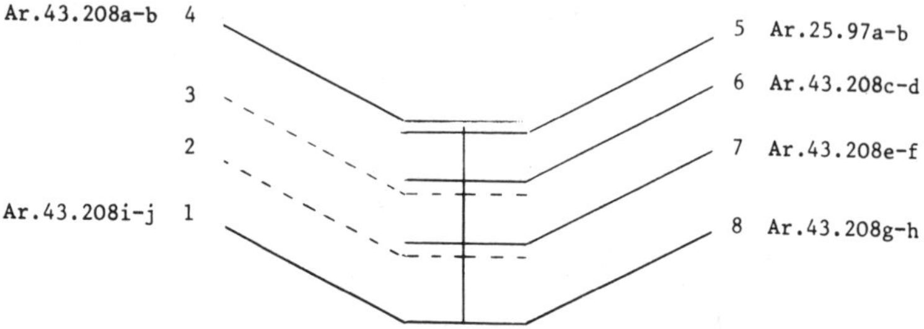

C. Cambridge University Library, *T–S* NS 168.1 and NS 91.35.

These two fragments belong together and indeed form a gathering of 3 sheets of 6 consecutive leaves (the last of which bears a catchword), some of which have sustained loss of text through staining and damage. They measure 19 cms × 14 cms, contain 20 lines of black ink on paper and cover folios 15a, l. 10 to 22b, l. 1 of MS. A. The text is written in a neat Oriental square hand possibly dating from the XIVth century. The chapters are numbered.

As is to be expected in view of their anteriority, the readings of the two Cambridge fragments are superior to those of the Bodleian manuscript and appear on the whole to be more complete. It is unfortunate that the Cambridge manuscripts have not restored the missing part of the introduction to the Bodleian text.

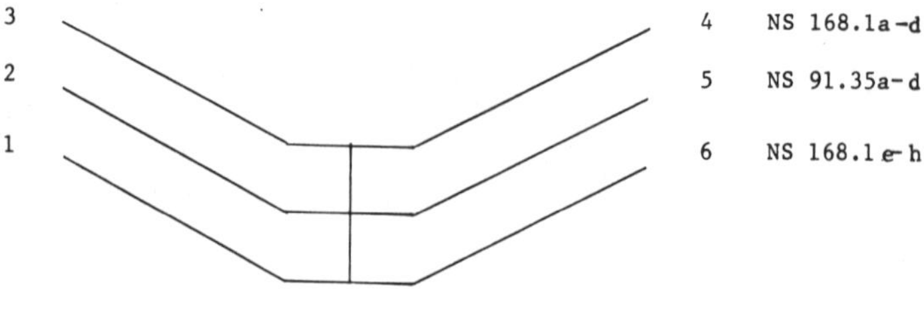

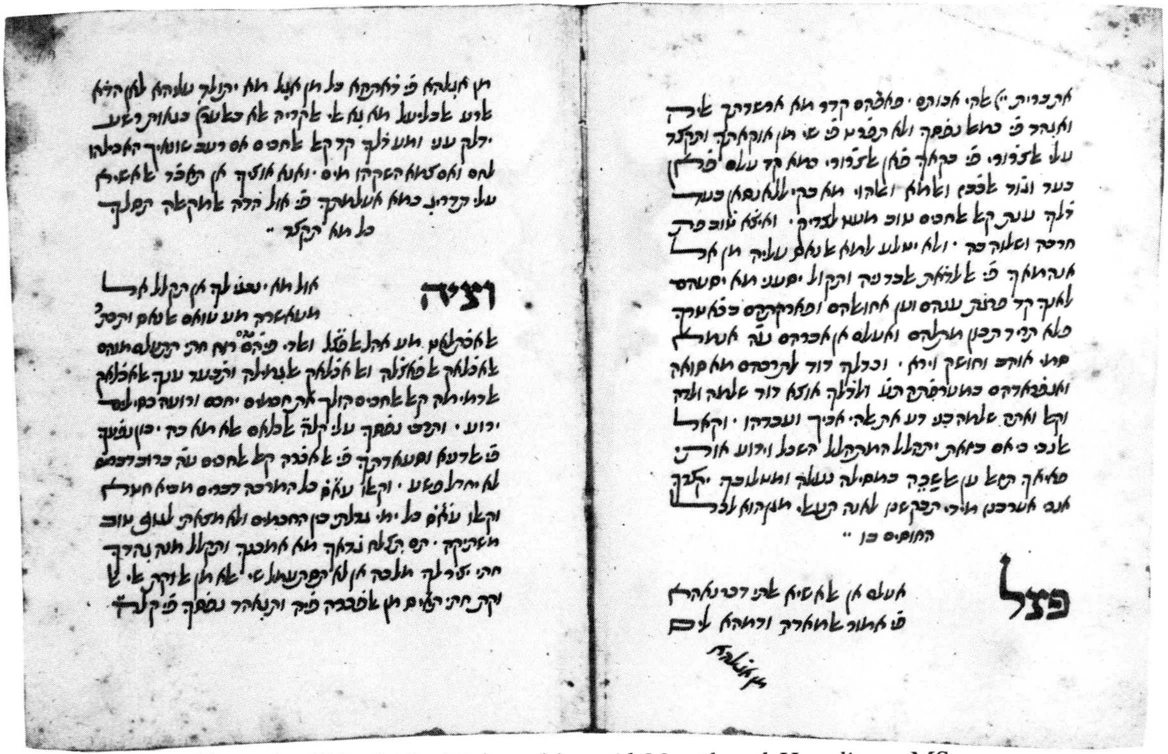

Plate I ‘Obadyāh Maimonides *Al-Maqāla al-Ḥawḍiyya* MS. Bodl. Or. 661, f° 18b–19a.

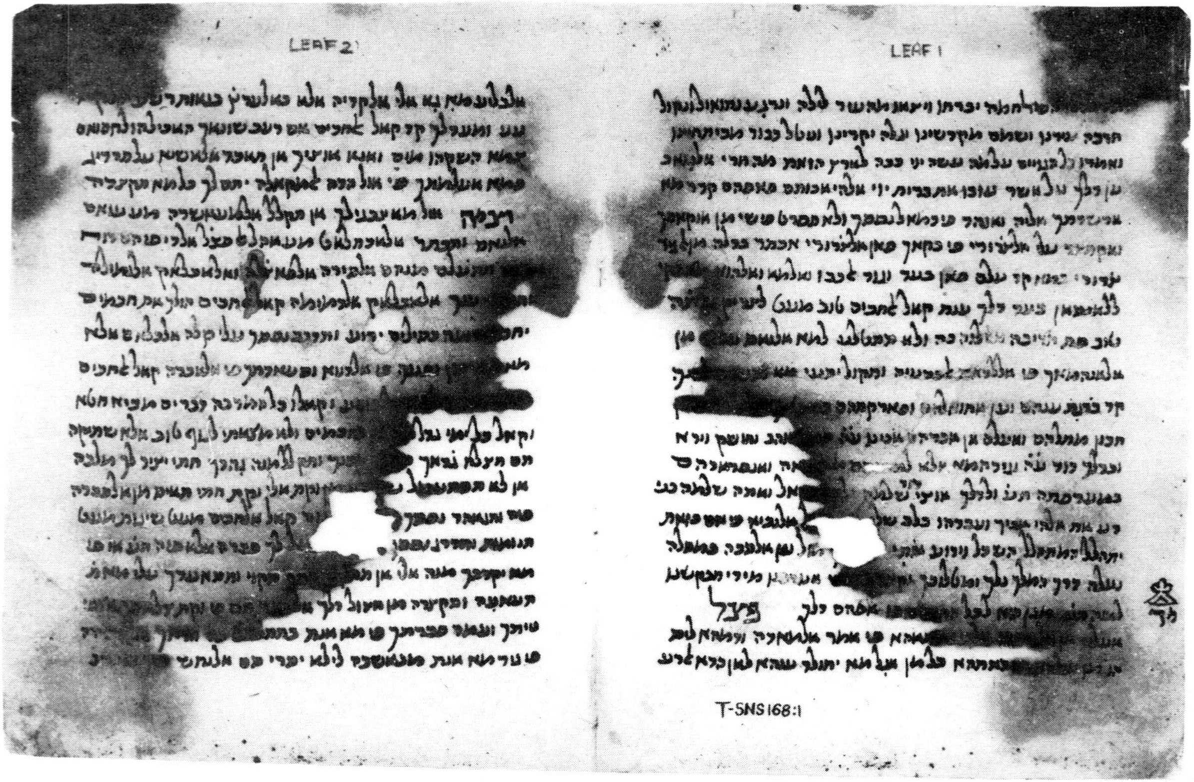

Plate II MS. Cambridge University Library, *T–S* NS 168.1, f° 1b–2a.

Plate III MS. Cambridge University Library, *T–S* Arabic Box 43.208, f° 2b–3a.

vi. The Language of the Treatise

The Judaeo-Arabic idiom in which the *Ḥawḍiyya* is composed can make no claim to great literary value and is typical of the post-classical period when the influence of vernacular Arabic was making wider and wider inroads into the literary idiom. Since grammatical irregularities appear in all the manuscripts and thus cannot be attributed to individual scribal errors they must therefore have originated with 'Obadyāh. Indeed although the latter endeavours to adhere to the norms of Classical Arabic, he falls victim to the same orthographical and grammatical deviations as other Judaeo-Arabic authors of the pseudo-classical period. Although the language of this period has been masterfully studied by Blau (51), it will not be superfluous to point out the most salient irregularities typical of 'Obadyāh's style.

(1) The most frequent is the ubiquitous use of the relative *allaḏ̌ī* for both masc., fem. and pl. Similarly *hāḏ̌a* is often employed instead of *hāḏ̌ihi*, probably because the dialect had a single form for both, i.e. *'ellī* and *ḥ̌ād* respectively. (Blau, §51)

(2) More often than not the nominative is employed for the accusative, e.g. f° 12a, *fa-tūrīk nūr bāhir*, although the opposite also occurs, f° 7a, *fa-tarid ..... 'umūr*[an] *ilāhiyya*[tan] and 21b, *buyyina lahu šay'*[an]. (Blau, §219)

(3) The gender and form of the dual is disregarded, f° 8a, *waquwwatayn aḥ̌ar fahum maḥ̌ǧūbayn*. (Blau, §122)

(4) *mā* is used more often than not for the negative, regardless of the verbal tense although an irregular use of *laysa* is also met with: f° 3a, *lays ta'ūd*, 21b, *lays ḥaṣal*, 22b, *lays yatimm*. (Blau, §§204–6)

(5) The subject often changes from second to third person in the sentence and vice versa. (Blau §325)

(6) As usual in such texts there is an inconsistent disregard for gender and number in the agreement of the verb. (Blau §119)

(7) Non-concordance of numerals, e.g. f° 8a, *awlā'ika al-ḥ̌ams ḥawwāss*. (Blau, §140)

(8) There are several examples, typical of vulgar Arabic, of asyndetic constructions where *an* is omitted before the verb, especially after verbs of desire, possibility and necessity, as well as after the verbs *ḥaṣala* and *raǧʿa*, employed with their colloquial meaning 'to become'. (Blau, §§327–8)

(9) Other usages are outright colloquial phenomena such as the addition of a prosthetic *alīf*, in the Vth form (Blau, §75), e.g. f° 3a, *itṯabbat*; the prefix of the vulgar particle *bi* to the indicative: f° 27b, *bi-tataqaddam* (Blau, §65); the loss of *nūn* in the indicative plurals; the use of *wa-lā* in the sense of 'or': f° 22a, (Blau, §203) and irregular use of the VIIth form, e.g. f° 23a *inbanā*.

(10) In addition the following colloquial and unusual expressions have been noted:

f° 4a	*matātī*	'flexible, receptive'	cf. *Guide* III: 8, Qāfiḥ p.470
9b	*yata'affafu*	'to be reluctant'	cf. *Guide* III: 53, Qāfiḥ p.686
10a	*yušaḥiḥu*	'to abstain rigorously'	cf. *Guide* I: 71, Munk. I p.334
10b	*tastarqid*	'to put to sleep'	cf. Dozi, *Dict.* I p.546
10b	*ayyāka*	'beware'	cf. Blau, § 252
12a	*yašfī ġalīlak*	'to slake one's thirst'	cf. Dozi, *Dict.* I p.771
13b	*amyā'*	plural of *mā*, 'water'	cf. Skoss, *JQR*, XVIII, pp.188–90.
13b	*yaǧbur fā'itahu*	'defect which cannot be remedied'	cf. *Guide* II.3b, Qāfiḥ p.402; Dozi; *Dict.* I p.170
14b	*yufāriq*	intransitive: 'to leave,' or 'to die'	cf. *Chapter on Beatitude*, p.35
18b	*'anita*	'to be difficult'	
19b	*'ammar*	'to fill' or 'instruct'	
19b	*manašab*	'to be attached to'	cf. *Kifāya,* Intr. p.38

20a	*ḥaṭṭa*	'to place'	
21a	*'awwal 'alä*	'to undertake'	
22b	*ḥalba*	here: 'a series of sayings'	
25a	*bi-l-marra*	'very'	cf. *Kifāya*, Intr. p.39
25b	*qawā' im*	'feet'	cf. Wieder, p.46 and *Chapter on Beatitude* p.7
26a	*taḍabbuṭ*	'attachment'	
27a	*mašä 'alä ğarīḥ*	'to offend'	
27b	*lahağ*	'to meditate' or 'desire'	cf. Wieder p.46 and *Chapter on Beatitude,* p.7

Most interesting is 'Obadyāh's use of Sufi technical terms, a list of which will be found in the Appendices to the present volume.

vii. Orthography

(1) The spelling in the three manuscripts collated is more or less uniform and diacritical points and vocalisation are very parsimonious. In A the *ğīm* (dot below) and *ġayn* (dot above), *ṣād* and *ḍād*, *fā'* and *peh* are always distinguished but the *dāl* and *ḏāl, kāf*, and *ḫā'* only occasionally. Confusion between *ẓā'* and *ḍād* and even *ḏāl* often occurs, e.g. f° 4a, *aẓ-ẓahr*; f° 12b, *yanḍaf*; f° 14b, *'aḍīm* but also same page, *'aẓīma*; f° 15b, *ḥaḍḍaru'*; f° 20a, *yaqḍatih*; f° 24a, *biḍ-daḍ*. (Blau, §23)

(2) Long *alīf* is indicated by a *ṣēre* beneath the following consonant, e.g. f° 3a, אפֵה; f° 11b, אלאכׄרה. (52)

(3) Curiously this sign is also employed to designate the *šadda*, e.g. f° 11b, אלקוֵה; f° 16b, ושבֵה; f° 18b, אלסכֵה; f° 20a, מודֵב.

(4) Elsewhere, as in MS. B and C, the *šadda* is indicated by redoubling the letters concerned: f° 7a, וקוות; f° 11b, אלמתכׄיילה; f° 21b, בויין. (Blau, §§30,31.)

(5) In MS. B *ḥā'* and *kāf, ğīm* and *ğayn, ḍād* and *ṭā'* are generally distinguished, whereas in MS. C only the *ḍād* and *ẓa, ğim* and *ġayn* are furnished with diacritical points.

(6) In all MSS. *tā' marbūṭa* is generally written ה although sometimes it is written ת : f° 12a, לכת̇רת; f° 27b, אלחוצ̇יה̈ אלמקאלת. (Blau, §27.) Conversely ה̈ is mistakenly written for ת : e.g. f° 11a, ארתבטה̈; f° 15a, אט̇רבה̈; f° 19b, צחה̈. The writing of *ta' marbūṭa* as an *alīf*, typical of late Judaeo–Arabic MSS. frequently occurs in MS. A: f° 9a, סאלמא; f° 13b, צ̇רוריא; f° 16a, אליקצ̇א; f° 22b, אלג̇אהליא. (Blau, § 27, 3c.)

(7) *Alif maqṣūra* is generally represented as a *yā'* although it does occur as an *alīf*: f° 26b, יבקא; we also find *alīf* represented as a *yā'*: f°8, אלי תרי.

(8) *Scriptio plena* where *wāw* serves as *mater lectionis* for short *u* is quite frequent: f° 7b, וצוו; f° 10b, תורי; f° 14a, פצונה; f° 15a, פדום; f° 15b, חולי; f° 20a, תנפור; f°21b, בויין.

(9) Similarly *yā'* is retained where it should normally be suppressed: f° 4b, קוי; f° 7b, פאעתני; f° 14a, פאצפי; f° 17b, ופיק; f° 26b, פאסתחי.

(10) The otiose *alīf al-fāṣila* is sometimes irregularly added: f° 3a, פתנג̇וא but often omitted: f° 15a, כאנו. (Blau, §43.)

(11) In the Vth form a prosthetic *alīf* is added: f° 3a אתת̇בת. (Blau, §75.)

(12) *Tanwīn* is represented orthographically as a final *nūn*: f° 23b, תאמלאן

The spelling of Biblical quotations are generally *plene* but otherwise conform with the standard Ben Ašer text. Sometimes however, there are marked deviations from the latter. As these do not seem to follow any particular recension but result from the author's quoting from memory they have been corrected to conform with standard texts and the variant readings indicated in the notes.

In the establishment of our text we have preferred to retain vernacular forms and orthography except when the latter are obviously erroneous and interfere with the better understanding of the text. In this case, as in the case where we have preferred the readings of the alternative MSS. to the Bodleian text, amendments have been made directly in the text and the original readings are indicated in the notes.

At the same time in order to co-ordinate the different systems of punctuation and to facilitate reading we have furnished diacritical points for all the consonants to be distinguished and for convenience we have supplied numbers, in accordance to what appears to be the correct sequence, to the various chapters in the translation. Furthermore in the latter, with the exception of Biblical quotations, the italicisation of words indicates that they were in Hebrew in the original and not in Judaeo-Arabic.

NOTES ON THE INTRODUCTION

Judaism and Sufism

(1) See for example on the Jewish sources of the early Ṣufi Mālik ibn Dīnār, S.D. Goitein in *Tarbiz* VI, pp.89–101, 510–22. It is interesting to note that the Rabbinical legends (*'Aggadōt*) were submitted to symbolical hermeneutics in Sufism, as they were in Jewish esotericism. It is likewise noteworthy that there existed in pre-Qabbalistic times mystical Judaeo-Arabic commentaries on the *'Aggadōt* as the Genizah fragment *T–S* Arabic 46.213 indicates.
(2) Cf. al-Qušayrī (*ob*. 1073) *Risāla* II, p.490; the same tale is found in al-Gazzālī (*ob*. 1111) *Iḥyā'*, II: 8, p.294; *Risāla*, II, pp. 686–7, related also by al-Yāfi'ī (*ob*. 1367), *Rawḍ ar-rayāḥīn*, edn. Cairo, 1874, p.130, and al-'Aṭṭār (*ob*. 1230) *Tadkirat al-awliyā'*, q.v. Mālik ibn Dînār.
(3) On Sa'adya (882–942) in the East, see I.Efros, 'Saadia's general ethical theory and its relation to Sufism' in *The Seventy-Fifth Anniversary Volume of the Jewish Quarterly Review*, Philadelphia, 1967, pp.166–177. The philosophy of Ibn Gabirol is thought to have been influenced by the school of the Andalusian Sufi, Ibn Masarra, cf. M.Asín Palacios, *The Mystical Philosophy of Ibn Masarra*, Leiden, 1978, p.130. A Sufi aspect of his poetry has been (unwittingly) touched on by A.Parnas, 'Remembrance of God in the poems of Solomon Ibn Gabirol' in *Keneset*, VII, 1942, pp.280–293 (in Hebrew). The ascetic ideal which Ibn Ġayyāṯ presents in his commentary on *Ecclesiastes*, entitled significantly *Kitāb az-Zuhd* (ed. Y. Qāfiḥ in *Ḥamēš Mĕgillōt*, Jerusalem, 1962, pp.161–296), smacks of Muslim pietism. As for Yĕhūdāh ha-Lēvī, although he freely employs Sufi vocabulary (cf. I.Efros, 'Some aspects of Yehudah Halevi's Mysticism' in *PAAJR*, XI, 1941, pp.27–41), his criticism of ascetic solitude in the *Kuzarî*, III: 1, pp.90–91, is most certainly directed against Sufism.
(4) Cf. G.Vajda, *La théologie ascétique de Bahya Ibn Paqouda*, Paris, 1947, and A.Lazaroff, in *JJS*, XXI, 1970, pp.11–38. However, much new material has come to

light since the publication of these studies.
(5) *Hidāya*, p.26.
(6) Cf. *Inkišāf al-asrār wa-ẓuhūr al-anwār*, ed. A.S. Halkin, Jerusalem, 1964, p.258, and *Risāla*, II, pp.614–5. G.Vajda had suggested (in *REJ*, CXXIV, p.187) Daylami's *'Atf al-alīf* as a source for these definitions.
(7) Cf. A.S. Halkin in *PAAJR*, XIV, 1944, pp. 120, 146. See also p.67.
(8) It is indeed a moot point whether or not Maimonides himself was influenced by Sufi trends and it seems obvious in view of his extensive Arabic culture that he at least had knowledge of them. On the other hand many of his ideas, especially in the concluding chapters of the *Guide*, could be of Sufi provenance. A. Heschel, who discussed several points of similarity in doctrine, had intended to devote a study to the subject, cf. his article in the *L. Ginzberg Jubilee Volume*, (Hebr. sec.) p.186. It is also clear from Maimonides' *Ṯamāniya fuṣūl*. Ch. IV (Arabic text, ed. Wolff, p.10) that there already were Jewish Sufis in his day. He expresses disapproval of the excesses of Sufi practice and rebukes 'those of our co-religionists ... who imitate the followers of other religions ... when they torment their body.' (tr. J. Gorfinkle, New York, 1912, p.64). On the previous page Maimonides gives details of some of those practices (p.62): 'When at times some of the pious ones deviated to one extreme by fasting, keeping nightly vigils, refraining from eating meat or drinking wine, renouncing marriage, clothing themselves in woollen and hairy garments, dwelling in the mountains and wandering about in the wilderness, they did so partly because of the immorality of the townspeople ... when the ignorant observed saintly men acting thus, not knowing their motives, they considered their deeds of themselves virtuous and so blindly imitating their acts, thinking thereby to become like them, chastised their bodies with all kinds of afflictions imagining that they had acquired perfection and moral worth and that by this means man would approach nearer to God, as if He hated the human body and desired its destruction ...' Even if this account is a projection into the past, at least some of Maimonides' examples are taken from contemporary Sufi practices.
(9) Cf. G. Scholem, *Les Origines de la Kabbale*, Paris, 1966, pp.244–6, 270. Although quite distinct, these two movements can be construed as a simultaneous attempt to revive an ancient theosophical ideal.
(10) Cambridge University Library, *T–S* 10 Ka1.1., published by H. Hirschfeld in *JQR*, XV, pp.176–7, 180; notes thereon by I. Goldziher, ibid., pp.526–8. Cf also *T–S* 8 Ka 3, sayings by al-Hallāǧ, published by Hirschfield, ibid., p.181, and *ENA*2462, f° 55, poems by al-Ḥallāǧ and other Sufi authors.
(11) *T–S* Arabic 43.190 and 309, and *BM* Or. 5554 B, f° 11. *T–S* Arabic 37.78 is the beginning of Ibn Sina's mystical treatise *Al-Kalima al-Ilāhiyya*.
(12) *T–S* Arabic 43.247, a page from as-Suhrawardī's *Kalimat at-Taṣawwuf*; NS 223.9, some of his sayings together with a mystical poem; Kaufmann Genizah Collection 205[b], a mystical litany by the same; *T–S* Arabic 44.201, quotation from Abū Ḥafs as-Suhrawardī, on *raqṣ*, 'the ecstatic dance.'

(13) *T–S* Arabic 51.52, eight pages from an unidentified Sufi treatise on love transcribed into Hebrew characters. Kaufmann Genizah 205[e], *Lawāmi' anwār al-qulūb*, a more complete manuscript of which, also in Hebrew characters, is to be found in the Vatican Library, cf. Levi Della Vida, *Elenco ... della Bibl. Vat.*, p.281, no. 32, sec. 3.
(14) *T–S* 8 Ka 6.4, a mystical poem by al-Ġazzālī, sometimes ascribed to al-Ḥallāǧ, as in *Bodl.* Heb. e. 76, f° 62, was edited by H. Hirschfeld in 'A Hebreo-Sufic poem' in *JAOS* XLIX, 1929, pp.168–73. The same poem is to be found in *Bodl.* Heb. e. 98 f° 105, together with other mystical poems of (Jewish) Sufi origin, some of which were published by S.M. Stern in *JQR*, L, pp.355–7; *T–S* 8 Ka 3, published by H.Hirschfeld, in *JQR*, XV, p.181, also contains a quotation from al-Ġazzālī's *Munqiḏ min aḍ-Ḍalāl*; a larger fragment of the latter written in a most elegant hand is to be found in *Bodl.* Heb. d.58, f[os] 64–72. Furthermore *T–S* Misc. 29.29 contains a fragment of his *Kimiya' as-Sa'āda*. In a Genizah letter dealing with a purchase of Hebrew and Arabic books (*T–S* NS 264.22) among the titles mentioned is al-Ġazzālī's esoterical treatise *al-Maḍnūn 'alā ġayr ahlih*. For an idea of al-Ġazzālī's extensive influence on Jewish thought, see article *Ghazali* in *EI*[2], vol. 7, 538–40, and Steinschneider, *Hebräische Uebersetzungen*, pp.296–348.
(15) E.g. *T–S* Arabic 41.1, a correspondence between the two Sufi masters Abū l-Ḥusayn an-Nūrī and al-Ǧunayd.
(16) E.g. *T–S* 10 J 13.14, a letter from the Pietists of Alexandria to Abraham Maimonides; *T–S* 12.289, a letter of reproach to a follower of Abraham Maimonides, both published by S.D. Goitein, in 'Rabbi Abraham Maimonides and his Pietist Circle' in *Tarbiẓ*, XXXIII, pp.181–97. *T–S* 13 J 9.12, a letter from Benjamin, a Pietist, to Rabbi Ḥayyim, published by E. Ashtor, *Jews in Egypt and Syria*, vol. III, pp.28–32. *T–S* 20.148, a letter in Hebrew to Rabbi Abraham he-Ḥasīd, discussed by the present writer in *JSS*, XXVI, 1981.
(17) E.g. *BNU* MS. Heb. 4110, f° 69, a *ḏikr* arranged according to the hours of the day. *ENA* 3523, f° 1, a confession.
(18) E.g. *T–S* Arabic 44.3 and 47.58 on Prayer; and *BNU* MS. Heb. 4110, f° 61 on 'renouncement' (*taḥallī*).
(19) E.g. *Bodl.* Heb. f. 106, f° 755–7 and *T–S* Arabic 43.78 are both part of a compendium describing the degrees of *tawḥīd, zuhd* and *maḥabba*, quoting al-Ǧunayd, aš-Šiblī and other Sufi authorities. *ENA* 2943.36, definitions of *murāqaba* and *mušāhada* for novices (*murīdīn*). Quite remarkably this MS. seems to be a copy of Ma'mar al-Isfahāni's *Nahǧ al-Ḫāṣṣ*, of which only one other MS. is recorded to exist. Cf. S. de Beaurecueil, in *Mélanges Taha Hussein*, Cairo, 1962, pp.46–76.
(20) *Bodl.* Heb. c. 28, f°s 45–6, published by S.D. Goitein, in *JJS*, X, pp.105–114.
(21) MS. *Bodl.* Hunt. 382 f° 7b, *sulūk dereḵ ha-ḥasīdūt* 'traversing the Path of Piety.'
(22) Ibid., f°s 46b, 54a and 56a. Also *dereḵ ha-šem*, f°s 10b, 25b, 38a. See also *T–S*

NS 189.9v, *al-maqām aš-šarīf a'anī mĕsillō la-šem.*
(23) *Ḥawḍīyya*, f° 18b. *Kifāya*, I, p.146 and II, p.44 etc.
(24) On the latter see S. Safrai 'The teachings of Pietists in Mishnaic Literature', in *JJS* XVI, pp.15–33. Baḥya, *Hidāya*, III:4 p.149, interestingly equates the *ḥasīd* with the highest degree of devotion, that of the 'prophets and saints.'
(25) Their example is often evoked in support of their new reforms, e.g. the author of a chapter on prayer, *T–S* AS 165.135, quotes the authority of 'the first *ḥasidîm* who would tarry an hour before prayer that they may direct their hearts to God.' (*Mišnāh Bĕrākōt* V).
(26) MS. Hunt. 382 f°s 4b–6b, *vide infra*, note 86.
(27) In his explanation of Ex. XXIII:3 'neither shalt thou favour a poor man (*dal*) in his cause,' quoted by Abraham Maimonides (*Comm.*, p.361), Rabbi Abraham he-Ḥasīd interprets the verse to refer to the Pietists, as if the Hebrew word *dal* were the equivalent of the Sufi term *faqīr*, cf. Wieder p.36. In MS. *BNU* 4110, f° 61b, which we have reason to believe is also from Abraham he-Ḥasīd, the Pietists are referred to as *mĕbaqqĕšē ha-šem*, 'seekers of the Lord,' equivalent of the Sufi term *ṭālib*.
(28) *Kifāya*, I, p.134. See also *Guide*, III 53, Qāfiḥ, p.687.
(29) *T–S* K15.68, published in *Tarbiẓ* XXXIII, pp.181–4. Yōsef b. Šĕlōmōh ha-Lēvi, the scribe of this document, is known to us from other Pietist's writings; he is also the author of *T–S* NS 98.20 and *Bodl.* Heb. f.61, f°10, both of which are dated 1298.
(30) On the latter see A. Obadyah, *Sinai*, II, pp.96–98; Wieder, pp.32–37. His newly discovered writings are dealt with in our 'Some Judaeo-Arabic fragments of Rabbi Abraham he-Ḥasīd, the Jewish Sufi' in *JSS*, XXVI, pp. 47–72, 1981. These include a mystical treatise on gnosis, which, as suggested in our article, may be identical with a lost work which bore the typically Sufi title *Tāğ al-'Ārifīn*, 'The Diadem of the Gnostics.' Although this work is attributed to Abraham Maimonides by the chronicler Yōsef Sambarī (cf. *Mediaeval Jewish Chronicles,* ed. A. Neubauer, Oxford, I, p.134), the latter may have confused the two scholars both of whom were called Abraham he-Ḥasīd.
(31) *Kifāya*, II, p.290, according to Leningrad MS.
(32) In a Genizah letter, *T–S* 20.44, he is referred to as 'the head of the Pietists.'
(33) The writer has recently discovered in the Genizah fragment *T–S* Arabic 43.372, a page from the missing third chapter of the *Kifāya*, 'On communion', which concluded the fourth part of the work. A large part of this work has unfortunately been lost. Part of the surviving fragments have been edited by S.Rosenblatt, see bibliography for details.
(34) *Kifāya* II, p.320.
(35) Ibid., p.266.
(36) Ibid., p.322.
(37) The Prophet's Companions are always included in Sufi historiographies. See

also J.S. Trimingham, *The Sufi Orders in Islam*, 1973, p.72.
(38). *Kifāya*, I, p.146, II, p.324, *Ḥawḍīyya* f° 22b and MS. Hunt. 382, f° 4b 'he who attains perfection is called a "man of piety" and a "disciple of the prophets"' and f° 26b, 'the path of piety and the disciples of the prophets.' Cf. the use of the expression in *Hidāya*, p.374, *Kuzarī*, III:1, p.91 and *Yĕsōdē ha-Tōrāh*, VII:5.
(39) *Kifāya*, II, p.298. The Leningrad MS reads 'were pious and could be of the degree of Prophets.'
(40) *Kuzarī*, I: 47, 95, 103. Cf. I. Goldziher in *REJ*, L, pp.32–41. On the kindred theory of the 'Muhammadan light' see *idem* in *Zeitschrift für Assyriologie*, XX, pp.328–36 and Rubin in *IOS*, V, pp.62–119.
(41) Rabbi Abraham he-Ḥasīd, quoted in *Comm.*, p.379, adduces Ex. XXIV:10 'They saw the God of *Israel*' (i.e. Jacob.) as an indication that the Israelites had reintegrated the patriarchal tradition at Sinai. Cf. our article in *JSS*, XXVI.
(42) *T–S* Arabic 18 (1). 179. It is quite clear from the vocabulary employed that the source of this Pietist doctrine is Yĕhūdāh ha-Lēvi's *Kuzarî*.
(43) *T–S* Arabic 16.60. Incidentally, an Arabic (Pietist) translation of Ex. XIX:6 conserved in *ENA* 2406.11 renders 'kingdom of priests' as 'kingdom of saints' (*awliyā'*). Cf. *Comm.* p.303.
(44) Joel XI:1
(45) *Iggeret Tĕmān*, ed. A. Halkin, New York, 1952, p.80. Cf. A. Heschel in *Louis Ginzberg Jubilee Volume*, New York, 1945, (Heb. sec.) pp.183 ff. An indication of the popularity of this belief is afforded by the Yemenite scholars cited by Halkin (*op. cit.*, p.xii), one of whom even considered Maimonides as the awaited renovator. Cf. also G. Cohen in *PAAJR*, XXXVI, p.55. The fragment *T–S* NS 164.159 is a popuar speculation on this Maimonidean tradition; while most significant in this context is al-Ḥarīzī's laudative praise of Maimonides in *ENA* 7025 f°s 16–18, (quoted by S.Stern in *Hagūt 'ibrīt bĕ-Europāh*, ed. M. Zohori and A. Tartakower, Tel Aviv 1969, p.95), 'he was among the few saints (*awliyā'*) who have approached the degree of prophecy.' It is noteworthy also that a similar Muslim tradition held that prophecy was to be restored in Islam in the year 500 of the Hiğrah. Indeed al-Ġazzālī (*ob.*1111) saw his Sufi inspired 'Revival of the religious sciences' as a renovation of Islam, while the great Sufi philosopher Ibn 'Arabī, (*ob.*1240) who bore the title *Muḥyī d-Dīn* 'Reviver of Religion', was later to consider himself the last of the saints (*ḫātim al-awliyā'*).
(46) *Kifāya*, I, p.138. *Comm.*, p.325, 'only the perfect ones among your descendants may attain (the ways of prophecy).' The more immediate aim however of the Pietist movement was to attract back to the Jewish fold the intellectual dissidents. Their use of Sufi teachings was in no way a concession to Islamic inroads, as G. Cohen would have it (*PAAJR*; XXXVI, p.54) for they sincerely believed the tenets of Sufism to have been of Jewish origin. The most eloquent indication of this is Abraham Maimonides' use of purely Jewish sources in the exposition of his Sufi-inspired doctrines, in contrast to Baḥya's great dependence on Islamic models.

(47) *Kifāya*, I, p.142. No doubt this ternary corresponds to the Sufi *maḥāfa*, *maḥabba*, *ma' rifa*, 'fear', 'love' and 'gnosis'.
(48) Cf. G. Vajda, 'La pensée religieuse de Maimonide, unité ou dualité', *Cahiers de Civilisation Médiévale*, IX, pp.29–49, and I. Twersky, 'Some non-Halakhic aspects of the Mishneh Torah' in *Jewish Medieval and Renaissance Studies*, pp.95–118.
(49) *Kifāya* I, p.145.
(50) Published by S.D. Goitein, in *JJS*, XVI, pp.105–114.
(51) Cf. S.D. Goitein, 'New documents from the Cairo Genizah' in *Homenaje a Millas Vallicrosa*, Barcelona, 1954, I, pp.707–720.
(52) Some of the practices mentioned here have already been discussed in masterly fashion by Wieder, whose *Islamic Influences on the Jewish Worship* first brought attention to this aspect of the Pietist movement.
(53) Cf. Wieder, p.10 ff. and S. Eppenstein, in *Festschrift Israel Lewy*, Breslau, 1911, pp.42–43. 'Obadyāh twice mentions the act of ablution in his *Ḥawḍiyya* (f° 8b) 'if he be not in need of immersion then let him carry out the ablution of hands and feet in order that the natural heat circulate in the body and arouse thereby the soul' and (f° 19b) 'for this reason it is fitting to prepare oneself before (prayer) with the ablution of one's hands and feet so that the soul may be aroused and restored.' See also *T–S* AS 161.34, 'ablution of the hands and feet.'
(54) Cf. Wieder, p.68. Several types of prostration were distinguished and enacted at special prayers such as the *qaddiš, qĕdūšāh, bārkū*, etc. Cf. Wieder, p.47 ff. In addition the Pietists would remain standing in parts of the liturgy where the custom would be to remain seated. Thus Abraham Maimonides states in the *Kifāya* (Eppenstein, *loc.cit.*, p.53) in connection with the *qaddiš* 'At every *qaddiš*, I choose to stand in honour of the glory of His name. Others have followed me in this and in respect of other parts of the liturgy, as I have explained. The first to have acted thus was Rabbi Abraham he-Ḥasîd, of blessed memory, and indeed to conduct oneself in this manner is in keeping with the fear of His Name.' It is apparent from the Genizah document *T–S* Arabic 51.111, published by Goitein in the article referred to in note 51, that the profusion of bowings and prostrations was one of the aspects of Pietist practice that met with distinct disapproval in conservative circles.
(55) Wieder, pp.65–67.
(56) Ibid., pp.79–82.
(57) Ibid., pp.45 and *Kifāya*, II, p.404.
(58) As a conscious departure from Muslim custom, the normal practice in Oriental Jewish houses of prayer is to sit along the walls, cf. Wieder, pp.68–78. Moreover Abraham Maimonides mentions that he had introduced this practice together with Rabbi Abraham he-Ḥasīd, cf. Wieder, p.93.
(59) *T–S* Glass 20.44. Another letter emanating from the group alludes to the same practice, *T–S* 10 J 13.8, published by Goitein in *Tarbiẓ*, XXXIII, p.187, 'and the

group who fast and stand in prayer.'

(60) On Baḥya's recommendation of nocturnal vigils see *Hidāya*, pp.390–1.

(61) *Kifāya*, II, p.417.

(62) *Hidāya*, p.331.

(63) This term, which signifies direct knowledge of God, was extensively employed by al-Ġazzālī, e.g. *Kimiyā' as-sa'āda*, pp.16–17. Cf. Trimingham, *The Sufi Orders*, p.136, and the relevant references in note 2.

(64) *T–S* 13 J 9.12, published by E. Ashtor, *History of the Jews in Egypt*, vol. III, 1970, pp.28–32. Both he and Goitein, (*Tarbiẓ*, XLI, pp.77–79) failed to recognize the mystical significance of this letter, whose Pietist author was an acquaintance of 'Obdayāh Maimonides, as we shall presently see, cf. note 6, p.66. On the significance of journeying (*safar*) in Sufism see *Iḥyā'*, II:7, p.244, *'Awārif al-ma 'ārif*, Ch. 26–7. A fragment dealing with the journeys of the Prophets is conserved in *ENA* 2160.3.

(65) *'Awārif al-ma 'ārif*, Ch. XXVI. Cf. also the article *khalwa* in *EI²*, IV, 990–991 (Landolt), and E.Bannerth 'Dhikr et Khalwa d'après Ibn 'Ata Allah' in *Mélanges de l'Institut Dominicain des Etudes Orientales*, XII, 1974, pp.65–90. In Jewish, as in Islamic tradition, the number forty corresponds to spiritual or physical maturity, as in the forty days required for the formation of a foetus (cf. *BT Niddah*, 30b). Thus the *'arba'īn* symbolize the rebirth of the devotee. For a further interpretation of Moses' sojourn in the mountain, see H. Corbin, *Trilologie Ismaelienne*, Paris, 1961, p.181.

(66) M. Berger, *Islam in Egypt today*, Cambridge, 1970, pp 83–4. Cf. also E.W. Lane, *The Modern Egyptians*, end of Ch. X.

(67) On this synagogue see S.Assaf, *Texts and Studies*, Jerusalem, 1946, pp.155–62. Abū Ṣāliḥ in his *Churches and Monasteries of Egypt*, translated by B. Evetts, Oxford, 1895, f° 67a, mentions that this synagogue indeed had lodgings attached to it. N. Golb (*JNES*, XXIV, pp.255–6) has suggested that they were for wayfarers. It is possible that they were cells for meditation. It is known that 'Obadyāh Maimonides died in the Dammūh synagogue, where he could well have retired in order to practice *ḫalwa*. It can be inferred from the words of Abraham Maimonides [(*Kifāya*, II, p.392) 'Now as for retirement in houses and places of worship and so forth, the first to assume that . . . was our father Jacob'] that retirement to places of worship was practised in his day too.

(68) E.g. the Ġarība synagogue on the island of Djerba.

(69) *Kifāya*, II, p.418, 'This path is the last of the elevated paths and is contiguous with communion . . . and that which is last is considered more important than all ' Cf. *BT Mĕgillah* 32a. There is an error in Rosenblatt's translation.

(70) This distinction is already made by Baḥya, *Hidāya*, IX:3 pp.360–3. Abraham Maimonides' definition of internal seclusion comes very close to that of al-Ġazzālī in his *Iḥyā'*, II:6, p.227, 'internal seclusion is the emptying of the heart and thought of all else except Allah and their being filled with Him', *Kifāya*, II, p.384. Cf.

Comm., p.307.

(71) Quoted by Abraham Maimonides, *Kifāya*, II, p.418. This interpretation is also quoted in the name of Abraham he-Ḥasīd in the remains of a chapter on *ḫalwa* preserved in *T–S* NS285.10. On this aspect of *ḫalwa*, see *Iḥyā'*, III:2, p.76: 'The senses can be curbed properly by seclusion (*ḫalwa*) in a dark place, or, short of that, by wrapping his head in his garment', and *Ğāmi'a al ḥaqā'iq*, p.35, 'the first step toward communion (*wuṣūl*) is to sojourn in a dark room.'

(72) Abraham Maimuni, *Responsa*, ed. A. Freimann, Jerusalem, 1937, no. XXX, p.39, and *Kifāya*, II, p.394. Cf. *supra* note 67. It is interesting to note that until recent times, incubation was practised in the crypt of the so-called Maimonides Synagogue situated in the former Jewish Mousky quarter of Cairo.

(73) '*ḏikr* of the tongue', not that of the 'heart', which would be practised during *ḫalwa*.

(74) Extremely significant in this respect is a Genizah letter, *BM* Or. 5542.13, published by Goitein in *Jewish Education in Muslim Countries*, Jerusalem, 1962, pp.60–1, in which a schoolmaster strongly denies the accusation that he conducted a *zuhdī*, a Sufi dance, with his pupils. On the other hand the communal singing of Jewish litanies in both Hebrew and Arabic was not uncommon and the later ceremony of the *baqqašōt*, adopted in Egypt and elsewhere under the impulse of the Qabbalistic liturgy, incorporated many Sufi elements as we have pointed out in our articles 'Baqqašōt d'Orient et d'Occident,' *REJ*, CXXXIV, pp.101–121, and 'Attitudes to Music in the Later Qabbālāh,' Paper read at the *Seventh World Congress of Jewish Studies*, Jerusalem, 1977, Music section.

(75) *T–S* Arabic lb.27, published in our article 'Some Judaeo-Arabic fragments of Rabbi Abraham he-Ḥasīd' in *JSS*, XXVI, pp.47–72, 1981.

(76) Cf. *BT Bĕrākōt*, 33b.

(77) *Ḥawḍiyya*, f° 27a–b. The last part of the passage is the only certain quotation from Sufi sources that we have been able to locate. It is a saying generally attributed to the mystic al-Ḥasan al-Qazzāz. Cf. *Risāla* I, pp.265–6, *Luma'*, p.301. Al-Ġazzālī (*Iḥyā'*, II:2, p.76) reports that these virtues are the attributes of the saints (*abdāl*).

(78) *Ḥawḍiyya*, f° 14a–b. Cf. also *Kifāya*, II, pp.264 and 278, where Abraham states that 'the prophets condescended to marriage lest their celibacy be emulated by the people and bring about the extinction of mankind'. It seems that David Maimonides also subscribed to this attitude. Cf. *Midraš Rabbi David*, I, p.101, 'since man does not attain perfection (*kamāl* in the Arabic) until he has reached the age of forty, which is the age of maturity (*sinn al-wuqūf*, the second after-growth, *sinn an-numū* of the four traditional stages of man). Consequently Abraham sought a wife for Isaac only after he had reached perfection and attained the age of forty years.' Cf. *supra*, note 65.

(79) On Baḥya see *Théologie*, p.109. On Sufi opposition to marriage see al-Huğwīrī, *Kašf al-Maḥğūb*, trans. Nicholson, pp.360–6 and *Iḥyā'*, II:2 p.33.

(80) *Kifāya*, II, p.266, 'We have adopted in emulation of them (the Sufis) the wearing of sleeveless garments and the like.'

(81) *Ḥawḍiyya*, f°s 22a and 22b. See also the article on *taqīya* by Goldziher in *ZDMG*, LX, p.213–226.

(82) See Introduction, pp.44–46.

(83) From their letter *T–S* 10 J 13.14 published by Goitein in *Tarbiẓ*, XXXIII, pp.184–6, it seems that they were also the object of strong opposition on the part of the local communal dignitaries. See also Abraham's *Responsa*, ed. Freimann and Goitein, no. LXII, pp.62ff., for another letter addressed to him concerning Pietist practice.

(84) *Kifāya*, I, p.125.

(85) *T–S* 8J26.19, published by Goitein in *JQR*, XLIV, pp.41–49.

(86) Cf. Wieder, p.57–64.

(87) Al–Ḥarizī mentions a Pietist of Bagdad, 'Amram al-Hītī, who practised *ṣiyām wa-qiyām*. Cf. S.M. Stern in *Sĕfunot*, VIII, p.153.

(88) *Fawāt al-wafayāt*, I, pp.123–5, translated by I. Goldziher, 'Ibn Hud the Mohammadan mystic and the Jews of Damascus' in *JQR*, VI, pp.218–20. Cf. Goitein, *JQR*, XLIV, 39–40. Furthermore 'Abd as-Sayyid al-Isra'īlī, the famous physician of Damascus (*ob.* 1315), was reported to have had theological discussions with a Sufi šayḫ before his conversion to Islam, cf. I. Goldziher in *REJ*, LX, p.38.

(89) MS. Hunt. 382, which has been briefly but penetratingly analysed by F. Rosenthal, 'A Judaeo-Arabic work under Sufic influence' in *HUCA*, XV, pp.433–484. His sources and mystical exegesis well deserve a further study. Among his Sufi sources the following are the most outstanding: as-Sarraǧ's *Kitab al-Luma'*, Suhrawardī's *Hikmat al-Išrāq* and *Kalimat at-Taṣawwuf*, al-Ġazzali's *Iḥyā'* and the Andalusian Sufi Ibn 'Arīf's *Maḥāsin al-Maǧālis* (his reflection on patience, *sabr*, in MS. *Hunt.* 489, f° 49b, is taken from *Maḥāsin*, see the edition by Asín Palacios, Paris, 1933, pp.80–81).

(90) Rosenthal gives a late date for this author whom he surmises is of Syrian origin. Another of his works is preserved in MS. Hunt. 489, further fragments of which have been discovered by the present writer in the Genizah which could date from the 'classical period'. If this were the case then the interest of this mystico-philosophical treatise, which bridges the gap between the Pietist movement and the writings of the early Qabbalists, would be considerably enhanced. F° 148a–b, wherein the words of 'Obadyāh Maimonides are quoted, corresponds, for example, with the Genizah fragment *T–A* AS 163.23–26.

(91) E.g. Zĕkaryāh b. Sulaymān in his commentary on the *Song of Songs* in *Ḥameš Mĕgillōt*, ed. Qāfiḥ, Jerusalem, 1962, p.27, and Ḥōṭer aḍ-Ḍamāri in both his *Commentary on Maimonides' Thirteen Principles*, ed. D. Blumenthal, pp.336–338 and his *Sirāǧ al-'uqūl*, ed. Kohut, p.40.

(92) Cf. M. Idel, *Abraham Abulafia's works and doctrine*, Doctoral thesis, Hebrew University, 1976, p.257.

(93) *mĕḥīqāh*, which is the equivalent of the Sufi term *maḥw*. Cf. *Luma'* p.355 and al-Kāšānī, *Dictionary of the Technical Terms of the Sufis*, ed. A. Sprenger, Calcutta, 1845, p.53–56. This passage is quoted from the work *Ša'arē Ṣedeq*, thought to have been composed in the East. Cf. G. Scholem, *KS*, I, pp.127–8 and *idem, Major Trends in Jewish Mysticism*, New York, 1961, p.147.

(94) Jellinek was the first to point out the influence of Sufism on Isaac of Acco in his *Beiträge zur Geschichte der Kabbalah*, Berlin, 1852, II, pp.45–7, 'Sufismus und Kabbalah'. Indeed Isaac's doctrine of solitary devotion (*hitbōdĕdūt*) set out in both his *Mĕ'īrat 'Eynayīm* (ed. Erlanger, Jerusalem, 1975, pp.281–2) and his *'Oṣar ḥayyim*, while containing techniques of a universal nature, utilizes a particular vocabulary that betrays a Sufi source. For example his definition of *hitbōdĕdūt*, quoted from the *'Oṣar ḥayyim* by E. Gottlieb in *Proceedings of the IVth World Congress for Jewish Studies*, 1969, II, p.330, is identical with the traditional Sufi definition of *ḥalwa*: 'those that practise solitary contemplation endeavour to extinguish their corporeal senses and divest their soul of the thought of all sensible objects, clothing it with the spirituality of the intellect'. Cf. *supra* note 70 and G. Scholem, *Major Trends in Jewish Mysticism*, pp.96–7.

The anecdote concerning *hištawwūt* (equanimity in the face of blame or praise, in Arabic, *istiwā'*) that Isaac adduces in the name of the oft-quoted but otherwise unknown Qabbalist, Rabbi Abner, originates in al-Makki's Sufi manual *Qūt al-qulūb*, II, pp.547–8, where the 'virtuous man', referred to by Isaac, is in fact the Prophet Muḥammad, although the selfsame anecdote is also to be found in Baḥya's *Hidāya*, V:5, p.246. It is not impossible that Isaac gleaned his ideas on solitude directly from Sufi sources, since he had a good knowledge of Arabic, as is proven by his translation and commentary of Yĕhūdāh Ibn Malka's *Uns al-ġarīb*, although doubt about their attribution to him is expressed by G. Vajda in *REJ*; CXV, pp.25–6. His ideas on *hitbodĕdūt* enjoyed a certain amount of popularity among his successors and demonstrate quite strikingly the penetration of Sufi doctrine into the later Qabbālāh. As has already been pointed out by G. Scholem in his *Kitĕbē Yad ba-Qabbālāh*, Jerusalem, 1930, pp.225–30, al-Buṭīnī's (*ob.* 1519) theory of meditation found in his *Sullam ha- 'aliyāh* (*Ladder of Ascension*, a title which in itself smacks of Sufism, cf. *infra* note 25 on the Translation) were borrowed from Isaac, who may also have been the source of Yōsef Caro's (*ob.* 1575) quotation of the *hištawwūt* anecdote in his *Maggid Mēšarīm* (pericope *bĕšalaḥ*, ed. Vilna, 1875, p.38). On the other hand Elijah de Vidas in his *Re'šīt ḥokmah* (II:3, edn. Venice, 1613, f°. 82b), written in 1575, explicitly cites Isaac in his discussion of *hitbodĕdūt*. The same author (III:4, edn. cit., f° 93a), quoting perhaps from Isaac's *'Oṣar ḥayyim*, relates in the latter's name another anecdote, the Hebrew of which is manifestly based on an Arabic original, about the lover who through 'solitary meditation and extreme desire divested his soul of sensible forms and united with the intelligibilia.' He goes on to say that among other tales of the saints, Isaac mentions the (Sufi) idea that 'he who hath not loved a woman hath no phenomenal model for worship of

God.' Cf. Ibn 'Arabī, *Fuṣuṣ al-ḥikam*, XXVII, ed. 'Afīfī, p.217: 'The contemplation of God through woman is the most perfect of contemplations.' Cf. also *al-Futūḥāt al-Makkiyya*, Ch. CVIII, p.251. Another outstanding Qabbalist and moralist, Eli'ezer Azikri (*ob.* 1600), in the concluding chapter of his *Sefer ha-Ḥarēdīm* (edn. Lublin, 1909, p.101) advocates solitude and invokes the authority of Isaac of Acco 'who relates that several saintly persons were wont to practise solitude in his time.' Finally, Ḥayyim Vital (*ob.* 1620) may have had Isaac's testimony in mind when he refers in the introduction to his *Šaʻarē qĕdūšāh*, to the 'early Pietists who followed the ways of the prophets, remaining aloof from their fellow men, some in caves and in the wilderness and some in the solitude of their houses.' An anonymous Qabbalistic treatise on contemplation, combining Sufi and Qabbalistic elements, has been discussed by G. Scholem in his 'Note on a Kabbalistical Treatise on Contemplation' in *Mélanges Henry Corbin*, Teheran, 1978, pp.665–70.

(95) Quoted from the Paris MS. of his commentary on Genesis by G. Vajda in *AHDLMA*, XXIII, p.135. The extraordinary figure of Sarmad (*ob.* 1661), the Persian Jew who became a wandering Sufi in India, lies beyond the scope of the present survey. On him see W. Fischel in *PAAJR*, XVIII, pp.137–77. Likewise the Persian Sufi sect which J. Wolff mentions in his *Narrative of a Mission to Bokhara*, London, 1845, I, p.11 and II, p.181, and his *Research and Missionary Labours among the Jews*, London, 1835, pp.128–384, lies outside our scope. On the latter see M. Weinstein, 'A Hebrew Qur'an manuscript' in *Studies in Bibliography and Booklore*, X, 1971, pp.19–52, especially, pp.19–20. Suffice it to say that the copying into Hebrew characters of Persian Sufi poetry, such as that of Rūmi and Sa'adī, greatly contributed to the circulation of Sufi ideas amongst Persian Jews.

(96) *'Omer ha šikḥāh*, Leghorn, 1748, f° 135a.

(97) See our article, 'A Jewish Sufi on music' in *Yuval*, IV, and the articles referred to in note 74 above. A. Danon, in *Šīrē Yisrā'el be-ereṣ ha-qedem*, ed. B. ben Yōsef, Constantinople, 1921, pp.8–10, contends that the proficiency of Eastern Jews in music was stimulated and modelled after the Sufi orders in Turkey. Moreover certain later Qabbalists are known to have had regular contacts with Muslim mystics, such as the Moroccan Qabbalist, Ḥalīfa Ibn Malka (*ob. c.* 1750) as related in Y. Benaim, *Malkē Rabbānān*, Jerusalem, 1931, 80a. The outstanding mystic, Ḥayyim Vital (*ob.* 1620) relates in his diary that his theological discussions with Islamic dignitaries even prompted him to acquire a better grasp of the Arabic tongue, cf. *Sefer ha-ḥezyōnòt*, ed. A. Aešcoly, Jerusalem, 1954, pp.86, and 12, 37, 243.

(98) The Sabbatians later included certain Dervish poems in their mystical litanies which were conducted to the music used during Sufi ḏikrs. It seems, on the basis of Sabbatian tradition, that not only did Šabbatai Ṣĕbī himself take part in Dervish *ḏikrs*, but he was also acquainted with the great Sufi poet Niyāzī al-Miṣrī (*ob.* 1694) in whose *tekkiyyeh* he would stay during his visits to Constantinople. Cf. G. Scholem, in *Zion* VI, 1941, pp.143–4 and *idem Sabbatai Ṣevi: The Mystical Messiah*,

London, 1973, pp.836–7.
(99) The former in his *'Abodat ha-Lewi*, (cf. A. Harkavy in *Ḥadašim gam Yĕšanim*, X, Warsaw, 1896, p.78) and the latter in the introduction to his commentary on the *Midraš Rabbāh*, *Imrē Yōšer*, Warsaw, 1874.
(100) Despite their particularist nature, the Jewish writings of the time did engage the interest of Muslim readers as proves the above-mentioned instance of Ibn Hūd, who studied Maimonides' *Guide*, cf. *supra*, note 88. Indeed, even in Maimonides' lifetime, the *Guide* attracted the attention of no less a scholar than 'Abd al-Laṭīf al-Baġdādi (*ob*. 1231), who read the *Guide*, apparently in Hebrew characters, cf. Ibn Abi Uṣaybi'a, *'Uyūn al-aḫbar*, II, Cairo, 1884, pp.205–6. Likewise Yōsef Ibn Kaspī in his *Sefer ha-Mūsar* (ed. I. Last, Pressburg, 1903, p.70) relates in 1332 that the Muslims of Fez and other localities studied the *Guide* together with Jewish teachers in their Madrasas. The fact however that the Pietists' writings greatly depended on the exegesis of the Hebrew Bible and that they were written in the Judaeo-Arabic idiom, greatly restrained their possibility of influencing Muslim Sufis. With the disappearance of their adherents, there was even less likelihood that their works be translated into Hebrew. Notwithstanding the foregoing, it is nonetheless likely, as we have indeed seen, that some at least of their ascetic practices were assimilated by the nascent Qabbalistic trends.
(101) Indeed the growth of Qabbālāh, coupled with the decline in the mastery of the Classical Arabic idiom, account for the fact that the great intellectual activity inaugurated by the *'irfānī* school of Ibn 'Arabī and the *isrāqī* school of as-Suhrawardī *al-maqtūl* have left no imprint on the texts so far known, with the exception perhaps of the *Maqāla fī derek al-ḥasidūt*, whose combination of Qabbālāh and Sufism clearly indicates a significant turning point in Pietist thought.

'Obadyah Maimonides and the Treatise of the Pool

(1) Or in Arabic, 'Abdallah ibn Ibrāhīm Maymūnī. The name 'Obadyāh had been that of several forebears of the Maimonides family. Cf. Sa'adyah Ibn Danan's Chronicle in *Fas we-ḥākāmēhā*, ed. D. Obadyah, Jerusalem, 1979, vol. II, p.20. On David Maimonides, see A. Ashtor, *History of the Jews in Egypt*, I, pp.117–143.
(2) Cf. the Genizah memorial list (now *Bodl.* Heb. f.56 f° 69) published by A. Neubauer in *JQR*, III, p.559, and the list from Tripoli published in *ha-Ṣĕfirāh*, XIV, 1887, no.185, p.559, where 'Obadyāh is styled 'his honour and splendour, our dear master and teacher, 'Obadyāh the son of (Abraham) the Pious'. In his 'Genealogy of the Maimonides family' in *Alūmmāh*, Jerusalem, 1936, pp.17–25, A. Freimann has discussed a number of genealogical lists and particularly (p.17) Vatican, Neophyti 11, f° 125, whose account of 'Obadyāh reads as follows: 'The pious Rabbi 'Obadyāh was born on the eve of Sabbath at the New Moon of Nisan in the year 1539 Sel., and died on account of our numerous sins on Sabbath eve, just after night-

fall in the synagogue of Dimtah [read Dammūh] on the 12th of Šĕbaṭ, 1574 Sel. Thus he lived for 35 years less 50 days and was buried in Old Cairo beside his father.' A further list containing information about 'Obadyāh, with some inexactitudes, has been published from a Moussayef manuscript by A. Habermann in *Tarbiẓ*, XX, p.227.

(3) Extracts from his *Dibrē Yōsef* containing details about 'Obadyāh were published by A. Berliner, *Quellenschriften zur jüdischen Geschichte und Literatur*, I, Frankfurt-am-Main, 1896, p.10, and A. Neubauer, *Mediaeval Jewish Chronicles*, Oxford, 1887 (repr. Jerusalem, 1967), I, p.120 and p.135. These are discussed by Brann, *MGWJ*, XLIV, pp.18–19 and 138–9 in conjunction with a further memorial list from the Sulzberger collection, similar in content to the list quoted in the preceding note.

(4) On this synagogue see *supra*, note 67. Sambari however says nothing about his being buried in Cairo alongside his father. His brother David Maimonides was buried in Tiberias; at least that is where his tombstone was discovered this century. Cf. Assaf, *Texts and Studies*, p.14.

(5) E. Ashtor, *op. cit.*, p.169 and M. Steinschneider in *MGWJ*, XLV, p.133. Moses de Rietti in his commentary to his *Miqdaš Mĕ'at*, ed. Vienne, 1851, p.101, also credits 'Obadyāh with offspring, evidently mistaking him for one of David Maimonides' descendants who bore the same name. Cf. Freimann, *Alūmmāh*, p.20. Correct also A. Halkin, *EJ*², X, p.421.

(6) *T–S* 13 J 9.12, published by Ashtor, *op. cit.*, III, pp.28–32. Cf. *supra*, note 64. The letter is addressed to Rabbi Ḥayyim, whose father was a judge at David Maimonides' court and presumably also a Pietist. Greetings are sent to both David and 'Obadyāh.

(7) Cf. Goitein in *Tarbiẓ*, XII, pp.78–79. The same scholar has also found in *CUL* Or. 1080 J.179 what seems to be a letter of condolence to David Maimonides on the death of 'Obadyāh, in which there is an indication that there may have been a third brother, who, though a doctor, attained no rabbinical renown. See *Tarbiẓ*, XXXIV, pp.251–3.

(8) In several documents (e.g. *T–S* 12.152 and 13 J 9.12) David is designated as 'the Crown of the Pietists' and his son is likewise styled *he-Ḥasīd*, cf. Mann, *Texts*, I, p.425, n.24. The commentary on the *Pirqē Abōt*, published in Alexandria, 1901, (Cairo, 1932, Heb. trans. *Midraš Davīd*, Jerusalem, 1944) and ascribed to David Maimonides, has no mystical content. On the other hand, in his collection of sermons, *Midraš Rabbī David*, (first section published in Alexandria, 1914; tr. Jerusalem, 1947; Genesis and Exodus published in translation by A. Katsh, Jerusalem, 1964–8), David adduces philosophical and even mystical notions. Cf. ed. Katsh, I, p.2–3, his description of the *Perfect Man*, pp.49, 96. Cf. also A. Katsh, in *JQR* XLVII, pp.14–1, and *supra* p.61, note 78. Moreover, Katsh claims in his introduction to volume I, p.22–23, that David is the first mediaeval author to quote the Zōhar. However, the quotations in question could have originated in some midraš,

if they are not interpolations. Before a more definite reply can be given to his all-important question, a careful examination is required of all the midraš manuscripts of which there are many more than those enumerated by Katsh (Introduction pp.11–12): e.g. a complete MS. is to be found in *BNU* Heb. 4031–5 (dated 1476), an incomplete one in *T–S* Arabic 16.68, in addition to tens of pages disseminated throughout the Genizah. It is most noteworthy however that in the following generation knowledge of the Qabbālāh is already patent in the works of the Rabbis of the East. Indeed the doctrine of the *Sĕfīrōt* permeates both the *Tōrat ha-Minḥāh*, completed in the East before 1336 by Jacob as-Siqillī, who is thought to have been a disciple of David Maimonides (cf. E. Hurwitz in *Sinai*, LIX 1966, p.38) and Šem Tōb Ibn Ga'ōn's *Baddē ha-'Arōn*, completed in Safed in the year 1325. Besides its importance for the elements of popular philosophy it employs, David's exegetical method is of no mean interest in itself and now and again it will be evoked, for the elucidation of some of 'Obadyāh's interpretations.

(9) In *Der Israelit des Neunzehnten Jahrhunderts, Literaturblatt des Israeliten*, 1846, p.138. He had earlier mentioned the manuscript in his *Wissenschaftliche Zeitschrift für Jüdische Theologie*, V, 1846, p.443.

(10) In his article *Zur Literatur der Maimoniden* in *MGWJ*, XLV, pp.132–3, and in *Die Arabische Literatur der Juden*, p.225, n.161.

(11) 'The Mystical Doctrine of Rabbi Obadyah, grandson of Moses Maimonides' in *JJS*, VI, 1955, pp.213–225. Cf. also his 'Un opuscule inexistant d'aš-Šāḏilī' in *Arabica*, VIII, p.100 and *L'Amour de Dieu dans la Théologie juive du Moyen Age*, Paris, 1957, *Obadyah Maimonïde*, pp.147–8.

(12) See Steinschneider, *ALJ*, p.173–5 and the new information in our note 90, *supra* p.62.

(13) f° 148; by chance this reference to 'Obadyāh has also been preserved in a Cambridge Genizah fragment of this anonymous work, *T–S* AS 163.23.

(14) *Dibrē Yōsef*, ed. A. Neubauer, I, p.134.

(15) As already suggested by E. Wiesenberg in his introduction to *Comm.*, pp.40–43.

(16) A Sufi technical term meaning 'to grasp through mystical experience', Cf. *Risāla*, I, p.220. Moreover the term is frequently used by the Jewish Sufis to designate the esoteric sense of a verse. See nos. 47 and 58 of our 'Some Judaeo-Arabic Fragments, and H. Corbin, *L'Archange Empourpré*, pp.341–2. Apropos Gen. XXVII:39, Abraham Maimonides remarks (*Comm.*, p.83) 'this mystery (*sirr*) can only be comprehended by him who has intuition (*dawq*) of the sort that the prophets sought when they said (Ps. CXIX:66) "Teach mě a good reason (*ṭa'am*)."' More than once Abraham mentions in his *Responsa* that the Torah contains mysteries which are not to be freely divulged (No. 30, see also Nos. 16, 24 and 43). In the last responsum, he replies to a question on cosmology. 'The explanation of the true meaning (*ḥaqīqa*) of "firmament" and "water" above it, belongs to the secrets of the Torah and the mysteries of the account of Creation (*ma'aseh bĕre'šīt*). These

mysteries and the divulging of their doctrine are subject to conditions which are not fulfilled in the circumstances of the present responsum.' It is possible that Abraham is alluding to the Sufi symbolism bound up with the three worlds, cf. Wensinck, *On the relation between Ghazali's Cosmology and his Mysticism*, in *Med. Kon. Ak. Wetensch.* Amst., LXXV, no.6. Cf. also *Guide*, II:30, Qāfiḥ, p.383. Moses Maimonides claimed in the introduction to his third volume of the *Guide*, Qāfiḥ, p.449, that he had arrived at the comprehension of some of the esoterical mysteries of the Torah, the knowledge of which had practically disappeared. Cf. A. Altmann in *MGWJ*, LXXX, pp.305–330. It is not impossible that Abraham Maimonides and the Pietists identified the mysteries of the Torah with their own Jewish Sufi doctrines. Cf. Cohen, *PAAJR*, XXXVI, p.35.

(17) Both Moses (*Guide*, I:8, Qafiḥ, p.33) and Abraham Maimonides (*Kifāya*, II, pp.258, 410 and *Comm.*, p.313) invoke these verses as proof of the necessity of spiritual preparation. The Pietist author of *T–S* NS 189.9 likewise quotes the verse of Ecclesiastes, adding 'One must surely exercise caution when advancing along (the spiritual path) for every step could result either in supreme felicity or perdition.'

(18) The same warning is uttered by both Moses (*Guide*, I:5, Qāfiḥ p.33) and Abraham Maimonides (*Comm.*, p.311) and even David Maimonides (*Midraš Rabbi David*, II, 86). It is worth mentioning that Abraham (*Kifāya*, II, p.406) sees an allusion to the progressive advance of the devotee along the spiritual path from one spiritual station to another, in the verse (Ps. LXXXIV:7) 'They shall go from strength to strength.'

(19) Cf. *Guide*, III:12, Qāfiḥ p.486, and *Kifāya*, II, pp.144, 169, 318. Cf. *Hidāya*, p.371, *Midraš Rabbi David*, I, p.123.

(20) *Comm.*, p.67.

(21) *Ḥawḍiyya*, f° 25a, *Comm.*, p.58 and *Kifāya*, II, p.388.

(22) As we have seen, Baḥya regards monasticism as an extreme (*Hidāya*, 360–1) as does Maimonides in his introduction (*Ṯamānīya fuṣūl*, ed. Wolff, p.16) and *Commentary on Aboth* (II:5). However the latter admits in his *Guide*, III:51, Qāfiḥ, p.677, that seclusion and solitude (*ḫalwa wa-infirād*) are conducive to the love of God. *The Chapter on Beatitude*, p.17, proposes the following interpretation of Ps. XLV:14 'All the glory of the King's daughter is within', 'the perfection of the rational soul is accomplished through seclusion and solitude' (*bil-inqiṭā' wal-ḫalwa*). Rabbi Abraham he-Ḥasīd, quoted in *Comm.*, p.379, construes the spiritual preparation prior to the Sinaitic revelation as a supreme example of *ḫalwa*.

(23) *Kifāya*, II, p.318. Cf. *Hidāya*, p.373. On the following page Abraham quotes an interpretation of Rabbi Abraham he-Ḥasīd, who, in connection with the ragged garb of the prophets, specifically states that this 'resembles the attire of the Sufis in our day.'

(24) *Kifāya*, II, 264 and 320, *Ḥawḍiyya*, f° 14b.

(25) Cf. *Comm.*, p.53, and *supra* p.61, note 78.

(26) On the interpretation of 'house' as 'the body', cf. *Midraš Rabbi David*, I, p.3.

Further sources indicate that the Pietists infused the religious precepts with their own teachings. Fragments *T–S* NS 186.46 and NS 229.43 are all that remain of a beautifully written treatise that apparently dealt with the inner significance of the Jewish festivals. Thus the Sabbath was instituted to curb worldly preoccupations in order to give oneself over to worship and seclusion (*ḫalwa*), 'to delight in God's recollection (*ḏikr*) and to fill one's thoughts with Him.' The Day of Atonement is similarly a moment of withdrawal from worldly pursuits in order to devote oneself to acts of sincerity (*iḫlāṣ*) and to purge oneself of the 'impurity and veils of matter.' Similar conceptions of the inner meaning of the festivals are exposed by the Jewish Sufi author of MS. Hunt. 489, f°s 142–148 and the mystical treatise *Risālat al-asrār*, *Bodl.* Poc. 186, f°s 25–26.

(27) The personification of the 'evil instinct' as the enemy of the little city is indeed ancient and may already be found in Talmudic sources. Cf. *BT Nĕdārim*, 32b, *Qōhelet Rabbah* IX:22. 'Obadyāh takes his inspiration from Baḥya, *Hidāya*, V:5, p.233. Further references are given by Steinschneider, in *MGWJ*, XLV, pp.136–7.

(28) A kinship is here assumed between the Hebrew words *ḥamōr*, 'ass', and *ḥōmer*, 'matter'. A similar association is to be found in *Chapter on Beatitude*, p.15.

(29) Cf. *Guide*, I.2, Qāfiḥ, p.27.

(30) Cf. *Guide*, III:9, Qāfiḥ, p.474.

(31) Cf. *Guide*, III:51, Qāfiḥ, p.683. *Kifāya*, II, pp.146 and 158.

(32) *Ḥawḍiyya*, f° 7b. Muḥammad too is equated in Sufi sources with the Intellect; see note 44 on the Translation, p.120.

(33) Cf. *Exodus Rabba*, IX:10. A similar idea that dissipation can pervert a high spiritual state is expressed by the Qabbalist, Isaac of Acco, in his *'Oṣar ḥayyim*, f° 7a, quoted by E. Gottlieb in *Proceedings of the IV World Congress for Jewish Studies*, II, p.33 'all depends on one's thought; if the latter be attached (*dibbūq*) to any creature, even if it be a hidden spiritual being far superior to mundane creatures . . . this is but idolatry.' The passage follows on from Isaac's speculations on *hitbodĕdūt,* cf. *supra* note 94 p.63, and could well be of Sufi inspiration. The Qabbalist Ibn Malka also refers to the Cherubim in his *Uns al-ġarīb*, MS. *Bodl.* Or. 661, f°158b, the same MS. incidentally as the *Ḥawḍiyya*, as 'Matter (*hayūlā*) which causes the doubts that impede one's comprehension of the Divine.' Cf. *Judah ben Nissim*, p.32 and G. Vajda in *REJ*, CXV, p.54.

(34) *BT Yōmā'*, 75b. The Zōhar (*Bĕšalaḥ*, II, f° 61b) construes the Manna as a spiritual nourishment. Yōsef Ibn Ǧiqaṭilla's remarks are typical of mediaeval exegesis. Cf. his commentary on the *Guide*, printed in Abarbanel's *Šĕ'ēlōt Sā'ūl*, Venice, 1574, II, f° 27a; '"Man did eat the bread of the mighty" signifies an intellectual sustenance of supreme splendour that was created through the Divine Will and served to purify their intellects'. Cf. also *Midraš Rabbi David*, II, p.207.

(35) Maimonides already intimates (*Guide*, III:7, Qāfiḥ, p.464, and also *Guide*, II:47, Qāfiḥ, p.442) that this verse is vital to the understanding of the *Merkābāh* and that it is a figure of speech, without however specifying its interpretation.

'Obadyāh's thought must be close to that of Rabbi Abraham he-Ḥasīd who saw in the verse (*Bodl.* Heb. e. 74, cited in Wieder, pp.34–5) an allusion to 'the revelation of the intelligible world . . . the rending of the veils and the illumination of the individual by the lights from the realm of Holiness.'

(36) 'Obadyāh says of the termination of the Exile that it will be (*Ḥawḍiyya*, f° 25a) a time when conjunction (*ittiṣāl*) and perfection (*kamāl*) will be made possible. A strange interpretation of the Messianic era is set forth in the *Kifāya*, II, pp.406–8. Herein Abraham conceives of the rebuilding of the Temple, which is to be rebuilt as the place of *ḫalwa*, *par excellence*, in which it will be possible to achieve the ultimate state of prophetic communion (*wuṣul nabawī*).

(37) Cf. *Comm.*, p.71, where this enigmatic statement is to be found: 'The name of the well was *'eseq*, "occupation", and in this is a great mystery, for in spite of their great wealth, the Patriarchs were not concerned with worldly affairs. Their real preoccupation, and inner devotion in which their time was spent, was their religious achievements . . . therefore the well was called "occupation" (*'eseq*).' The motif of the well also plays an important role in the Qabbālāh where it symbolizes the entrance to the spiritual world, the *Sĕfirāh Malkūt*. Cf. *Zōhar*, I, f° 141b: 'He who beholds this well will perceive a supernal mystery and this is the reason why the Patriarchs busied themselves with the digging of wells of water.'

(38) Both Moses (*Guide*, I:2, Qāfiḥ, p.28) and Abraham Maimonides (*Comm.*, p.45) interpret this verse as 'an unveiling of the inner vision' (*kašf baṣīra*).

(39) In Qabbalistic literature *bĕ'ēr*, 'the well of Good', and *bōr*, 'the pit of Evil', are often constrasted. See Ibn Ǧiqaṭilla's commentary on the *Guide* in *Sĕ'ēlōt Šā'ūl*, II, f°s 20b–21a, where he points out that the word *bĕ'ēr* comes from a Hebrew root meaning to 'explain' or 'reveal' and that a *bĕ'ēr* has a spring, whereas a *bōr* has not.

(40) *Iḥyā'*, IV:10, p.528–30. Cf. also the article *ḥawḍ* in *EI²*, III, 286 (Wensinck).

(41) *Iḥyā'*, III:1, pp.2 ff., *al-Ma'āriǧ al-qudsiyya*, edn. Cairo, 1927, pp.98 ff., *Rawḍat aṭ-Ṭālibin*, Cairo, n.d., pp.122f. At-Tirmiḏī also wrote a work entitled *Bayān al-farq bayn as-ṣadr wa-l-qalb wa-l-fū'ad wa-l-lubb*, ed. N. Heer, Cairo, 1958, devoted to the heart as the instrument of spiritual knowledge, which seems to have influenced al-Ġazzālī. The importance of the heart is also exposed in a Jewish Pietist work which, although anonymous, betrays the style of Rabbi Abraham he-Ḥasīd and may be identical with the lost work known as the *Tāǧ al-'Ārifīn*. By coincidence the passage is to be found in more than one manuscript: *BNU* MS. Heb. 4110.61 *ENA* 3453.17 and *T–S* Arabic 1a.25: 'The access to His door and the arrival at His proximity (*qurb*), presence (*ḥudūr*) and illumination (*išrāq*) are achieved by the cleansing of God's shrine (*maḥall*) of its impurities and arousing it from its slumber . . and God's shrine is the heart . . . which contains His mystery, light, image and likeness (*ṣelem wa-dĕmūt*).'

(42) *Iḥyā'*, III:1 p.20. This symbolism is repeated in volume III:2, p.76: 'Solitary devotion (*ḫalwa*) has the advantage of dispelling worldly cares and regulating one's

hearing and sight which are the corridors of the heart. Indeed the heart is comparable to a pool (*ḥawḍ*) into which flow the polluted waters of the senses. The object of moral discipline (*riyāḍa*) is to empty the pool of these waters and the dregs that they carry so that the pure and clean water may spring forth from the source of the pool.'

(43) *Ibid.*, p.19. 'The Truths contained in the mirror of the Tablet are revealed in the mirror of the heart, the forms of one mirror being reflected in the other ... when the veils (of the sensual world) are lifted from the heart's vision, then something of what is inscribed in the "Well-Guarded Tablet" is revealed to it.' The expression "Well-Guarded Tablet', which originates from the Qur'ān (*Sūra* LXXXV:22) is identified in mystical literature with the Active Intellect or the Universal Soul. It signifies more particularly in al-Ġazzālī's cosmology the centre of the eternally active ideas (see Wensinck's article cited above). The correspondence between the two parables of the cleansing of the heart, the organ of divine knowledge, as well as between the vocabulary involved, is a clear indication that al-Ġazzālī was a major source of Sufi ideas to both 'Obadyāh and indeed to the Jewish Pietists generally. It is noteworthy that the idea of the heart as the *locus* 'of the Ark in which lie the two Tablets of the Testimony' is to be found in the *Chapter on Beatitude*, p.2, and in the apocryphal letter of Moses Maimonides to his son Abraham, *Musar nā'eh* in *Epistles of Maimonides*, Leipzig, 1855, f° 39d, although the latter is clearly derived from Abraham Ibn 'Ezra's commentary on Ex. XXV:40 and thus belongs to a different school of thought. In the Qabbalistic symbolism, on the other hand, the Tablets of the Law correspond to the *Sĕfirāh Malkūt*, and the letters thereof to the *Sĕfirāh Bināh*, which symbolizes the realm of Ideas and Archetypes.

(44) *BNU* 4110.62b.

(45) p.12.

(46) See Bacher, *JQR*, IX, pp.270–289, H. Davidowitz in the introduction to his edition, pp.xiv–xxii, and more recently G. Scholem in *Tarbiẓ*, VI, p.91.

(47) Wieder, pp.45–6.

(48) Steinschneider, in *MGWJ*, XLV, p.133.The manuscript still bears the following press-mark on the fly-leaf: Cod. Zunz 26.

(49) The whole manuscript has been described by G. Vajda, *Juda ben Nissim*, p.7.

(50) Part of f° 27a was copied into f° 15a and then subsequently scored.

(51) *A Grammar of Judaeo-Arabic*, Jerusalem, 1961 (in Hebrew).

(52) The conclusion that the *ṣerē* is used both for *imāla* and *šadda* as well as to indicate a long vowel is based on the observation of a system of vocalisation whose exact significance exceeds our competence. However other Genizah texts from more or less the same period exhibit a similar usage. Cf. *ENA* 2708 f° 10 where we read: נבוֵהּ, אמֵהּ and *T–S* 10J17 f° 10: אכֵרי, עלֵי, נְרֵי

TRANSLATION

TRANSLATION

[INTRODUCTION]

'. . . [3a] thy crown in this world and thy guide in the hereafter.' (1) 'For the Lord shall be thine everlasting light'. (Is. LX:20) 'My son, if sinners entice thee with the sweetness of their tongues, consent not' (Pr. I:10) for they shall not deal justly until they obtain from thee their designs. 'Walk not in the way with them and restrain thy foot from their paths'. (Pr. I:15) Set thine aim to be the perfection of thy soul, strive therein exceedingly and do not fret nor falter. If ever thou art hindered by an obstacle, do not yield, rather remain steadfast until it be cast aside, as Solomon hath said 'If the spirit of the ruler rise up against thee, leave not thy place' (Eccl. X:4) for thou shalt be sheltered from the adversity of being *hidden from His Face*. (2)

If, perchance, thou wert to attain such a state *(ma'anä)*, then thou shouldst be sheltered 'in the covert of the Most High and wouldst abide in the shadow of the Almighty'. (Ps. XCI:1) Indeed, the virtue to be acquired from this discipline (*fann*) is greater than that which accrueth to thee from the Purgative way (*muǧāhada*) (3) in subduing thine instincts, for thou wilt have attained to the state of 'presence with God' (*maqām al-ḥuḍūr*) (4) and contemplation (*mušāhada*). (5) For if man's soul were to secure praiseworthy qualities, then his evil instincts would be cast aside and the obstacles that impede him from attaining human perfection would disappear, for these are but one's sins as the Prophet hath explained, 'Your iniquities have separated between you and your God.' (Is. LIX:2) (6)

Having attained to this state thou wilt no longer be troubled by the superfluities of food, or drink, or shelter, or attire, in which the vulgar indulge and thou wilt be preserved [3b] from great wrong. Upon being guided by Reason thou shalt escape the contingence and vicissitudes of this world, with which the Lord hath threatened the evildoers, as it is said 'In that day, I shall surely hide My face for all the evil which they shall have wrought, in that they turned unto other gods'. (Deut. XXXI:18) Likewise it is said of him that hath forsaken the soul in order to indulge in material (pleasures), 'Thou hast cast Me behind thy back (lit. "body")'. (1 Kings XIV:9) Beware of thine enemy's hold over thee, and thine enslavement to him through the continual thought of the *Cherubim* (7), who guard the way to the *Tree of Life*, so that it may not be said of thee 'the eyes of a fool are in the ends of the Earth'. (Pr. XVII:24) Understand this well.

Chapter I

Know that all the sayings of the prophets and philosophers (that have come down to us), exhort us to heed the intellect and to forsake corporeal pleasures, in order to prepare a path for the intellect, that it might perceive what it can of the Creator. (8) Dost thou not see that our Forefather Jacob, peace upon him, was endowed with the name Israel in allusion to his possession of both worlds, as it is said 'For thou hast striven with angels and men, and hast prevailed'. (Gen. XXXII:29) (9)

Hence he was no longer subject to contingence, as the (Sages) of blessed memory have said concerning those that have truly (attained the state) of Israel 'There is no star for Israel'. (Šabbāt, 156a) (10) Since Reason is the bond (*wuṣla*) (11) between the Creator and His creatures, the individual who setteth his intent thereon, visualizing it [4a] as his goal, in the sense of David's words 'I have set the Lord always before me; surely He is at my right hand, I shall not be moved' (Ps. XVI:8) (12), will be protected from adversity by the emanation that floweth from God, as it is said, 'Because he hath set his love upon Me, therefore will I deliver him'. (Ps. XCI:14)

Consider how milk floweth from the breast of the nursing mother whenever she thinketh of her suckling; even though the latter be not with her, her compassion is moved 'as a father hath mercy upon his children'. (Ps. CIII:13) In a similar manner upon encountering a mutual affinity (*munāsaba*) (13) with a certain individual, Reason will abide with the latter and never forsake him, 'I will be with him in adversity', (Ps. XCI:15) 'Fear not for I am with thee'(Is. XLIII:5) 'when thou passest through the waters I will be with thee.' (ibid.:2) (14) Be then attentive of this noble discipline and engage therein all thy time, as it is said 'If a man would give all his fortune for love, no account would be taken of him'. (Cant. VIII:7)

Chapter II

It is surely a Divine grace, that one whose family responsibilities are few (15) and whose bodily complexion proveth compliant and receptive (16), happeneth to receive Reason's favour (*intibāh*); for all obstacles shall be cast aside before him, especially if his desire for this state be constant and he remaineth unperturbed by worldly affairs, as it is said, 'I have put off my coat [4b], I have washed my feet. How then shall I defile them?' (Cant. V:5) (17) His sole attachment will be his Beloved, to the skirt of his raiment will he only cling, as the Sage hath said, 'I am my beloved's and my beloved is mine'. (Cant. VI:3) Such a state is most difficult to attain, for how may impure and coarse beings such as we, cling to a luminous and most simple substance?

How then must a person fare, for if he desireth to draw near to

Him he must languish and if he turneth from Him he must perish? There remaineth for him but one resort—to strengthen the bond (*wuṣla*) between them and admit his incapacity (to unite with him) (18) as David hath said 'Lord my heart is not haughty, nor mine eyes lofty, neither do I exercise myself in things too high', (Ps. CXXXI:1) 'Teach me to do Thy will, for Thou art my God', (Ps. CXLIII:10) 'O send out Thy light and Thy truth'. (Ps. XLIII:3)

Let not thine intent (*himma*) falter upon seeing the difficulty and remoteness of the task. Say not that thou art the prisoner of lust, anger, hunger, thirst, heat, cold, fear or disease, thus weakening thy resolve to search. Rather fortify thy determination, toiling in thy labour, for whosoever persevereth in this pursuit is a true man (*al-insān 'alä l-ḥaqīqa*) (19), concerning whom David hath said 'Happy is the man whose strength is in Thee, in whose heart are the highways.' (Ps. LXXXIV:6) (20) 'Happy is the people whose God is the Lord'. (Ps. CXLIV:15)

It is proper that this verse is in the singular for this pursuit is the exclusive concern of the individual. But he who remaineth remiss (therein) is *considered a dead man*, (Nědd. 64b) for he will never find an authentic [5a] doctrine to which to adhere and concerning such a person, Solomon hath said 'He that perverteth his ways shall be found out'. (Pr. X:9) Whereas for him who passively accepteth belief (*taqlīd*) (21), it is better that he were never created, as the Sage hath said 'An untimely birth is better than he. . . .' (Eccl. VI:3) and 'He that heareth let him hear and he that forbeareth let him forbear'. (Ezek. III:27)

Chapter III

Know my son that, notwithstanding their numerous advantages for mundane affairs, commercial experience as well as (bodily) welfare and wealth have no bearing on this pursuit, since they deal with the mutual contracts and social dispositions which constitute the policy of the vulgar. (22)

This science (23) however, concerneth thee alone, as the Sage hath said 'Let them be only thine own and not strangers' with thee.' (Prov. V:17) (24) Whether it be through self-instruction or guidance, this science can only be attained after having mastered the exoteric revelation (*aš-šarī'a*), inasmuch as the latter is the axis (*quṭb*) of moral discipline and the ladder by which to ascend to the Most High (25), 'for they shall be a chaplet of grace unto thy head'. (Prov. I:9) Similarly the philosophers maintain that the study of Mathematics bordereth on Physics, which leadeth (in turn) to Metaphysics (26) of which it is said, 'Let him that glorieth, glory in this alone, that he understandeth and knoweth me'. (Jer. IX:23) Upon placing thine aspiration in Him [5b], thy destiny (*ḫatm*) (27) will be freed from worldly ambitions. Hence, upon being asked to occupy thyself with a worldly matter which concerneth thee, thou wilt reply, on account of thy (higher) preoccupations, *let the world depend on others* (28), as it is said 'I am my beloved's and his desire is toward me'. (Cant. VIII:11)

Know that if thou desirest to draw near to the Divine Presence (*al-ḥaḍra al-ilāhiyya*) (29) then thou must realize that thou art but an *insignificant, obscure and humble creature*, (Yĕs. ha-Tōrāh II:2) whose matter is that of a dumb animal. Hence thou must first purify thyself of all defilements such as that caused by *menstruation*, which is in fact the waste product of vital functions, similar to the excrement resulting from overeating. Then through *immersion*, thou must cleanse thyself of the *filth* with which the *Serpent* hath envenomed thy body (30) and which thou hast neglected to remedy with the theriac at thy disposal. (31)

Indeed the Scriptures have said of one such as thee 'I passed by the field of the slothful and by the vineyard of the man void of understanding'. After having described the field's state, the passage continueth 'then I beheld and considered well' and mentioneth the remedy, 'yet a little sleep, a little slumber . . . so shall thy poverty come as a runner and thy wants as an armed man'. (Prov. XXIV:30–34) Next, thou must cleanse thyself of worldly vanities that veil the *Tree of Life*, as the prophet hath said 'Wash you, make you clean, put away your evil doings'. (Is. I:16) Thereupon thou wilt be fit to draw near to the divine service 'and the priests also that draw near to the Lord shall purify themselves', (Ex. XIX:22) as the Sage hath said 'Guard thy foot when thou goest [6a] to the house of God'. (Eccl. IV:17) Remember (in this respect) the impetuousness of the *Nobles of Israel* and the punishment they consequently incurred on account of their inadequate spiritual preparation. (32)

Hence it behoveth the wise man not to ascend to a state which is too elevated for him but to be aware of the extent of his soul's (capacity) and advance gradually, as is the wont of nature, which assimilateth things progressively. The Sage said in this respect, 'Only he who hath eaten his fill of bread and meat is fit to stroll in the orchard'. (Yĕs. ha-Tōrāh IV:13) Similarly it is written in allusion to the very same principle 'Thou shalt not go up by degrees upon mine altar.' (Ex. XX:23) (33)

Be heedful of thy soul, so that when thou farest upon the Path, thou wilt be free of fear, 'For the ground upon which thou standest is holy'. (Ex. III:5) Mark these my words.

Chapter IV

O thou that meditatest this treatise, know that the matter to which we have here alluded, cannot be more overtly expounded. Thus, upon happening on a verse that can be interpreted in several manners, my goal is merely to open the gate and rely upon the disciple's comprehension. If he be endowed with insight and intuition (*d̮awq*) (34), he will then arrive at the true significance through his own resources. This is the meaning of the Sages' saying 'Except he be wise and understandeth of himself, and then only the headings of the chapters are entrusted to him'. (Ḥagīgāh 13a) (35) [6b].

Chapter V

Know that the creator's constant emanation to all creation floweth first upon the Intelligences, in accordance with the degrees of the individual entities, and then continueth throughout the spheres (*al-aflāk*) until it reacheth the object of its providence (*'ināya*). As long as man's intellect (36) meditateth God's created works, then this providence will abide with him, parting his company (only) if he turneth his attention from it. 'Wilt thou set thine eyes on it? It is gone, for it maketh itself wings like an eagle that flieth towards heaven'. (Pr. XXIII:5) For in such case it will return to its element, leaving that individual 'a fugitive and a wanderer in the land' (Gen. IV:14) with none to protect him 'and it shall come to pass that whosoever findeth him will slay him'. Be then diligent to satisfy its behest, perchance wilt thou gain its intimacy and an affectionate affinity (37) will be established between you.

Thine aim should be ever to accomplish and fulfil its design. Bestow upon it that which thou cherishest 'perhaps thou wilt find grace in his eyes' (Gen. XXXII:6) and through it, thou wilt be aided in all thy pursuits. It will not cease to be thy companion until thou departest (this life); and thereupon will it wax strong on account of the disappearance of the corporeal matter which kept thee hitherto from perception.

Chapter VI

Know that there is nought to prevent man from perfection as there is nought to prevent [7a] him from transgression as it is said in the Holy Torah, 'Behold man is become as one of us, to know good and evil'. (Gen. III:22) Likewise Jeremiah proclaimed, 'Out of the mouth of the Most High proceedeth not evil and good'. (Lam. III:38)

The Sages too have stated in this respect 'Whosoever cometh to purify himself is aided thereunto and whosoever cometh to defile himself, the way is opened before him'. (Šābbāt 104a) It is then clear that there existeth no pre-determinism (*ğabr*) (38) and therefore man should close his thoughts to all and awaken his intellect, devoting himself to it, since it is the bond (*wuṣla*) between him and his Creator. Were he continually to think of Him, he would not fail to find Him as the prophet hath said, 'Seek ye the Lord while He is to be found. Call ye upon Him, while He is near. Let the wicked forsake his way and the man of iniquity his thoughts and let him return unto the Lord and He will have compassion upon him, and to our God, for He will abundantly pardon'. (Is. LV:6) Upon returning to the Lord, all obstacles will be dispelled, since the sole hindrance to reaching Him is man's obscure substance called 'darkness, cloud and thick darkness' (Deut. IV:11) (as it is said) 'He made darkness his hiding place'. (Ps. XVIII:12) (39) However, all that which dwelleth with the Creator, may He be extolled, is but pure, bright light as it is written, 'And the Earth did shine with His Glory'. (Ezek. XLIII:2)

Were an individual to remain steadfast and persevere continuously until he achieved this state, then the phenomena that were previously concealed from him and others, would be revealed to him. Reason's will shall strengthen and reveal that which is inscribed on the Tablet (*al-lawḥ*). (40) Divine visions will be manifested to him without his knowing whence they came. [7b] He will walk by the light of his intellect, directed by its guidance. So take heed of thy soul and safeguard its form (41), for the former hath no lasting beatitude unless accompanied by Reason.

It is on this account that Solomon enjoined us to 'find them about thy neck, write them upon the table of thy heart, thereupon shalt thou find grace and good favour in the sight of God and man'. (Prov. III:3) Thou wilt be sustained with that with which thine ancestors were nourished in the wilderness, as it is said, 'man did eat the bread of the mighty ... and gave them of the corn of heaven'. (Ps. LXXVIII:25) (42) Similarly it is stated 'the heavens were opened' (Ezek. I:1) (43), 'open to me the gates of righteousness, I will enter them and give thanks to the Lord. This is the gate of the Lord; the righteous shall enter it'. (Ps. CXVIII:19) The generation of the wilderness attained perfection through the excellent master in their midst, who showed neither greed nor grudge in their instruction, imparting to each individual in accordance with his capacity of understanding. This is similar to the manner in which Reason itself proceedeth (44), 'and when they did mete out with the omer, he that gathered much had nothing over and he that gathered little had no lack; they gathered each according to his eating'. (Ex. XVI:18) Thus he proceeded, until they had mastered what they could of the Word of the Lord. Moreover, he instructed them how to improve their moral qualities and how to utilise theriac (45) upon being bitten by the serpent, for this was a land of many serpents but little water, as Scripture relateth 'There were snakes, fiery serpents, scorpions and thirsty soil where was no water'. (Deut. VIII:15)

Likewise, when Israel was thirsty and craved for water, Moses beseeched the Lord (on their behalf) and He answered, 'Behold I will stand [8a] before thee, there upon the rock' (Ex. XVII:6) (46) It came to pass that when the water sprang forth, the serpents perished. Similarly we were promised in future times that 'a fountain shall spring forth from the house of the Lord and shall water the valley of Shittim'. (Joel IV:18) O thou who meditatest these verses, comprehend their profoundness; 'and it shall come to pass in that day, that the living waters shall go out from Jerusalem' (Zech. XIV:8) 'for the waters thereof issue out of the sanctuary'. (Ezek. XLVII:12)

Chapter VII

Know that man possesseth primary and secondary organs (47), and that each dischargeth a specific function which is ancillary to another organ, such as in the relation of the heart and the liver. The brain possesseth three main faculties: thought, memory and imagination, in addition to two other faculties: estimation and common sense. The latter remain latent during the activity of the five external senses on the surface of the body: sight, hearing, smell, taste and touch. When the activity of the latter is at rest, the (five internal faculties) begin to function (48), especially during sleep, inducing thereby truthful dreams when (the mind) is pure. Know that the prolonged consumption of harmful foodstuffs causeth acute ailments, which, defying medical [8b] treatment, eventually lead to leprosy, swelling and severe inflammation or cerebral disorders such as loss of vision and tinnitus. Likewise a man who neglecteth his soul, abandoning it to its illness through his indulgence in worldly affairs, spending night and day buying and selling and so forth, will have nought but fearful and alarming dreams (49) upon retiring to sleep.

It is for this reason that our pure and purifying Law hath cautioned us concerning all external and internal defilement. The former, such as *menstruation and nocturnal emission*, are to be cleansed through *immersion in a ritual bath*. Thus Aaron and *his descendants* were enjoined 'to wash their hands and feet, *that they perish not*' (Ex. XXX:21) this being the reason for the *act of purification*. For through the conviction man's soul acquireth after immersion that all veils, as it were, have been lifted, there ensueth a state similar to spiritual predisposition (*tahayyu'*) and communion (*ittiṣāl*) (50) with God. If not in need of *immersion*, then one must carry out the *ablution of hands and feet* in order that the natural heat circulate in the body and arouse thereby the soul. (51)

For a similar reason it is prohibited to enter the sanctuary in a state of intoxication, lest one's devotion be impaired by an error of substitution (*badl*), as it is said '(That ye die not) . . . that ye may discern between the holy and profane'. (Lev. X:10) Moreover it is said [9a] concerning the Priests, that 'They shall be holy unto their Lord', (Lev. XXI:6) while the whole of Israel were enjoined 'sanctify yourselves therefore and be holy'. (Lev. XI:44)

Internal purity (52) is (achieved) by refraining from prohibited aliments such as the flesh of horses, swine and camels, which produce toxin that corrupt the body, dull the mind and strengthen the body's propensity for vice, as it is written, 'Ye shall not make yourselves abominable with any swarming thing that swarmeth, neither shall ye make yourselves unclean with them, that ye should be defiled thereby'. (Lev. XI:43)

'Say not *we-niṭme'tem* and 'ye shall become defiled' but *we-niṭamṭem* 'and ye shall become feeble-minded'. (Yōmā' 39a) (53)

In a similar spirit, other prohibitions have been instituted by the religious Law (54) in order to restrain man's lust and keep him from resembling the beast. (55) Among these rank the class of *forbidden unions*, and (those not) *legitimately contracted*, for these concern (more particularly) the beast in man. Also belongeth to this group the precept of *circumcision* which is carried out on the physical organ through which marriage is consummated. As for the commandments concerning the wearing of *fringes* (*ṣīṣīt*) and *phylacteries* (*tĕfīlīn*) and the fixing of an *inscription* on the doorposts (*mĕzūzāh*) (56), they were instituted in order to remind the soul at moments of inadvertence of its purpose as it is said concerning the *fringes*, 'That ye may look upon it and remember all the commandments of the Lord'. (Numb. XV:39) Likewise, it is written concerning the phylacteries, 'And it shall be for a sign unto thee upon thy hand and for a memorial . . .' (Ex. XIII:9) The purpose of the commandments concerning the building of a *parapet* (Deut. XXII:8) and the covering of wells dug near a thoroughfare, is to safeguard public welfare and remove stumbling blocks. As for the *bread offering* [9b], the *Temple offerings, tithes, gleanings, forgotten sheaves, field corners, vineyard gleanings, charity for the poor* and so forth, their aim is to foster man's generosity until it becometh a natural (gesture). (58)

For when a person firmly acquireth a commendable trait, the opposite (evil) trait is dispelled. As for the commandments, 'If thou meetest (thine enemy's ox)', 'if thou seest (the ass of him that hateth thee)', (Ex. XXIII:4–5) 'ye shall not afflict any widow or orphan' (Ex. XXII:21) 'oppress not the stranger' (Ex XXIII:9) and similar injunctions, their intention is to establish in man the virtue of mercy.

The prohibitions 'thou shalt not wear a mingled stuff', (Deut. XXII:11) 'thou shalt not sow thy vineyard with two kinds of seed', (ibid.:9) 'they shall not make baldness upon their head' (Lev. XXI:5) and that concerning the *shaving of the corners of the head and beard* (Lev. XIX:27), were instituted in order to avoid the imitation of idolatrous practices and to affirm the principle of God's uniqueness—'thou shalt have no other gods' (Ex. XX:2)—and to establish in our souls the principle of His Existence. (59)

It is common knowledge that ere one expresseth the thoughts that occur in one's mind, they are known to the Lord, as David said, 'For there is no word in my tongue, but, lo, O Lord Thou knowest it altogether' (Ps. CXXXIX:4) and it is also stated 'I the Lord search the heart, I try the reins'. (Jer. XVII:10) All one's movements and stations, be they good or evil, are known and recorded by Him, inasmuch as our deeds are manifest to Him. For this reason, the God-fearing (60) are reluctant to uncover their heads, out of respect for Reason. Thus in moments of anger [10a] or lust of any kind, they show restraint firstly (out of deference for) the soul, with which man alone has been endowed and in virtue of which it is said that 'in the likeness of God, He made him'. (Gen. V:1) Secondly, they do so (out of deference) for Reason, which continually cleaveth and communeth with man, and on whose account it is said that 'in the image of God made He man'. (Gen. IX:6) And thirdly, they do so (out of deference for) the Creator, may He be exalted, before Whom man is ever present, while standing or sitting, thinking or speaking, be he in the highest or the nethermost of places, as it is said, '"Can any hide in secret places that I shall not see him?" saith the Lord'. (Jer. XXIII:24) How (carefully) then should a person demean himself and go about his business in the presence of the three above mentioned onlookers?

Consequently, the Sages, peace upon them, have rebuked those of haughty gait for 'the whole earth is full of His Glory' (Is. VI:3) and the Prophets have also stated 'that the high of stature shall be hewn down and the lofty shall be laid low.' (Is. X:33) (61) Were man to become distracted and forgetful of his being in their presence, on account of the necessity to attend to exigencies such as food and social intercourse, he should admit his failings and explain, 'I have sinned unto the Lord your God and unto you'. (Ex. X:16) But if he confesseth not then it will be said of him, 'Behold I will enter into judgement with thee, because thou sayest, I have not sinned'. (Jer. II:35) Take heed therefore of Reason and 'set his throne above the throne of the kings that are with thee.' (62)

Chapter VIII

Know O brother that if we be cast aside from His intimacy (*al-qurb*) (63) [10b] it is because we have severed the bond (*wuṣla*) between us and Him, through our indulgence in unnecessary matters and animal-like pursuits. (64) We have turned aside from the soul so that it hath become tarnished like a mirror that no longer reflecteth any light (65), inasmuch as it hath sinned by forsaking moral improvement. Therefore do I recommend thee to seek the face of the Lord in moments of respite from the burden of corporeal matter. When Satan is slumbering, arise in the dead of night and turn to the Most High in prayer and supplication, as it is said 'Arise, cry out in the night at the beginning of the watches, pour out thy heart like water before the Face of the Lord'. (Lam. II:19) (66) Ever turn toward the Gate which faceth the *sanctuary*, 'thy gates also shall be open continually, day and night, (they shall not shut)', (Is. LX:11) 'ye that are the Lord's remembrancers, take ye no rest'. (Is. LXII:6) This verse urgeth us to turn continually (toward the sanctuary) *day and night*, so beware not to be distracted, 'for there is but a step between me and death'. (67) (I Sam. XX:3)

Furthermore, reflect on how thou mayest meet thy Master through this creed. (68) (Reflect) also upon how even the Prophets, peace upon them, and their vicegerents—who undoubtedly are the Sages—did fall into the hands of their enemies, whenever they succumbed to the body's demands. How then will we fare, we who are devoid of knowledge, spiritual preparation and purity?

Upon becoming pure, our soul will draw near to that state described as 'the righteous seated with their crowns upon their heads, delighting in the splendour of the Divine Presence. What are their crowns? Their good and comely deeds, wrought in this World, the reward for which is stored up for them in the World which is truly good.' (Bĕr. 17a) [11a]. And if our soul desireth to join their company, they would say unto it 'From there also shalt thou go forth with thy hands upon thy head' (Jer. II:37) that is, it shall be more ashamed than the woman (referred to in this verse) upon her return from among them. (69)

It therefore behoveth thee, O brother, to tarry at the Gate, as Solomon said 'Happy is the man that hearkeneth to me, watching daily at my gates'. (Pr. VIII:34)

Be not forgetful of thy soul and commend this unto thy heart. Take heed that it hear nought but that which concerneth His Truth (*ḥaqq*). Melt thy couch with thy tears and reflect upon how thou hast returned evil for good, refusing the instruction of intellect and soul, who are God's envoys and messengers with which He hath favoured you, placing them among the soul's faculties. (70) Thus thou shalt be capable of uniting with Reason, so that, when thou departest this world, thou shalt be at ease. Deal kindly with thy soul, and it shall be said of thee, 'And thy righteousness shall go before thee, the glory of the Lord shall be thy rearward . . . then shall thy light rise in darkness'. (Is. LVIII:8,10)

Chapter IX

The present chapter not only constituteth the very purpose of this treatise but is also a preliminary to that which followeth, so apply then thine attention in understanding it.

Know that man is the élite (*ṣafwa*) of this lower world for he is the last of its composite beings to have been created. He is called a Microcosm (*al-'ālam aṣ-ṣagīr*) (71) on account of the rational faculty implanted in him, concerning which the Prophet said 'Yet thou hast made him but little lower than the angels and hast crowned him with glory and honour'. (Ps. VIII:6) [11b] Man was subjected, on its account, to positive and negative precepts, reward and punishment. This (rational) faculty is superior to all the transient faculties in that each organ is limited to a particular function. However when this (rational) faculty is united with a seemly matter, a *woman of valour* (72) through its illumination (*išrāq*) of man's (intellect), it will perform wonders, providing that he accord it its due and withhold it not from its labour. For the wise man is he who rendereth to every man his desert, as it is said, 'The righteous giveth and spareth not'. (Prov. XXI:26)

Moreover (the rational soul's) task is to acquire science and knowledge and to apprehend as much as possible of Reason's knowledge of the Creator. (73) If it remaineth steadfast and the obstacles hindering its task be lifted, then it will have access to the knowledge of hidden mysteries; unlike the imaginative faculty, whose knowledge is defective. (74)

For (the rational) faculty is sound (*ṣaḥiḥ*) and devoid of doubtfulness, when its possibilities are actuated. If thou aidest it in this pursuit then thou wilt obtain quietude in this world and the next. As for this world, every mystery herein shall be revealed to thee, according to the hidden meaning of the verse, 'the heavens were opened and (I saw visions of God)' to which we have hitherto referred. (Ezek. I:1) (75) If this Gate be opened to thee, then thou wilt continue to frequent the palace all thy life long. Be not careless in the company of thine enemies, lest thou become one of those of whom it is said, 'So He drove out the man' (Gen. III:24); for as soon as they discern any dissipation (on thy part), they 'hiss and gnash their teeth . . . (certainly this is the day we have waited for)' (Lam. II:16) and it will prove [12a] tiresome to be rid of them. Meditate this allegory and it will quench thy thirst, for if thou cleavest to the Gate, which is the (Garden of) Eden, the source of His mercy (76), and settest thy mind thereunto, then upon encountering any *positive deed*, thou wilt eagerly (accomplish it) on account of the ardent desire with which 'thou cravest after her beauty in thy heart'. (Pr. VI:25) Indeed thou wilt say, 'ask me much dowry and gift (and I will give as ye say unto me), but give me the damsel to wife', (Gen. XXXIV:12) 'perhaps I will find grace in his eyes.' (ibid.:11) Dost thou not see the desire of our lord David to build the *Temple*, a *place for the Lord*, when he said, 'Surely I will not come into the tent of my house... (until I find a place for the Lord)'? (Ps. CXXXII:3) So he donated gold, silver, brass and iron for the edifice, in order that the Divine Light might abide therein, as it is recounted in the book of Kings. Is this not the height of love, 'With all thy heart, with all thy soul and with all thy might'? (Deut. VI:5) Likewise, thou shalt hasten with great love to accomplish any favour which thy beloved shall request of thee 'for love is as strong as death'. (Cant. VIII:6)

When thou remainest alone with thy soul after having subdued thy passions (77), a Gate will open before thee through which thou wilt contemplate wonders. When thy five external senses come to rest, thine internal senses will awaken and thou wilt behold a resplendent light emanating from the splendour of Reason. Thou wilt perceive mighty and awesome voices which leave a man bewildered. 'He maketh lightnings with the rain and bringeth forth the wind out of his treasuries'. (Jer. X:13) Know that wind (*ruaḥ*) is an ambiguous term (78), as are the metaphorical expressions used in the following allegories; 'and He opened the doors of heaven', (Ps. LXXVIII:23) 'the doors of heaven were opened', (Ezek. I:1) 'open ye the gates' (Is. XXVI:2) which are but allusions (*tanbīh*) (79) to this mystery. It is on account of (the latter) that a [12b] hierarchy hath developed among the mystics (*as-sālikin*) (80) that pursue this Path, for it is the manner in which the individual conducteth himself when he drinketh, eateth, sleepeth and thinketh, (in short) in all his activities, that determineth the effort required in moments of spiritual preparation (*tahayyu'*). Solomon hath said 'whoso guardeth his mouth and his tongue, keepeth his soul from sorrow'. (Prov. XXI:23) Reflect upon this saying of the Rabbis, may peace be upon them, which also alludeth to the aforementioned diversity of spiritual states among the wayfarers, 'Unto Abraham, whose power was strong, (the Angels) appeared as men, whereas unto Lot, whose power was weak, they appeared in the likeness of Angels.' (Gen. Rabbāh L:3) (81) Indeed the Sages have explained all the preliminaries required for the pursuit of this Path. It is still needful to expound yet another allegory in the coming chapter.

Chapter X

Know that if thou desirest to comprehend the allegories contained in this treatise then thou shouldst pay attention to the examples given herein. Fix in thy mind that everyone entrusted with a certain mission is called an angel. (82)

Imagine a certain person who, possessing a very old pool, desireth to cleanse the latter of dirt and mire and to restore it. Certainly a Divine favour hath been bestowed upon him. He must therefore ensure that the pool cease to be polluted, occupying himself with its gradual cleansing until it is completely purified. Only after having ascertained that there remaineth therein no impurity [13a], can the *living waters that go forth from the House of God* flow therein, concerning which it is said, 'And a source from the House of God'. (Joel IV:18) The foregoing is an allegory alluding to the purification, cleansing and purging of the heart, the correction of its defects and failings and its being emptied of all but the Most High. He who accomplisheth this will comprehend invaluable notions which were hitherto hidden from him, deriving therefrom that which none else can acquire (even) after much time and with plenteous knowledge, as Solomon hath said, 'above all that thou guardest keep thy heart; for out of it are the issues of life'. (Prov. IV:23)

Therefore thou must remain steadfast for a long period, reducing thine indulgence in unnecessary occupations until doing so no longer requireth effort but cometh naturally to thee. When thou wilt have persevered in this effort, thine imaginative faculty will be purified and all that is graven on the 'well-guarded Tablet' (*al-lawḥ al-maḥfūẓ*) (83) will be manifested to thee. Thou wilt speak of hidden mysteries, inasmuch as thy mind will be immersed in the pursuit of this goal. Be however extremely mindful that no residue remain in the pool and beware that no impurity seep into the water which floweth therein.

For any (impurity) remaining there will be restored to thee by the imaginative faculty when thou sleepest or when thou awakest or at times of solitary devotion (*ḥalwa*). (84) Thou wilt think it an object from without, whereas it is part of the dregs left in the pool. (85)

The rabbis have warned us against this (error) in the account of the four who entered Paradise: 'Rabbi 'Aqîba said unto them, "Upon reaching the marble stoned floor, do not utter 'Water, water', for it is written [13b], 'He that speaketh falsehood shall not endure before mine eyes'".' (Ps. CI:17) (Ḥagīgāh 14b) (86)

Ever strive toward the bountiful and salutary waters which quench man's (thirst) and withhold thyself from all others which only increase man's thirst, lest 'the disciples who come after you drink thereof and die, and the Heavenly Name be profaned', (Abōt I:11) or lest it be said of thee 'they have forsaken Me, the fountain of living waters and hewed them out cisterns, broken cisterns, that can hold no water'. (Jer. II:13) (87) Reflect upon this.

[Chapter]

O my son, honour him that mediateth between thee and thy Creator, may He be extolled inasmuch as he intercedeth for thy good, since he is 'the interpreter between them'. (Gen. XLII:23) (88) Take great pains to retain (his mediation) for its loss is irretrievable. (89) If thou neglectest it, then it will disappear, 'as the sun waxed hot, it melted', (Ex. XVI:21) 'wilt thou set thine eyes upon it? It is gone'. (Prov. XXIII:5) Therefore, grieve nor weary not, (in thine effort) as David hath said in this respect, 'For Thy sake we are killed all the day'. (Ps. XLIV:23)

Lo, after having attained to this state, so passionate will be thy rapture, that thou shalt not suffer to be separated from Him, even for an instant. And as thy bliss increaseth, so will thy passion increase and thou wilt no longer delight in food nor drink nor rest. In the end, however, thou alone art the one to gain (from this), 'if thou growest wise thou growest wise for thyself'. (Prov. IX:12)

Realize that the state to which thou hast attained or to which thou hast drawn near is to be likened to the case of one who hath found a precious object [14a]. If he be conscious and appreciative of the value of his find, then he will evermore be beholden unto the Most High, who hath bestowed upon him this (gift) without (his having suffered) neither effort or hardship. Then he will utilize it in perfecting his soul, for the sake of Him who hath been merciful towards him. A fool however will imagine that this valuable object is obtainable at any time. He will fail to recognize his find as having been bestowed by the One 'who maketh poor and He who maketh rich' (I Sam. II:7) as a Divine grace in return for his personal merit, though none is innocent of having sinned by inadvertence, 'For there is not a righteous man upon earth (that doeth good and sinneth not)'. (Eccl. VII:20)

Safeguard then this (gift) O Seeker, for it is a most precious and valuable commodity, 'bind them about thy neck, inscribe them upon the table of thy heart', (Prov. III:3) 'let them be only thine own, and not strangers' with thee (Prov. V:17) (90) Remain sincere to it and withdraw from those occupations that turn thee aside from it whilst thou art among thy people and thy kinsfolk. Do not believe, like the poor in spirit, that seclusion (*inqiṭā'*) (91) is meant for the mountains and caves and that by merely withdrawing thereunto they will accomplish aught, for it is not so. Spend the time which passeth in striving (*muǧāhadāt*) towards the goal to which I have guided thee, thereby wilt thou obtain thy heart's desire. At present, I shall expound to thee what people have said concerning this Path.

Chapter XI

Know that the true adepts who pursued this Path (92) endeavoured to perfect themselves before marriage for they knew that after having acquired wife and child [14b] there is no real respite, for if opportunities for achievement arise, they do so but rarely and after much difficulty. (93) Did not Abraham, peace be upon him, find a wife for his son Isaac only after the latter had attained spiritual perfection? Accordingly it is specifically stated in the Scriptures that when Eleazar arrived with Rebecca he found him contemplating (*tahayy'a*) in the desert, as it is said, 'And Isaac went out to meditate in the field at the eventide.' (Gen. XXIV:63) (94) He was at that time forty years old, which is a suitable age (for marriage) and he departed not from (the desert), as it is said 'and Isaac dwelt by Beer-lahai-roi' (Gen. XXV:11) for he had achieved the state of permanent (perfection). (95) Similarly Jacob busied himself with perfecting his soul whilst in his father's house as the Scriptures state, 'And Jacob was a *perfect* man, dwelling in tents' (Gen. XXV:27) (96) and hence he merited the blessing rather than Esau. He fled from the latter and took refuge with Laban, and when Rachel emerged and he made her acquaintance, he beheld the well and realized the amount of effort the individual must deploy before reaching the water. It is said 'and the stone upon the well's mouth was great' (Gen. XXIX:2) as though in allusion to the great obstacles that impede man from reaching the *Tree of Life*, for (Jacob) was to suffer throughout his sojourn (with Laban) saying, 'and now when shall I provide for mine own house also?' (Gen. XXX:30) It befitteth thee therefore to follow the example of the virtuous; and if this be their doctrine then it is this after which thou must strive. The Scriptures say in this respect, 'What man is there that hath built a new house and hath not dedicated it?'. (Deut. XX:5) He hath tarried in obtaining its initiation which is the perfection of (the body's) entelechy. [15a] (97)

It is clear then to thee that thine ultimate aim is the perfection of (the latter). I have taught thee that if thou honourest that which thou hast in thy hand at the outset, keeping thyself from all doubts that wreak destruction on the majority of creatures and thou endeavourest to expel from the city all thine 'enemies and adversaries', then (the city) will prosper and be inhabited (98) and the King's orders carried out therein. But if perchance thou hast overlooked one of those enemies then it will be the cause of thine affliction. ('But if ye will not drive out the inhabitants of the land from before you) then shall those that ye let remain of them be as thorns on your eyes and as pricks in your sides (and they shall harass you)'. (Num. XXXIII:55) For if those inhabitants are expelled from the (city) then the latter will prosper and its sovereign will be established in his citadel and his tenets will be executed throughout the (land). Justice will prevail therein and its inhabitants will be safe from belligerent enemies, fearing the king and revering him; 'Fear thou, my son, the Lord and the King'. (Pr. XXIV:21) Persevere in this doctrine and thou wilt possess both worlds as did Rabbi 'Aqība. If however thou waverest and thou inclinest toward the Cherubim (99), then thou wilt end up as Eliša' the Apostate or his companion, who 'gazed upon the (Divine secrets) and became demented'. (Hagīgāh 14b) (100) . . . [15b]

It is for this reason that the Sages have warned us against indulging in this discipline prior to being (first) fully versed in the Revealed Law (*aš-šarī'a*), as it is said, 'only he who hath eaten his fill of bread and meat is fit to stroll in the orchard.' (Yĕs. ha-Tōrāh IV:13) For the (Revealed Law) prepareth one's character to accept this discipline.

Having attained this state, thou wilt experience a constant bliss, from which thou wilt not bear to be separated, even for a moment. Thou wilt remain guarded and protected by this experience for it shall be thy honour and thy crown as it is said, 'And thou hast crowned him with glory and honour' (Ps. VIII:6) and 'in that day shall the Lord of Hosts be for you a crown of glory, and for a diadem of beauty unto the residue of His people'. (Is. XXVIII:5)

If thou attainest to this degree then all veils will be lifted and thou wilt behold naught but the Souls and the Intelligences and thou wilt perceive the prophets and saints in comely form. Thou wilt progress therein until thou attainest an even higher state which man's tongue is incapable of describing. (101) But this can only be obtained through perseverance and practice (*tikrār*). For if thou weariest or indulgest thy fancy in some worldly object and thy lower soul induceth thee into (thinking) that this pursuit is possible whenever thou pleasest to apply thyself thereunto, then thy soul hath lured thee [16a] into an absurd situation. Indeed thou wilt be likened unto him who sayeth, 'I shall sin and thereafter I shall repent'. (Miš. Yōmā' VII:9) For thou knowest that were a man to prepare himself and devote his whole life to this aim, until he had waxed old, he would ever pursue his quest because this state (*maqām*) hath no limit; 'Who can express the mighty acts of the Lord, or make all his praises to be heard?' (Ps. CVI: 2) 'If a man would give all the riches of his house for love, he would utterly be contemned'. (Cant. VIII:7) Similarly it is said; 'O that I had wings like a dove, then would I fly away and be at rest', (Ps. LV:7) 'my soul yearneth, even pineth for the courts of the Lord', (Ps. LXXXIV:3) 'for a day in thy courts is better than a thousand, I would rather stand at the threshold of the house of my God'. (ibid.:11)

Chapter XII

Know that it is impossible to expound and discuss the subject to which I have hinted and alluded throughout (this treatise), by reason of its extreme abstruseness, the intricacy of its meaning and the remoteness of its essence. Consequently, not all men are suited to it nor initially capable of receiving it except after having acquired certain preliminaries. Hast thou not observed how the Pentateuch and Prophets have expressed these notions in the form of parables in order that they may be comprehended? In the same manner the Sages have alluded thereto with allegories, and the Philosophers with conciseness. For these questions are at (first) manifest and then hidden (102) inasmuch as man's grasp of them dependeth on the measure of his labour and passion.

Bearing in mind this preliminary, art thou aware of the parable mentioned in the book of Ecclesiastes, 'there was a little city with few men within it [16b] and there came a great king against it'. (Eccl. IX:14) (103) Man's matter is (here) likened to 'a little city with few men within it', whereas the *evil inclination* is compared to a 'great king'. The reprehensible vices are the 'bulwarks and nets' (Eccl. VII:26) which he built against it. The plight of Reason, which governeth matter, is likened to that of 'a child, poor and wise' (Eccl. IX:15), whom none heedeth nor hearkeneth to his words, as it is said, 'nevertheless the poor man's wisdom is despised and his words are not heard'. (ibid.:16) His humiliation, misery and his isolation suffice not but 'they hated him and could not speak peaceably unto him'. (Gen. XXXVII:4) Yea, they sought to destroy and slay him, saying 'come now therefore and let us slay him'. (Gen. XXXVII:20) (Indeed, they accomplish their design with ease) on account of the scarcity of (Reason's) followers and supporters, i.e. the intellectual faculties, who are 'poor, needy and destitute', whereas the *evil inclination* is called 'a great king' because of his numerous auxiliaries, i.e. the corporeal faculties. Thus David the *Anointed of the Lord of Jacob* proudly declared his conquest and destruction (of the evil inclination), saying 'he smote the two altar-hearths of Moab; he went down also and slew the lion in the midst of a pit in time of snow'. (II Sam. XXIII:20) The Sages of blessed memory have likewise said, 'Who is mighty? He who subdueth his passions as it is said, "He that ruleth over his spirit is better than he that taketh a city".' (Abōt IV:1; Pr. XVI:32)

Hast thou not seen the (evil inclination's) struggle with the Patriarch Abraham on his way to sacrifice (Isaac) as the Rabbis related, 'Satan came to our father Abraham, . . .?' (Genesis Rabbah LVI:5) Consider the *Evil One*'s audacity against a formidable opponent (104) such as this lord, how then (may we fare), we who do not pay regard to (the evil inclination) and are not wary of him, but let the reprehensible vices hold sway over our souls and rule them? [17a]. Yet despite this we stand and implore mercy from our Lord saying, 'Forgive us O Father and prithee look upon our affliction' (105), forgetful of the prophet's warning, 'but your iniquities have separated between you and your God'. (Is. LIX:2) So that we resemble those of whom it is said 'and they beguiled him with their mouth'. (Ps. LXXVIII:36)

O fellow creatures, 'as one mocketh a man would ye mock him?', (Job XIII:9) like the prophet said unto us, 'When ye come to appear before Me, who hath required this at your hand, to trample My courts?' (Is. I:12) 'Yea when ye multiply your prayers, I will not hear . . . (ibid.:15) bring no more vain oblations', (ibid.: 13) 'add your burnt-offerings to your sacrifices and eat ye flesh. For I spoke not unto your fathers, nor commanded them in the day I brought them forth out of the land of Egypt, concerning burnt-offerings or sacrifices, but this thing I commanded them saying: Hearken unto My voice and I will be your God . . . that it may be well with you'; (Jer. VII:21–24) 'after the Lord shall ye walk', (Deut. XIII:5) 'thou shalt love the Lord thy God with all thy heart', (Deut. VI:5) 'for the Lord searcheth all hearts . . . if thou seek Him, He will be found of thee', (I Chr. XXVIII:9) 'He judged the cause of the poor and needy . . . is not this to know Me? saith the Lord'. (Jer. XXII:16) The latter verse alludeth to what we have already mentioned concerning the attention given to the destitute child, 'poor and wise', his reign and the defence of his rights before his claimants.

It is for this reason that the prophet Isaiah alluding thereunto rebuked us saying, 'they shall not judge the orphan, nor shall the widows' cause come unto them', (Is. I:23) 'it hath been told thee, O man, what is good and what the Lord requireth of thee, only to do justly'. (Micah VI:8) Awaken from the slumber of indifference and clear thy head of the intoxication of ignorance (106); fathom thy soul and purge thine intellect of thy passions, so that it rule over them and thy deeds become praiseworthy (17b). Awaken from thy drunkenness and deliver thyself from the sea of stupidity. Persist in that which I have indicated to thee and thy soul will be delivered from perdition and it will have rest and serenity in its abode, 'where the weary are at rest'. (Job III:17)

In the coming chapter I shall now undertake to guide thee in the disciplining of thy corporeal matter, showing thee (firstly) what comportment to adopt in order to throw off the evil inclination and (secondly) what course to follow in the care of thine intellect.

Chapter XIII

Know, o brother, how vigilant a man would be, if he were to know that he hath an enemy who, not content with destroying and suppressing him, is resolved to seize his wife, dishonour her in his presence and destroy his children. He would be ever vigilant, even while eating and drinking, sleeping or waking, to ward off his (enemy). He would be ever mindful of the (latter) in order to arrest him from accomplishing his design. He would not even have a moment's respite, because if the (Evil One) overpowereth him, he would 'not be left so much as a single man-child' (I Kings XVI:11) 'and none of them shall remain or escape' (Jer. XLII:17) but he would be left 'shut up and forsaken forever'. (I Kings XXI:21)

As for the course to be followed (concerning the intellect), thou must install the intellect in the centre 'upon the throne of his kingdom'. (Deut XVII:18) Then appoint the soul as his minister, the principal organs as close commanders and the secondary organs as servants in waiting (107), having each member carry out that which thou deemest appropriate. In this way, thou wilt condemn thine enemy [18a] and bind him 'in fetters' and thou shalt 'give judgement against him'. (Jer. XXXIX:7, 5)

Understand how thou mayest escape his cunning and cursed perfidy, for he is subtle and guileful. He can think like the noble when in their company and knoweth how to escape their grasp. Therefore be sure to learn all the artifices with which he defendeth himself. 'Neither shall thine eye pity him', (Deut. XIII:9) for to be merciful toward evildoers is (to show them) inclemency (108), as the Sage hath said, 'For the mercy of the evil is cruel', (Prov. XII:10) 'but thou shalt surely slay him; thy hand shall be first upon him to put him to death'. (Deut. XIII:10)

If thou achievest this then the state of the city's inhabitants will improve and order will be restored, through the rule of the king who is fitting to govern it. Thereupon it will be said of that city, 'Happy art thou O land if thy King is a free man (109) and thy princes eat in due season'. (Eccl. X:17)

I beseech thee never to deviate from this doctrine in any manner, 'for it is thy life and the length of thy days'. (Deut. XXX:20) In short, I assure thee that as long as the king remaineth instated, then 'the city of Sihon will be built and established'. (Num. XXI:27)

But if the order be disturbed then 'a fire will go out of Heshbon' (ibid.:28) (110) and it will be said of the (city) 'woe to thee O land, if thy king be a boy, and thy princes feast in the morning!' (Eccl. X:16) If, moreover, perversity should spread abroad therein, it will be said 'then a breach was made in the city and all the men of war fled and went forth out of the city by night'. (Jer. LII:7) Thereupon we shall cry in lamentation, 'our city hath been laid waste, our sanctuary is desolate, exiled is our splendour and the glory hath been removed from the house of our life' (111) 'And even all the nations shall say: "Wherefore hath the Lord done thus unto this land? what meaneth the heat of this great anger?"' (Deut. XXIX:23) and answer, 'because they forsook [18b] the covenant of the Lord, the God of their fathers'. (ibid.:24)

Understand then the significance of that to which I have guided thee and strive to perfect thy soul. Be not intemperate when eating and content thyself with what is necessary for thy survival, for it is well known that essential commodities are easier to procure than that which is superfluous. (112)

Indeed men find difficulty in procuring (only) that which is beyond bread, water and air, as the Sage hath said, 'Better is the little of the righteous (than the abundance of the wicked)', (Ps. XXXVII:16) 'better is a dry morsel with serenity therewith (than a house full of feasting with strife)'. (Prov. XVII:1) Regard not the vulgar's indulgence in bodily pleasures, saying 'I can behave as they do' (113), for thou hast turned aside and parted company from them in thy mind (or interior) and thou no longer desirest to resemble them. Know that Abraham as well as David were named 'friend', 'lover' and 'God-fearing' (114) solely in virtue of their having forsaken all else but Him and their having withdrawn (*li-infirādihim*) (115) within the knowledge of Him. For this reason, David commanded his son Solomon saying, 'and thou Solomon my son, know thou the God of thy father and serve Him (with a whole heart and with a willing mind).' (I Chron. XXVIII:9) (116) And did not the Prophet say, 'But let him that glorieth glory in this, that he understandeth and knoweth Me?' (Jer. IX:23) Beware lest thou departest from thy path and destination, 'we shall go by the road of the King', (Num. XX:17) 'we will go up by the highway'. (Num. XX:19) 'I will be surety for him; of my hand shalt thou require him', (Gen. XLIII:9) for the Most High 'is a shield unto them that take refuge in Him'. (Ps. XVIII:31) Be heedful of this.

Chapter XIV

Know that what we have mentioned concerning the subject of matter and the condemnation thereof, is not [19a] on account of the former's essence but because of what is derived therefrom, for *evil* only besetteth the *city* in an accidental manner, 'through the arrogance of wickedness the poor is consumed'. (Ps. X:2) Yet hath not the Sage said (of the evil inclination) despite its (adversity), 'If thine enemy be hungry then feed him bread, and if he be thirsty then give to drink'? (Pr. XXV:21) (117). I conjure thee to proceed cautiously as I have instructed thee at the beginning of this treatise; thereupon thou wilt achieve all that thou desirest.

Exhortation

Firstly it behoveth thee to reduce thine intercourse with common folk and increase thy frequentation of men of virtue, who possess the *spirit* so that thou mayest emulate their upright conduct and excellent morals and dispel thy blameworthy traits, as the Sage hath said, 'He who walketh with wise men shall be wise, but the companion of fools shall worsen'. (Pr. XIII:20)

Then thou must inure thyself to speak little except that which causeth thee gain in this world and happiness in the hereafter. The Sage hath said, 'In the multitude of words there wanteth not sin (but he that refrainest his lips is wise).' (Pr. X:19) 'Whoso is profuse of words causeth sin . . . my whole life long I have grown up amongst the wise and I have found nought better for the body than silence'. (Abōt I:17) Next thou must amend thy diet as much as thou canst, decreasing thy relish until thou becomest accustomed to partake infrequently of food, so that thy thoughts desist therefrom. Strive also to reduce [19b] thy slumber, as Solomon the Wise hath said, 'a little sleep, a little slumber'. (Pr. VI:10) Then train thy soul progressively to think of nought else but Him or that which draweth thee near to Him until thy soul waxeth strong enough to help thee to obtain the end to which thou aspirest. Furthermore, at prayer time, purify thine intention (*niyya*) (118) and be thoroughly mindful of what thou utterest. Beware not to harbour thoughts of ought else but the object of thy devotion, lest the serpent's venom penetrate thee at a moment of inattention and render thy supplication unacceptable and of no avail. Consequently, as a preliminary to prayer, it is fitting to prepare oneself through the *ablution of one's hands and feet* (119), restoring and arousing thereby the soul. Furthermore, always recite a preliminary *Psalm* so that thy concentration (*kawwanah*) be engaged and avoid praying in ruined places (120) lest thou entertain foreign thoughts. If thou achievest this (state) and remainest steadfast therein with the help of thy master, then praise the Lord and give thanks unto Him for such a grace. Pay no attention to people who content themselves at prayer time with *concentrating on the first verse of the Šema' and the first paragraph (of the 'Amīdāh)* for the Truth shall show the Path. (121) Rather turn thyself to the attainment of thine objective and let not the world beguile thee with its beauty, for 'grace is deceitful and beauty is vain, but a woman that feareth the Lord, she shall be praised'. (Pr. XXXI:30) And when thou arrivest at thy heart's desire then 'give unto her from the fruit of her hand and her deeds shall praise her in the Gates'. (ibid.:31) Then wilt thou exclaim 'for now I know that thou art a woman of fair form' (Gen. XII:11) and it shall be said concerning thee 'I will multiply thee exceedingly [20a] and kings shall come forth from thee' (Gen. XVII:6) (122) 'and I will establish My covenant with thee ... to be for thee as a God and unto thy seed after thee'. (ibid.:7) Understand all this.

CHAPTER XV

Realize O my son how much the matters we have mentioned are alien and repulsive to the body and even the mind. The latter will at first refuse to acquiesce, since the body's nature spurneth such (matters) and the mind's faculties shrink before them. This may surely be compared to the case of a small child who was commended to a tutor to be taught the religious Law. Because the tutor began supervising its diet, sleep and speech in order utterly to reform them, the child became grieved and would fret, for his conduct which had hitherto been unrestricted, had now become governed by the tutor. However when the child grew up and matured he appreciated the value of what the tutor had done for him and rewarded him, where the latter had been successful. The corporeal matter will react similarly to Reason, for it hath also been accustomed to the habits contracted during its upbringing, of which it will prove difficult to break it. Consequently, proceed by degrees, in imitation of the manner in which Nature worketh, lest thou come to grief. For if ever the corporeal matter refuseth to relinquish one of its former habits, it is because it hath been too hastily changed. Thus I have urged thee to advance progressively [20b], in order to train the matter of the body (*qālib*) (123) from the outset, so that it become not refractory and troublesome, thereby defeating the purpose. (124) The Sage hath said in this respect, 'Be not too righteous . . . (Be not too wicked nor foolish; why shouldst thou die before thy time?) It is good that thou shouldest take hold of the one; yea also from the other withdraw not thy hand.' (Eccl. VII: 16–18) (125)

Know my son, that if thou desirest to achieve the state of solitude (*ḫalwa*) (126) and a worldly affair crosseth thy mind whilst thou art seated in contemplation, I urge thee to expel and banish it from thine abode and bar the door in its face; 'above all that thou guardest, keep thy heart'. (Pr. IV:23) Pursue thy task strengthening thy zeal, and thou wilt not find it difficult to remove this worldly thought from thy mind, for if it be a necessity then it will come of (itself). Indeed the fundamentals of existence are linked to one another and thou wilt have no difficulty in obtaining them when needed, for the necessary commodities can be acquired without the least effort and all else is superfluous. So turn thy thoughts from them and consider rather our *forefather* Jacob who requested but 'bread to eat and raiment to don'. (127) (Gen. XXVIII:20) Indeed 'this is the way that is becoming for the study of the Torah: a morsel of bread with salt thou must eat; upon the ground thou must sleep and a life of toil thou must live the while thou toilest in the Law.' (Abōt VI:4) (128)

The sole aim of the Sages in the composing of their works for us was that we should heal therewith our souls (129) and thus allay the difficulty of the task ahead. Indeed, none may travel this path save he that hath subdued and dominated this beastlike matter. But deal gently with it lest it resist thee (130) as happened to Balaam who resorted to violence and therefore the Angel rebuked him for having smitten his corporeal matter 'these three times'. (Num. XXII:32) Be then exceedingly wary of resistance, as [21a] I have warned thee aforetime, and keep watch lest it be said of thee, 'Surely now I might have slain thee and saved her alive'. (ibid.:33) For thou art entrusted with its guidance 'and unto thee is its desire, but thou shalt rule over it'. (Gen. IV.7)

Know thou that the Path which thou walkest is fraught with serpents in search of prey, and so thou must have much water. Consider the Patriarchs, peace upon them, whose sole pursuit and labour were for (water), as it is said, 'And Isaac digged again the wells of water which they had digged in the days of Abraham his father'. (Gen. XXVI:18) Israel acted likewise whilst in the wilderness; because of their great thirst 'the people murmured against Moses saying: "What shall we drink?"' (Ex. XV:24) 'And water came forth abundantly, and the congregation drank and their cattle'. (Num. XX:11) Similarly had Hagar not found more water when her flask was spent, her child would have perished, 'but God opened her eyes (and she saw a well of water)'. (Gen. XXI:19) If thou proposest to dig a well as did thy forefathers, then do so, 'drink waters out of thine own cistern, and running waters out of thine own well. Let thy springs be dispersed abroad.' (Pr. V:15) (131)

Chapter XVI

Know O my son that the intellect formeth the bond between thee and Him, may He be exalted, (132) and that the nourishment that sustaineth (the intellect) is the knowledge of the unalterable things, without which it would be unable to subsist or exist. Just as the body cannot subsist without salubrious and suitable food, so the intellect is sustained only by true knowledge through whose permanence it itself remains permanent. (133)

However there is no perpetuity or gain, neither in this world nor the hereafter, for him who studieth the sciences without comprehending their deeper significance. [21b] For in this world he would have lacked the gratification of having grasped their meaning since 'he hath not derived one proposition from another' (Šābbāt 31a) and in the hereafter his studies will disappear with his own disappearance on account of his having derived no spiritual instruction therefrom. Now God hath bestowed upon us a perfect Law which leadeth us to perfection. (134) Indeed it fortifieth our moral and intellectual strength, inasmuch as sound reason is the perfect Law and the Divine Law is sound reason, as it is written in the revealed book, 'Unto thee it was shown, that thou mightest know that the Lord, He is God; there is none else beside Him'. (Deut. IV:35)

The Sages have required of the wise man that he be, amongst other things, 'virtuous, exempt of ire and drunkenness, forbearing, gentle of speech to his fellows and middle-aged.' (Qiddūšīn, 71a) Take a Sage who is most proficient in the penetration of the mysteries of the Law and who, on account of his experience and wisdom, hath elucidated some of its secrets. Were such a person to be initiated (135) into the Law, then, providing he be 'wise and intuitive . . . and the headings of the chapters are imparted to him', (Hagīgāh 13a) he will eventually grasp all the mysteries necessary for the fulfilment of his aim and purpose, inasmuch as all is contained therein, as he who knoweth it well hath declared, (136) 'the Law of the Lord is perfect, restoring the soul'. (Ps. XIX:8) Similarly, the Rabbis of blessed memory have said, 'Turn it and turn it again for everything is therein; contemplate it and stir not from it, for thou canst have no better rule than this'. (Abōt V:25)

Exhortation

Know O my son that if some mystery be revealed to thee, either through thine own effort or through guidance, then [22a] ascribe not any merit to thyself nor disparage those lower than thyself lest thou come to harm, as the Sage hath said, 'He doeth it that would destroy his own soul', (Prov. VI:32) and it is said, 'neither shalt thou go up with steps unto My altar, that thy nakedness be not uncovered.' (Ex. XX:23) (137)

We have already warned thee, that none should share this pursuit with thee (so that) none may hold thee back from it. If (peradventure) thou betrayest thyself then the unimaginable will befall thee on its account. (138) Thou wilt be as the man stricken with poverty and known for his continual penury and his acceptance of alms from his fellow men who happened upon a treasure. Following this occurrence he became haughty toward his fellow men and avoided them, rebuffing them with word and deed. Consequently, his companions began to enquire after him and his situation and when they understood that he had come across a treasure, they denounced him to the king and all his belongings were confiscated. Thus he found himself reduced to a predicament harsher than his former state of poverty.

Hence it behoveth him that hath grasped a little of what we have alluded to, that he conceal and not disclose it to anyone except those worthy thereof (139) and not depart from the outward manner (*ṣūra*) to which he had been hitherto accustomed. Let him hold intercourse with his fellow men and endure their vulgarity whilst he contemns it in his heart. Let him be watchful of himself lest his language resemble theirs, either overtly or allusively. Moreover, let him ward his speech, (140) as the Lord hath commanded, 'therefore shall ye keep my charge' (Lev. XVIII:30); the Sages having explained this to mean 'appoint a guardian over my charge'. (Yĕbāmōt, 21a) Employ dissimulation (*kitmān*) (141) as the Sage hath said [22b] in a similar sense, 'I adjure you, O daughters of Jerusalem ... (that ye awaken not, nor stir up love until it please)'. (Cant. II:7) However upon acquiring the habit (*malaka*), this situation will pass, 'and the Lord whom ye seek, will suddenly come to His temple'. (Mal. III:1) If thou hast not what thou desirest, then desire what thou hast. (142) In this way, diminishing thy diet will not prove difficult. Grasp the capital that is with thee 'and to Him shalt thou cleave', (Deut. X:20) and put it to use to the extent of thy capacities 'until the Lord look forth and behold from heaven'. (Lam. III:50)

Chapter XVII

Know thou that in days of yore, the virtuous would strive to establish schools for their disciples. There they would instruct them in the doctrine (*mādda*) that would edify them and assist in the study of the Law and in the knowledge of the acquisition of its particulars, its ends and lofty goals, which surpass the comprehension of the masses. If I perceive of their words that which will likewise benefit our purpose, I shall divulge a part thereof in accordance with the consideration 'give to a wise man and he will be yet wiser'. (Prov. IX:9) These (Sages) were known as the 'disciples of the prophets' (143). However since our science has waned, the ways of the prophets have ceased from amongst us and ignorant nations have gained sway over us through this interminable exile which we are to endure 'until the coming of Shiloh'. (Gen. XLIX:10) (144) We since rely on those that lead the prayers and expound 'general principles' (*ra'šey dĕbārīm*). If we grasp something thereof (so much the better) but if not, we discard them and this is (in reality) the opposite of their purpose. [23a] Our observance of the commandments of the Law hath become a matter of rote, for which God hath rebuked us through his prophet saying, 'And their fear of Me is a commandment of men (learned by rote)'. (Is. XXIX:13)

Thou knowest that the practice of the precepts is intended as a preliminary moral discipline for man with a view to his being granted the true Torah (*at-Tōrāh al-ḥaqīqiyya*) (145) which is intended for him. Therefore strive in order to acquire those preparatives and discard thy reprehensible traits, 'they shall not dwell in thy land, lest they make thee sin against Me . . . for they will be a snare unto thee'. (Ex. XXIII:33) Consider that which is written thereafter, 'And unto Moses He said: "Come up unto the Lord".' (Ex. XXIV:1) (146) And now fathom the following observation, upon which the purport of this treatise is founded.

Observation

I wish to draw thine attention to the comprehension of Scripture and how to read it as a 'lover' (*muštāq*) and a 'seeker' (*ṭālib*) and not as it is read nowadays by people who consider not what they read but simply recite (the text), as if its purpose were solely to be read (*talāwa*). (147) Or (they think that the purpose of the Scriptures) consisteth in the knowledge of interchangeable (*ḫalaf*) (148), simple (*ḫafīf*) or double letters (*ṯaqīl*) (149) or the personal interpretation of a word, explained differently by others. This has nothing to do with their (real) purpose, which consisteth in their committal to memory, until thy mind happeneth upon one of the doctrines to which I have drawn thine attention. Thou wilt meet with a verse which correspondeth to that doctrine, and thou wilt infer therefrom a further meaning, ascending from one meaning to another until thou reachest the object of thy quest. [23b] The sages alluded to this (procedure) in their statement in the *Midraš*, 'How may the words of the Torah be described prior to their elucidation by Solomon? Her waters were deep and cool and none could drink therefrom. What did the discerning man do? Joining rope to rope and cord to cord, he drew from it and drank. Thus proceeded Solomon, joining one parable to another and one meaning to another until he penetrated the mysteries of the Torah.' (Cant. Rabbāh I:8) (150) Similarly Solomon hath said, 'counsel in the heart of man is like deep water; but a man of understanding will draw it', (Pr. XX:5) 'a wise man will hear and will increase learning ... to understand a proverb and the interpretation; the words of the wise and their riddles'. (Pr. I:5–6) Indeed, an apprentice of any science proceedeth in a similar manner. Firstly, he retaineth the fundamentals (*uṣūl*) thereof, then he proceedeth to learn its (true) meaning. Upon attaining this (level), he undertaketh the quest for its ultimate goal. Thou needst approach the words of the Sages in a similar fashion. If thou desirest to comprehend their allegories, then meditate attentively their sayings and, if thou understandest not, then study them with an expert master, well versed in their words and held in honour. However as a general rule it is well to receive the truth from whosoever uttereth it, so that thou mayest derive therefrom that which thou requirest for thy Path, as the Sage hath said, 'Who is wise? He who learneth from all men, as it is said, "From all my teachers I have gotten understanding".' (Ps. CXIX:99) (Abōt IV:1)

Despite the numerous Paths which the Sages opened up and strove to clear and disencumber, 'the dove hath found no rest for the sole of her foot' (Gen. VIII:9) 'had it not been for the Lord who was on our side' (Ps. CXXIV:1) 'Who hath left us a remnant on earth' (Gen. XLV:7) in the form of the Law which we possess, then we would [24a] have perished as have perished other nations of the past. The Lord hath said, 'And yet for all that, when they are in the Land of their enemies, I will not reject them (neither will I abhor them to destroy them utterly)', (Lev. XXVI:44) 'if My covenant be not with day and night, if I have not appointed the ordinances of heaven and earth (then will I also cast away the seed of Jacob)'. (Jer. XXXIII:25)

Chapter XVIII

The chapter upon which we are now about to enter is a kind of conclusion. I (first) preferred not to include it in the (present) treatise but it is nevertheless meet to do so on account of the wondrous things it containeth, so be heedful of them.

Know that the rational faculty with which man alone amongst animals is endowed, is not a body, nor a faculty in a body. (151) On its account, it is said of man that 'in the likeness of God He made him'. (Gen. V:1) If (the rational faculty) graspeth an intelligible, it is elevated through it to a greater potentiality than that enjoyed prior to their conjunction.

If man devote his entire being to Reason, then he will think little of bodily matters and they will no longer bother him as before. It is for this reason that Adam was not aware of his nakedness, on account of his devotion to Reason. (152) It is possible for man to remain for days on end without requiring food because of his concentration on and his utter absorption with this pursuit. It is for this reason that thou seest those that have attained something of this (degree) scorning the suffering which attendeth it, as hath been said: 'I have contented my contempt, with my passion for Him.' (153)

Quite the opposite is he who hath opted for the (passions) of the body, since he is incapable of enduring hardships but complaineth and is irritated by [24b] affliction, for his lower soul is idle. However, were his soul to occupy itself with this pursuit then the pain would ease and his body would become insensitive to it, on account of the soul's higher preoccupations.

Therefore my son, take care to repulse the affairs of the body as much as possible, for this will ease the restlessness that thou wilt experience at the very beginning of thy Path (*sulūk*). Upon being delivered from the snare of the body, the soul hath been compared to a shred of silk that hath fallen among the thorns (154): 'as a lily among the thorns (so is my love among the daughters)'. (Cant. II:2) How shall the soul fare? The more one is attached to the world the wider is one's separation from the soul. Therefore the Sages have said, 'Lessen thy toil for worldly goods and busy thyself with the Torah'. (Abōt IV:12)

O my son, one cannot be called 'a lover' nor 'an ardent lover' unless one attacheth one's soul to this pursuit. (155) Thou wilt find those who, by dint of practice, have accomplished something of this end and have become lovesick (*hā'im*). The more they become attached to it, the more intense is their craving, as David hath said, 'As the hart panteth after the water brooks (so panteth my soul after Thee)', (Ps. XLII:2) 'my soul thirsteth for God, for the living

God'. (ibid.:3)

Consequently, thou wilt surely see those who are attached to Him withdrawing to the desert and the uninhabited wilderness. How right they are to do so, because the Cherubim are numerous there as thou knowest (156)—and because this act enhanceth their courage and their resolve to discard all the encumbrances and burdens of life. (157) Furthermore the Lord dealt with us in a similar manner; when He wished to perfect us, He led us in the desert [25a] for forty years. He likewise promised us that the Exile would come to an end, for with the end of the Exile, (spiritual) union (*ittiṣāl*) (158) and perfection will be possible. The Patriarchs also dwelt most of their lives in the desert, as it is said of Abraham, 'He dwelt at the tent door' (Gen. XVIII:1) (159), likewise it is said of Isaac, 'And Isaac went out to meditate in the field' (Gen. XXIV:63) and of Jacob, 'And Jacob sent and called Rachel and Leah to the field'. (Gen. XXXI:4) Furthermore, the accounts of Elijah and Elisha also refer to this practice. Similarly, Jeremiah said, 'Oh that I had in the wilderness a lodging place for wayfarers that I might leave my people'. (Jer. IX:1) They only frequented the cities out of necessity, or in order to accomplish the Divine Will or a prophetic mission (*risāla*), to the inhabitants thereof. However the individuals who attained this state were very scarce, as it is said, 'I have seen the sons of Heaven, but they are few', (160) (Sūkkāh 45b) *like a drop in the sea*, 'and they that are left of you shall pine away in their iniquity in your enemies' lands'. (Lev. XXVI:39) For thou wilt find in each era but a single individual, such as Noah in the generation of the Flood, his predecessor Methuselah, Enoch, Lemech, Shem, Eber, Abraham, Isaac and Jacob. After the Patriarchs the bond (*wuṣla*) was severed and there was no intercessor (*šafīʿ*) until the birth of the most glorious of beings and the noblest of creatures, our Master Moses, peace be upon him, who restored it, through the Divine Will. (161)

It is clear that he who hath not gained an intercessor to mediate between himself and his Beloved, is *considered as dead*. (Nĕd. 64b) (162) Once thou hast realized this principle, then thou wilt be ashamed to call on the Lord without having achieved this. [25b]

Indeed '*Who is he and where is he* who could bear to stand before the Lord' [Esther VII:5] without having recourse to a mediator, for this is sheer impertinence! Thus it is incumbent upon us to seek diligently after an intercessor and to find one without delay, for he is our guardian in the nether world and our guide to the world everlasting and think not otherwise.

Yet despite this (intercession) we must stand and implore (the Divine mercy) for ourselves, saying 'withhold not thy tender mercies from me O Lord' (Ps. XL:12) for we rely on His clemency. Whereas he (Reason) will intercede for *those that sleep in the dust* (163) and he will request mercy for Israel so that they may be delivered from *among the nations*. It is through his mediation that we will reach the most *holy of Holies*, as it is said, 'I will say, "It is my people": and they shall say, "The Lord is my God".' (Zach. XIII:9)

Consider the divine favour of this bond which the Lord hath fastened within us, by which, if it is strengthened, the divine power may be attached to us who are but '*a fetid drop, of little intelligence*'. (164) Were man to perfect his soul, he would be sure, upon following the latter, to arrive within the precincts (or protection) of the Master of the World (*rabb al-'ālamīn*) and remain with Him everlastingly. Gird upon thy loins and serve the Truth as is meet, if thou art a virtuous servant. But if thou art an unworthy servant then it will be said of thee, 'therefore shalt thou serve thine enemies (Deut. XXVIII:48) . . . because thou didst not serve the Lord thy God'. (ibid.:47) Thus take heed, *remember and forget not* 'He will be with thee, He will not fail thee neither forsake thee'. (Deut. XXXI:8) [26a].

Exhortation

The Sages, peace be upon them, made mention of a principle to which I thought I might draw thine attention. They said: 'Consider each text wherein mention is made of the greatness of God and His elevation, therein also shalt thou find his humility and modesty' (165) as in the verse, 'Extol Him that rideth upon the heavens by His name Jah . . . a father of the fatherless and a judge of widows'; (Ps. LXVIII:5–6) likewise 'I dwell in the high and holy place, with him also that is of a contrite and humble spirit' (Is. LVII:15) and 'though the Lord be high yet hath he respect unto the lowly' (Ps. CXXXVIII:6) and 'our God, who dwelleth on high, who humbleth himself to see (things in heaven and on earth)'. (Ps. CXIII:5–6) As for the verse, 'I dwell on high . . . to revive the spirit of the humble' (Is. LVII:15) (it meaneth) that the soul may turn to Him and become intimate through His Proximity (*qurb*) and the presence of the Divine Beauty (*ǧamāl*). But since man cannot remain in such a lofty state without either expiring or returning to (the demands) of his matter, he (must) therefore confess his sin and error before God, so (that) he may be forgiven, as it is said, 'For I will not contend forever, neither will I always be wroth'. (Is. LVII:16)

The whole significance of the foregoing is that the individual should not venture upon this task until he hath subdued his instincts, vanquished his passions and weakened his ambitions. For if he embark upon (this Path) while yet fettered to wordly affairs, he will not find success 'and he will bring upon himself a curse rather than a blessing'. (Gen. XXVII:12) However, if thou severest thy thoughts from the pleasures of this world, turning toward God in thy heart [26b] and departing not from His door, then wilt thou be delivered from the imperfection and accidents of this nether world. Upon being assailed by matter's exigencies, such as eating and drinking, thou shalt be confused with shame; yea, upon doing so the Perfect man (*aš-šaḫṣ al-kāmil*) (166) will 'mourn and cover his head' (Esther VI:12) and be *full of shame and confusion*. (167) It behoveth man when rising, resting, or walking, that his heart cease not to contemplate (168) the Almighty in the hope that this will safeguard him until he reacheth his destination and that He will intercede for him if he turn to Him.

[Final] Exhortation

It hath been repeatedly said to thee that true devotion stemmeth from the heart, as it is said, 'And to serve Him with all your heart and with all your soul.' (Deut. XI:13) (169) This is indeed the goal of the exoteric Law. If an individual turn towards Him, it needeth be with the totality of his heart. Few, however, accomplish such a thing, whether it be in prayer, in study or in listening to the reading of the Torah. Indeed they occupy themselves rather with serving that which distracteth them from His service, and with knowing that which distracteth them from this Knowledge. Even the sole concern of those renowned for their science is to hear the interpretation of a Biblical verse or a pleasant expression, such as a line of poetry, with which they can embellish their prayers; in short, something which will charm their listeners. (170)

Whereas the vulgar busy themselves with domestic economy (*'ōl bayīt*) and *worldly affairs*, and their elect (*ḫawāṣṣ*) engage in commerce (*massā' u-mātān*), the particular discipline concerned with the soul [27a], called worship (*'ibāda*), is reserved for the gnostic (*'ārif*). (171)

(What hypocrisy) for one to stand and recite in his prayer 'God breaketh enemies and humbleth the arrogant' (172) or 'pour out thy wrath upon the nations (who know Thee not)', (Ps. LXXIX:6) while he be one of them. Or that he proclaim at other moments, 'Happy is the people, whose God is the Lord' (Ps. CXLIV:15) while he be excluded from them, since he understandeth not what he sayeth but 'he addeth rebellion unto his sin'. (Job XXXIV:37) For he practiseth solely out of imitative tradition (*taqlīd*) (173), and custom. They have turned aside from the Truth and followed after superficial fancies which truly are none other than the *evil inclination*. 'Their deeds are in darkness' (Is. XXIX:15) and of them it is said, '(Thou art near in their mouth) and far from their reins.' (174) (Jer. XII:2)

Beware lest thou tread their path or follow their example or be lured by what hath led them astray. Follow rather the elect—but not the elect of the vulgar—and 'wallow amidst the dust of their feet'. (Abōt I:4) Consider how Joshua waited on Moses, Samuel on Eli and Elisha on Elijah. But beware not to incur their displeasure, lest thou perish, 'for their bite is the bite of a serpent (175) and their sting is the sting of a scorpion'. (Abōt II:15) They will neither be deceived by charm (176) nor will they tend thy wounds. Consider in this respect in what wretched circumstances Gehazi departed from Elisha. (177)

Therefore in their presence exercise humility, modesty and submission, both externally and internally. Clasp thy head and let fall thy tears, let purity follow in thy wake and spend thy days in fasting. Delight not in the joys of the vulgar and sorrow not at that which grieves them. In a word, be not sad with their sadness and rejoice not with their merriment. Despise frivolity and laughter, rather observe silence and speak not except out of necessity [27b], eat not except when indispensable and sleep not unless overcome. (178) All the while thy heart should contemplate this pursuit, and thy thoughts be preoccupied therein as it is said, 'I am asleep but my heart is awake' (Cant. V:2) (179) and likewise David said, 'Were I to awake, I would still be with Thee'. (Ps. CXXXIX:18) Strive to obtain that to which I have given thee guidance for nought compelleth thee from without 'Thy deeds draw thee near and thy deeds draw thee away'. ('Edūyōt V:7) Know that the discipline which thou undertakest is boundless and requires much spiritual predisposition and preparation as it is said, 'And let the priests also that come near to the Lord, sanctify themselves'. (Ex. XIX:22) Such a preparation hath the advantage of easing the difficulties arising from the preliminaries and moral training. 'Though it tarry, wait for it for it will surely come, it will not delay'. (Habbakuk II:3) 'His name is Shoot, and he shall shoot up out of his place.' (Zech. VI:12) 'Happy is he that waiteth and reacheth'. (Daniel XII:12) 'Neither hath the eye seen God, beside Thee Who worketh for him that waiteth for Him.' (Is. LXIV:3) (180)

Here endeth the Treatise of the Pool, attributed to Rabbi 'Obadyāh son of Abraham the Pious, of blessed memory, son of our master his excellency Moses son of Maymūn, may the memory of the righteous be for a blessing.

NOTES ON THE TRANSLATION

(1) Although the introduction is lacking, nothing essential seems to be missing. The opening words may be the last part of an interpretation of Prov. 1:19. See Sa'adya's interpretation *in loc.* ed. Derenbourg, p.16.
(2) On the notion of 'dereliction' cf. *Guide,* III:51, Qāfiḥ, p.682.
(3) This is a Sufi term, cf. *Risāla,* I, p.264. Abraham Maimonides gives the following definition in his *Kifāya,* II, p.306, 'Striving consists in giving one's intellect predominance over one's passions.'
(4) This is a Sufi term, cf. *Risāla,* I, p. 214, *K. al-Luma'*, p.240.
(5) See *Risāla,* I, p.226. Ibn Sīnā remarks in the penultimate chapter of his *Išārāt,* 'contemplation (*mušāhada*) is not like audience. For those that attain the source [the Arabic word also means "eye"] are to be distinguished from those that hear its echo (*aṯr*).'
(6) Cf. *Guide,* III:51, Qāfiḥ, p. 681, 'to remove the obstacles most of which stem from ourselves.'
(7) Cf. *supra* note 33, p.69, and *infra* f°s 15a and 24b.
(8) *Guide,* III:54, Qāfih, p. 695, 'man's perfection is to comprehend whatever he can of the Creator.'
(9) As in Qabbalistic thought, the names Jacob and Israel here represent the human and angelic states of man respectively. See also *Comm.,* p.109, who construes Jacob's struggle with the angel as a spiritual allegory, as does also Yōsef Ibn 'Aqnīn, *Inkišāf al-asrār,* pp.132–4.
(10) The righteous are delivered from astral determination, according to Abraham Ibn Ezra. Cf. Rosin in *MGWJ,* XLII, pp.52–4 and G. Vajda *Juda ben Nissim,* pp.110–121, and *idem* in *Homenaje a Millas Vallicrosa,* II, pp.483–500.
(11) On this term, in addition to the note given by G. Vajda in *JJS* VI, pp.223–5, see Goldziher, *Ma'āni an-nafs,* pp.26 and 36*.
(12) Cf. the similar idea in *Kifāya,* II, pp.380-end.
(13) The spiritual affinity necessary for the reception of Reason's grace, cf. *Kašānī,* p.69 and *infra* f° 6b.

(14) On Reason's Providence see *Guide,* III:51, Qāfiḥ p.683 and *Kifāya,* II, p.158.
(15) Lit. 'whose back is light.'
(16) Cf. *Guide,* III:8, Qāfiḥ p.470, 'When man possesses a receptive body that does not overpower him . . . he possesses a Divine gift.'
(17) Compare Ibn 'Aqnin's interpretation of this verse, *op. cit.,* pp.266–8.
(18) Cf. *Guide,* III:51, Qafih p.676, 'you have in your power to strengthen that bond.' Recognition of one's incapacity to apprehend the Divine constitutes in itself a degree of comprehension. Cf. *Guide,* I:59, Qāfiḥ p.147, *Ma'ānī an-nafs,* pp.12*–13* and G. Vajda, *Isaac Albalag,* pp.127–9.
(19) This expression recalls *Guide,* III:8, Qāfiḥ p.470, 'those who desire to be men in truth.'
(20) Cf. the explanation of this verse proposed by Abraham Maimonides, *Kifāya,* II, p.404, 'those that find strength in God and achieve communion in the course of internal meditation (*ḫalwa bāṭina*) by means of the paths of the heart and intellectual proofs.'
(21) On the Mu'tazilite disdain of *taqlīd* and its appearance in Jewish thought, see G. Vajda, *Théologie,* p.18. Cf. also *Iḥyā'*, III:1, p.101, 'He who advocates blind adherence to Tradition alone, to the complete exclusion of reason, is but a fool.'
(22) The ultimate source of this idea is Aristotle's *Eth. Nich.*, I, VIII, 2, 1098b, 13–15, where advantages are said to be of three types: external, corporeal and psychological. The mediaeval Arab philosophers related the first two to the vulgar and the latter to the élite, since the perfection of the soul was at once man's ultimate and most intimate possession. 'Obadyāh comes back to this idea on f° 26b where he states that the vulgar engage in domestic affairs, the notables in commerce but the gnostics in the service of the soul. A similar hierarchy is to be found in *Midraš Rabbi David,* I, p.3: in the Jewish Sufi work, MS. Bodl. Hunt, 489 f°s 6a-6b, and the Genizah fragment *T–S* NS 163.16 where the following is to be read 'There are three types of politics: that of the élite, that of the gentry and that of the vulgar. The first is man's government of his soul, like Abraham and Isaac . . . the politics of the gentry consists in governing one's family and relatives, like Jacob . . . and the politics of the vulgar consists in the governing of cities and states such as the government of Joseph.' This theory also served as a basis for Maimonides' discussion of the four perfections in *Guide,* III:54, Qafiḥ p.691. See A. Altmann, 'Maimonides' Four Perfections' in *IOS*,II, pp.15–24.
(23) The Sufis were wont to call their doctrine a science, *K. al-Luma',* p.19.
(24) Cf. *Guide*, III:54, Qāfih, p.693, and *Hilḵōt Yĕsōdē ha-Tōrāh*, II:12. This *locus probans* also had its place in the doctrine of Rabbi Abraham he-Ḥasīd, cf. Wieder, p.34.
(25) In connection with the ladder motif see A. Altmann, 'The Ladder of Ascension', in *Studies in Religious Philosophy and Mysticism,* London, 1969, pp.41–72.
(26) On the tripartite division of the sciences see *Hidāya,* p.4, *Théologie* p.14, *Guide,* Introduction, Qāfiḥ, p.8, and H. A. Wolfson, 'The Classification of the

Sciences', in *Hebrew Union College Jubilee Volume,* 1925, pp.285–294.

(27) On the meaning of the term *ḫatm* and its astrological significance, see the references given in note 10 above.

(28) Cf. the words of Ben 'Azzai in *Tosefta Yĕbāmōt,* VIII:5, *Tosefta ki-fĕšuṭṭāh,* VI: 75 and *BT Yĕbamōt,* 63b.

(29) A Sufi term, see *'Awārif al-ma 'ārif,* Ch. XXXII, p.151.

(30) On the Serpent's venom, which also played a part in Maimonides' thought (*Guide,* II:30, Qāfiḥ p.388), see *BT Šabbāt,* 146a, and *Yĕbāmōt,* 103b.

(31) Theriac was the mediaeval antitoxin against snakebite. Cf. *infra* f° 7b and *Kifāya,* II, p.150.

(32) Israel's impetuosity at Sinai and the necessity of adequate preparation are also invoked by Maimonides (*Guide,* I:5, Qāfiḥ, p.33; *Guide,* I:32, Qāfiḥ p.71), Abraham Maimonides (*Kifāya,* II, pp.258, 410 and *Comm.*, pp.311–3): 'this refers to an inward over-eagerness to meditate that which is too great.' This could result in a catastrophe as in the case of Ben 'Azzai (who 'gazed and became demented') and David Maimonides also mentions the theme in his *Midraš Rabbi David,* II, p.86. For the Rabbinic sources regarding the ensuing punishment, see *Wayiqrā' Rabba,* XX:7 and *Tanḥūma, Bĕha'alōtĕkā,* 16, *Aḥarē mōt,* 6.

(33) Compare Maimonides' literal exegesis of this verse in *Guide,* III:45, Qāfiḥ, p.631.

(34) Cf. Introduction, note 16.

(35) These recommendations relating to the divulgence of esoteric doctrines are also voiced by Maimonides, *Guide,* Introduction, Qāfiḥ, p.5; *Guide,* I:33, Qāfiḥ p.74; *Guide*, I:34, Qāfiḥ p.81 and *Hilkōt Yĕšōdē ha-Tōrāh*, IV: II.

(36) Cf. *Guide*, III:17, Qāfiḥ p.514. Unfortunately there is practically no distinction in our text between the rational soul, Reason and the Intelligences.

(37) Cf. *supra* note 13, p.118.

(38) On the notion of *ğabr* see the article *djabriyya* in *EI*², vol. II, p.365 (Montgomery Watt).

(39) Reminiscent of *Guide,* III:9, Qāfiḥ, pp.474–5, 'the phrase does not denote the darkness that surrounds God, for with Him there is no darkness but great light.'

(40) That is the Ġazzālian symbol of the 'Well-Guarded Tablet'. Cf. Introduction, note 43, p.71.

(41) i.e. Reason is the form of the soul. Cf. *Kifāya,* II, p.224.

(42) Cf. Introduction, note 34, p.69.

(43) Cf. Introduction, note 35, p.69 and *infra* f°ˢ 11b and 12a.

(44) Indeed in the *Kuzari,* V:10, ed. Baneth, p.200, God, or the Active Intellect, is described as 'bearing no avarice but bestowing on every object its due.' In the spurious *Mūsar nā'eh,* allegedly an epistle of Maimonides to his son Abraham, (*Epistles of Maimonides,* Leipzig 1858, p.39) an extreme allegorisation equates Moses with the Divine Intellect whereas Pharoah is the corporeal passion. Likewise it is stated in the *Chapter on Beatitude,* pp.32–33, that Moses attained to the 'degree

of the Active Intellect . . . bestowing the emanation on the whole of Israel.' Cf. *infra* note 88, p.123.
(45) Cf. *supra* note 31, p.121.
(46) For the symbolism employed here see above p.41. On the mediaeval interpretation of the word 'Rock' see *Guide,* I:16, Qāfiḥ, p.45, and *Chapter on Beatitude,* p.17.
(47) Cf. *Guide,* I:72, Qāfiḥ, p.201.
(48) See *infra* note 77, p.123.
(49) A similar idea is to be found in *Kifāya,* II, p.226.
(50) On the doctrinal implications of this term see I. Efros in *PAAJR* XI, p.33, and G. Vajda, *Amour de Dieu,* p.112, note 2.
(51) Cf. al-Ġazzālī, *K. al-'Arba'īn,* Cairo, 1909, p.30: 'external purity also has an influence on the illumination of the heart, for when thou accomplishest thine ablutions and feelest external purity, thine heart is uplifted and purified.'
(52) According to Abraham Maimonides (*Comm.,* 305–9) 'outward purity' is achieved by the removal of uncleanliness through ritual ablution, whereas inward purity is achieved by 'the purging of the heart and the emptying of the thoughts of all else but God.' Compare this with the four degrees of purity mentioned by al-Ġazzālī, *Iḥyā',* I:3, p.126, which culminate in the 'purification of the interior of all but God.'
(53) Quoted also by the *Kifāya,* II, p.311.
(54) The brief discussion of the reasons for the precepts is culled from the *Guide,* III Ch. 35 *et seq.*
(55) *Guide,* III:49, Qāfiḥ, p.655, XIVth class. Cf. also Qāfiḥ, p.588.
(56) *Guide,* III:44, Qāfiḥ, p.626, IXth class.
(57) *Guide,* III:40, Qāfiḥ, p.606, Vth class.
(58) *Guide,* III:39, Qāfiḥ, p.601, IVth class. Cf. also *Ṯamāniya fuṣūl,* p.13.
(59) *Guide,* III:37, Qāfiḥ, p.595, IInd class.
(60) The expression *al-muta'ayyadīn bil-Ḥaqq,* which literally means 'those that find strength in God', is also to be found in *Kifāya,* II, p.404.
(61) An allusion to *BT Qiddūšīn,* 31a. This whole passage is however largely derived from the *Guide,* III:52, Qāfiḥ, p.686. A similar idea is expressed by the Pietist author of *T-S* Arabic 44.3: 'How should one conduct oneself . . . when God is looking on . . .and thus the Sages look with disfavour on the baring of one's head and walking with a haughty gait.'
(62) The kings mentioned in this verse, which is a play on Jer. LII:32, no doubt refer to the faculties of the soul, over which reason is to gain sway.
(63) A Sufi term, cf. *Risāla,* II, pp.236–9. *K. al-Luma',* Ch. XXIX, p.56.
(64) Cf. *Guide,* III:51, Qāfiḥ p.677: 'thou breakest the bond between thee and God whenever thou turnest entirely thy thoughts to the necessities of food or other matters.'
(65) The comparison of the soul to a mirror was a popular motif in Arabic Neopla-

tonic literature and appears repeatedly in the *Ihwān aṣ-Ṣafā'* and in the *Liber de Castigiones,* ed. Bardenhewer, VII, p.61. It was also used by Sufis such as at-Tirmidī, *Riyāḍat an-Nafs,* ed. Arberry, pp.70–71, and is one of many light symbols that 'Obadyāh shares with al-Ġazzālī, in whose writings this simile is particularly common. Cf. H. Lazarus-Yafeh, *Studies in Al-Ġhazzali,* pp.312–20. See also T. Burckhardt, 'Die Symbolik des Spiegels in der Islamischen Mystik' in *Symbolon,* I, 1960. pp.12–16. Among the Jewish authors who employed this symbol, Baḥya, *Hidāya,* pp.350–1, (see *Théologie,* p.118), *Ma ānī an-nafs,* 52*, 65, the Pietist author of Hunt. 382 (f° 19) (cf. Rosenthal, *art. cit.,* p.461) and Ibn 'Aqnin, *Sefer ha-Mūsar,* p.80 (where *barzel* signifies 'mirror'), are the most significant.
(66) Cf. *Hidāya,* pp.390–1.
(67) On the notion of *tawaǧǧuh* see Trimingham, pp.213–4 and Anṣari, *al-Futuḥāt al-ilāhīyya,* p.132. The Pietist author of *T-S* NS 189.9 declares 'He who doth not tarry at the Gates of the King will not savour the sweetness of His royal company, as it is said (Prov. VIII:34) "to tarry daily at my Gates."'
(68) This expression is also employed by Maimonides, *Guide,* I:59, Qāfiḥ, p.146.
(69) The text is uncertain.
(70) The text is uncertain.
(71) These themes have been discussed by G. Vajda, in *AHDLMA,* XVII, pp.112–4.
(72) The 'woman of valour' of Prov. XXXI:10 as a metaphor for a 'submissive complexion' was first employed by *Guide,* III:8, Qāfiḥ, p.170, whence it became commonplace in mediaeval exegesis. Cf. *Midraš Rabbi David,* I, pp.81–82: 'whosoever possesseth a goodly and submissive corporeal matter hath found a woman of worth, for such a thing is indeed rare and he that hath found one, hath found beatitude.' Cf. also the author of AIU *Biblical Commentaries,* II B, 151a, I, 11–12 and *supra* note 16, p.119.
(73) Cf. *supra* note 8, p.118 and *Ṯamāniya fuṣūl,* p.16.
(74) Or 'which is surpassed by knowledge'; the text is uncertain.
(75) Cf. *supra* note 43, p.120.
(76) A word play on Eden and *ma'dan,* 'source'.
(77) This opening phrase recalls the famous passage of the *Theology of Aristotle,* ed. Badawi, p.22, 'Often I was alone as it were with my soul . . .' Cf. A. Altmann, 'The Delphic Maxim in Mediaeval Islam and Judaism' in *Studies in Religious Philosophy and Mysticism,* pp.33 ff. 'Obadyāh gives further details of the ecstatic vision on f°s 7a, 12a and 15b. 'The opening of the Gates' is also mentioned in the account given by Rabbi Abraham he-Ḥasīd in his *Commentary on the Song of Songs, T-S* Arabic 1b, 7, translated in our 'Some Judaeo-Arabic Fragments': 'If the Gates be opened, he will be enabled to perceive all that lies within. A vision will take place and he will behold wondrous secrets and comely forms . . . they are those alluded to in the verse (Gen. III:24) "the flame of the revolving sword." The perception of these forms and the beauty of the spectacle shall be commensurate with one's attain-

ment and capacity.' He also describes Reason as 'a resplendent light' as does Ibn 'Aqnin, *Sefer ha-Mūsar*, p.80. Absence from the sensuous world as a condition of entrance into the intelligible world is also evoked by the *Chapter on Beatitude,* whose account of the ecstatic experience (pp.7–8) is likewise inspired by the *Theology of Aristotle*. Cf. also al-Ġazzālī, *Kimiyā' as-Sa'āda,* p.14, 'Upon sleeping, the door of sensual perception is closed, whereupon an inner door is opened which reveals to the individual mysteries from the intelligible world (*'ālam al-malakūt*) and from the 'Well-Guarded Tablet' (*al-lawḥ*). See also Introduction, note 71, p.61, and *Ḥawḍiyya,* f° 8a. As for the comparison of the ecstatic state with the 'lightning' in the scriptural verse quoted, see *infra* note 102, p.125.

(78) On *rūaḥ* as an ambiguous term see *Chapter on Beatitude,* pp.1–2, where the editor refers to Ibn Ǧanāḥ's interpretation of the term as 'prophecy.'

(79) Cf. Introduction, note 35, p.69.

(80) Compare this with Maimonides' expression of the same idea *Guide,* Introduction, Qāfiḥ, p.6, 'It is in accordance with these states, that the degrees of perfection in men (*al-kāmilīn*) vary.'

(81) This refers to the midrašic explanation of the discrepancy between Gen. XVIII:2 and Gen. XIX:1. Abraham who had attained the angelic state thus perceived the Angels as equals, i.e. men. This midraš is also quoted by Maimonides, *Guide,* II:6, Qāfiḥ, p.288, who refers to it as a 'great mystery.'

(82) Cf. *Guide,* II:4, Qāfiḥ, p.285.

(83) On the symbols of the 'tablet', the 'pool' as well as the 'heart' as a seat of spiritual knowledge, all of which were probably borrowed from the writings of al-Ġazzālī, see Introduction, pp.42–43.

(84) Cf. Introduction, pp.15–16.

(85) Cf. *Guide,* II:38, Qāfiḥ, p.412, 'It may be that things perceived (by false prophets) are nothing but ideas which they had before and impressions of which were left in their imaginations . . . whilst some are effaced, certain images alone remain and are perceived as new and objective coming from without.' Maimonides adds that this is a dangerous error 'and many wise men perished thereby.'

(86) Cf. *Guide*, I:32, Qāfiḥ, 71–72, where Maimonides states, after having also alluded to the episode in *Ḥagīgāh*, 'a man should not be impetuous in his investigation of false conceptions.' It seems that Maimonides considered that he knew the real nature of this 'water', cf. *Guide*, II:30, Qāfih, p.384.

(87) Cf. Introduction, note 39, p.70. 'Obadyāh takes 'cistern', equivalent of the Arabic *ḥawḍ* 'pool', to refer to the *heart* in its Sufi connotation.

(88) This is a reference to Reason's role as a mediator between the sensual and intelligible worlds. Indeed in the *Ma'ānī an-nafs* the Active Intellect is known as the 'great interpreter' (*at-turǧumān al-a'ẓam*), p.54 and Goldziher's remarks pp.41*–43*. In Isḥāq Israeli's *Book of the Elements*, (ed. Fried, pp.52–3, *Isaac Israeli* p.135) Reason's role is compared to that of the prophet 'For when the Creator wishes to reveal to the soul what He intends to innovate in this world, He makes

Reason the intermediary between Himself and the soul, even as the prophet is an intermediary between the Creator and the rest of His creatures.' In Sufi literature Reason is sometimes personified as the Prophet Muḥammad himself, as in *al-Futūhāt al-ilāhiyya*, p.139, 'and the individual shall reach Him in this pursuit through Muḥammad, for he is the intermediary (*wāsiṭa*) between God and His creation.' Indeed we have seen earlier how 'Obadyāh, as well as other Jewish authors (*supra* note 44), establishes a parallelism between Moses and Reason. It is important to bear all these associations in mind in connection with 'Obadyāh's enigmatic remarks concerning the 'intercessor' on f° 25b, to which we shall later revert.

(89) On the Arabic expression *yağbur fā'itahu*, 'repair its loss', cf. *Guide*, II:36, Qāfiḥ, p.402.

(90) Cf. *supra* note 24, p.119.

(91) 'Obadyāh is alluding to the constant communion with God through the practice of 'solitude in the crowd' (*ḫalwa bāṭina*) spoken of by Baḥya, *Hidāya*, IX:3, p.361, Moses (*Guide*, III:51, Qāfiḥ, pp.678–9) and Abraham Maimonides (*Kifāya*, II, pp. 383ff.). Cf. Introduction, pp.15–16.

(92) Note the Sufi character of this expression *al-muḥaqqiqūn min ahl hādihi ṭ-ṭarīq*. Cf. *al-Futuḥāt al-ilāhiyya*, p.132, 1.2.

(93) Cf. Introduction, p.18.

(94) Cf. Introduction, p.38, *Kifāya*, II, p.388 and *Comm.*, p.59.

(95) According to Abraham Maimonides, *Comm.*, p.61, Isaac's place of devotion (*ḫalwa*) was situated by the well 'for he would forsake his residence and retire to the wilderness to the above mentioned well in order to devote himself to worship, for he preferred solitude after the manner of the saints and prophets.' Targum Onkelos translates Gen. XXIV:62 *be'ēr le-ḥay rō'ī*, 'the well at which the angel appeared.' An esoterical doctrine concerning the well, similar to that discussed in the Introduction, note 37, p.70, was also known to the first Qabbalists. Cf. Naḥmanides on Gen. XXIV:62 and XXVI:20.

(96) Cf. *Kifāya*, II, p.392.

(97) Cf. Introduction, p.38–39.

(98) For the allegory of the city whose king is Reason, see *supra* p.39. 'Obadyāh's terminology is close to that of al-Ġazzālī, *Kimiyā'as-sa'āda*, p.10: 'if the minister's command is obeyed then the city will be established and the kingdom will prosper.'

(99) It is clear from *Guide*, I:32, Qāfiḥ, p.71, which is certainly 'Obadyāh's immediate source, that the Cherubim here represent 'the inclination toward defects and vice . . . as a result of confusion.' Cf. Introduction, p.40.

(100) The scribe of MS.B apparently inserted here by error two passages which belong to f°s 16b and 27a-b, as they do not appear here in the other MSS. Since this part of the passage was subsequently barred, the interpolation has therefore been omitted in order to restore the integrity of the context. We have however recorded some slight variants which the passage contained. The verse Ex. XIX:22 which

occurs in the interpolated passage is also mentioned by Abraham Maimonides (*Kifāya*, II p.410), who cites it as a warning against the insufficient spiritual preparation which was the cause of Ben 'Azzai's downfall.

(101) Cf. *Kimiyā'as-sa'āda*, p.14, 'and he shall behold the spirits, the angels and the prophets as well as beautiful, comely and majestic forms.' See also *supra* note 77, p.122, and *Theology of Aristotle*, p.22, 'I beheld there such light and brilliance that the tongue is incapable of describing nor the ear of comprehending.'

(102) This expression describing the transient nature of the intuitive vision is taken from Maimonides *Guide*, Introduction, Qāfiḥ, p.6. The latter's use of the imagery of lightning recalls in turn al-Ġazzālī's comparison of inspiration (*waḥy*) to a sudden flash of lightning (*Iḥyā'*, III:1, p.19, *kal-barq al-ḫāṭif*). An identical comparison is also employed by as-Suhrawardī, *'Awārif al-ma'ārif*, (Ch. XXXII, p.153) and *Maqtūl*, *Hayākil an-nūr*, end; cf. Corbin's translation in *L'Archange Empourpré*, p.65 and note 118. Rabbi Abraham he-Ḥasīd also utilises this expression, no doubt borrowed from the *Guide*, in his *Commentary on the Song of Songs* to describe the fleeting experience of ecstasy (*T-S* Arabic 1b.7) 'which flashes as lightning and then disappears as it is said (Cant. V:6) "I sought him but found him not."'

(103) On the allegory of the little city, used, *inter alia*, by Baḥya, *Hidāya*, V:5, p.233, and the Pietist author of *T-S* 13J9.12, see Introduction, note 27, p.69.

(104) The source of this expression which signifies literally 'great tree' is Rabbi 'Aqiba's saying to R. Šim'ōn bar Yoḥai (*BT Pesaḥim*, 112a) 'To hang oneself one must find a high tree.' This midraš is also used by Maimonides, *Guide*, II:30, Qāfiḥ, p.387.

(105) Morning liturgy, cf. *Siddūr R. Sa'adia Ga'ōn*, p.18.

(106) The awakening of the soul from the slumber of indifference is a popular theme in Islamic and Jewish Neoplatonism from the *Iḫwān aṣ-ṣafā'* onwards. Cf. among others, Baḥya, *Hidāya*, VIII:3, p.327, and even Maimonides, *Guide*, II:10, Qāfiḥ, p.296, as well as Pseudo-Maimonides, *Ma'amar ha-yiḥūd*, p.4.

(107) The ultimate source of this allegory is Plato, *Republic*, 440a-441a.

(108) This proverb is to be found in the *Guide*, III:39, Qāfiḥ, p.605, and *Guide*, III:35, Qāfiḥ, p.586. Cf. also *Qōhelet Rabbāh*, VII:33.

(109) 'Free man' signified according to the mediaeval exegetes the individual who had dominated his passions. Cf. Ibn 'Aqnīn, *Sefer ha-Mūssar*, p.57, where he states that he had expounded this subject at length in his *Ṭibb an-nufūs*, which 'Obadyāh may have read.

(110) The foregoing allusions are based on the Talmudical allegory of the righteous and sinful cities, cf. *BT Baba Batra*, 78a.

(111) Liturgy for New Moon and Sabbath Mūsaf, *Siddūr R. Sa'adia Ga'ōn*, p.130.

(112) Taken from *Guide*, III: 12, Qāfiḥ p.486. Contentment with necessities is exemplified according to Maimonides by Jacob's request (Gen. XXVIII:20) 'but

bread to eat and raiment to don,' which is also evoked by Abraham Maimonides, *Kifāya*, II, pp.232, 168 and 184. The idea that the necessities of life are the easiest to procure is also expressed by Baḥya, *Hidāya*, II:5, pp. 120–1.

(113) Cf. *Hidāya*, VIII:3, p.324: 'Turn aside from the superfluities of this nether abode and pursue the necessities of the world to come. Say not "I can behave as the ignorant do."'

(114) The degrees of 'friend' and 'lover' are discussed by Maimonides in the *Guide*, III:51, Qāfiḥ, p.684, and *Hilkōt Tĕšūbāh*, X:6.

(115) On the term *infirād* see L. Gardet, 'Mystique naturelle et mystique surnaturelle en Islam', in *Rech. Sc. Rel.*, XXXVII, pp.335–342.

(116) Cf. *Guide*, III:51, Qāfih, p.676.

(117) Cf. 52a. A less favourable opinion of matter is expressed by Maimonides' *Guide*, III:8, Qāfiḥ, pp.467, 469, and 474. For a general survey of the conflict of matter and mind in mediaeval philosophy see *Juda ben Nissim*, pp.129–134, and H. Blumberg, 'Theories of evil in Medieval Jewish Philosophy' in *HUCA*; XLIII, pp.149–168.

(118) For al-Ġazzālī, *niyya* is a necessary requisite to ablutions and prayer, see *Iḥyā'*, IV:7, pp.362 ff. On the all important notion of *niyya* in Islam see the article *niya* in *EI*[1], III, pp.930–1 (Wensinck).

(119) See Introduction, p.13.

(120) On the prohibition of praying in ruined places see *BT Bĕrākōt*, 3a-b.

(121) Cf. *Guide*, III:51, Qāfiḥ, p.678, and *BT Bĕrākōt*, 14b and 34b. For the expression 'the truth shall show the way', cf. *Tamāniya fuṣūl*, p.16.

(122) The 'woman' portrayed here is a metaphor designating 'matter'. Cf. *supra* notes 16 and 72, pp.119, 122.

(123) On the term *qālib* as a synonym of 'body' see the words of an-Naẓẓām, quoted by aš-Šahrastani, *al-Milal wan-Niḥal*, ed. Cairo, 1968, p.55, 'Man in reality is the soul, the body being merely its instrument and shape (*qālib*).' The term was popular with al-Ġazzālī who liked to contrast it with *qalb*, seat of the spirit; cf. *Kimiyā' as-sa'āda*, pp.8 ff. and Wensinck on al-Ġazzālī's cosmology, quoted above, p.68.

(124) Cf. *Kifāya*, II, p.252: 'The removal of habits, especially where they are supported by natural impulse, at one stroke is impossible ... therefore remove thy habits and weaken thy ties (*al-'alā'iq*) gradually (*tadrīǧ*). Do not, however, be impetuous so thou wouldest fail and not prevail.'

(125) That is, one must not neglect material needs altogether. The same idea is expressed by the Pietist author of *T-S* 10 J 13.8, published by Goitein in *Tarbiz*, XXXIII, p.187.

(126) See Introduction, pp. 15–16 and *Hidāya*, VI, 6, p.257.

(127) Based on *Guide*, III: 12, Qāfiḥ, p.486. See *supra* note 112, p.125.

(128) Cf. *Hidāya*, IX:6, pp. 373–4.

(129) The notion that the traditional sciences are a remedy for man's spiritual ail-

ments is a frequent metaphor in the Middle Ages and one especially dear to al-Ġazzālī, cf. *Théologie*, p.121, *Ṯamāniya fuṣūl*, Ch. III–IV, and H. Lazarus-Yafe, *Studies in al-Ghazzali*, p.343.

(130) On the verb *tamarrasa* see Sa'adya's translation of Num. XXII:29. On the allegorisation of the Bala'am episode cf. Introduction, p.39.

(131) For the symbolism in the foregoing passage cf. *supra* p.49. In the concluding verse, the verb *FWṢ* 'to disperse abroad' was associated in Mediaeval exegesis with the Arabic word *fayḍ* 'emanation.' Cf. *Chapter on Beatitude*, p.10.

(132) Cf. *Guide*, III:51, Qāfiḥ, p. 677. That is, through his intellectual faculty, man constitutes the link between the sensual and intelligible worlds.

(133) That is, the acquisition of the intelligiblia guarantees the rational soul of ever-lasting life.

(134) This expression recalls *Ṯamāniya fuṣūl*, p.11.

(135) In connection with the consultation of Sages, there is a curious list of obscure Biblical verses in the Genizah (*T-S* 16.71) which is headed 'verses to be disclosed to a sage (*futiḥa bihā 'alä ḥākām*).'

(136) Expression taken from *Ṯamāniya fuṣūl*, p.11.

(137) Cf. *supra* note 33.

(138) The text is uncertain. The meaning could be 'thou pretendest to know that of which thou art ignorant', in imitation of the example given in *Hidāya*, V:5, p.256.

(139) Cf. *Chapter on Beatitude*, p.19, 'Do not disclose our words to those not worthy of them.' Both of these recommendations recall the titles of two of al-Ġazzālī's esoterical treatises that 'Obadyāh had no doubt read, *al-Maḍnūn bih 'alä ġayr ahlih*. See Introduction, note 14, p.56.

(140) In Arabic *sayyaǧ*, on which see Blau, *Responsa Maimonides*, I, p.198.

(141) 'Dispensation from the requirements of religion under threat of injury.' Cf. Introduction, note 81, p.62 and the article *takiya* in *EI*[1] IV, pp.628–9 (Strothman).

(142) See I. Davidson, *Thesaurus of Proverbs from Mediaeval Jewish Literature*, Jerusalem, 1957, no.2732.

(143) On this expression see Introduction, pp. 8–10.

(144) Maimonides was also of the opinion that the ancient sciences of the Hebrews had been lost as a result of the Exile; cf. *Guide*, I:71, Qāfiḥ, p.188; *Guide*, II:11, Qāfiḥ, p.300. These would be restored in the Messianic era, alluded to in the Biblical verse quoted, according to the midraš, *Genesis Rabbāh*, XCVIII:13.

(145) I.e. the observance of *šari'a* and *ṭarīqa* lead to *ḥaqīqa*, cf. *al-Futūḥāt al-ilāhiyya*, pp.136–7.

(146) I.e. having subjugated their lower passions, Moses and the Elders were fit to ascend to a higher spiritual plane. Cf. *Guide*, II:32, Qāfiḥ, p.395; *Guide*, III:51, Qāfiḥ, p.679, and *Kifāya*, II, p.390.

(147) Baḥya, *Hidāya*, III:4, p.144–5, esteems that those who consider only the literal or linguistic aspect of Scripture, are among the lowest degree of the adepts of the Torah. See also *Hidāya*, V:5, pp.236-7 and 255, and *Théologie*, p.42.

(148) Cf. W. Bacher, *Die Grammatische Terminologie des Jehuda b. Dawid Hajjuğ*, p.1117.

(149) Cf. L.Prijs, *Die Grammatikalische Terminologie des Abraham Ibn Esras*, p.53.

(150) This midraš is also cited by Maimonides in a similar vein, *Guide*, Introduction, Qāfiḥ, p.11.

(151) On whether the rational soul is a body see G. Vajda in *AHDLMA*, XVII, pp.115–119, *Guide*, I:72, Qāfiḥ, p.208, and *Midraš Rabbī David*, II, p.87.

(152) Cf. *Guide*, I:2, Qāfiḥ, p.27, 'Since Adam was yet guided solely by reflection and reason . . . he could not comprehend why to appear in a state of nudity should be unbecoming.'

(153) We have not been able to trace this saying.

(154) Perhaps this is a reminiscence of *BT Běrākōt*, 8a, 'as a thorn in a ball of wool', which according to Raši (*in loc.*) 'designates the (soul) within the body.'

(155) A reference to the terminology employed by Maimonides, *Guide*, III:51, Qāfiḥ, p.684.

(156) The text is uncertain but it seems that the Cherubim are here equated with the Intelligences in accordance with the interpretation of *Guide*, II:6, Qāfiḥ, p.287: 'The Intelligences are known as Cherubim.'

(157) The passage through the wilderness according to Maimonides, *Guide*, III:24, Qāfiḥ, p.554, and *Guide*, III:32, Qāfiḥ, p.677, was intended to prepare the Israelites for the conquest of the Promised Land, since 'hardship develops courage.' Abraham Maimonides, on the other hand, maintains that the sojourn in the wilderness was for purposes of *ḫalwa*, cf. *Kifāya*, II, pp.390–2. That life in the desert is conducive to boldness is an idea current among the Arabs. Cf. Ibn Ḫaldūn, *al-Muqaddima*, I.i:5, and S. Pines, 'Ibn Khaldun and Maimonides, in *SI*, XXXII, 265–74.

(158) See *supra* note 50, p.121.

(159) See Introduction p.38 and *Kifāya*, II, pp.388 ff.

(160) Cf. *Kifāya*, II, p.274 and *Sefer ha-Mūsar*, p.81.

(161) See Introduction, pp. 9–10. On the epithets of Moses used here cf. *Guide*, II:33, Qāfiḥ, p.397, and Maymūn's *Letter of Consolation*, ed. L. Simmons in *JQR*, II, p.12 and W. Bacher, *Die Biblexegese Moses Maimunis*, Budapest, 1896, p. 78 note 1.

(162) Contrary to Vajda in *JJS* VI p.221, who sees in the intercessor a *šayḫ* or spiritual mentor, we are inclined to believe that this passage must be construed as an allegorical reference to the intercessional role of reason. Cf. *supra* note 88, p.123. The Hebrew term *mēlīṣ* discussed there is taken by Maimonides (*Guide*, III:23, Qāfiḥ, p.540) in the context of Job XXXIII:23, to mean 'intercessor.' It would seem that the eschatological functions ascribed to the intercessor here are to be interpreted figuratively. See also the following note. On Moses' role as an intercessor, see *Kifāya*, I, p.202.

(163) The verse is here used figuratively to designate 'those that inhabit the material body'.
(164) Taken from *Hilkōt Yĕsōdē ha-Tōrāh*, II:2.
(165) *BT Mĕgīllāh*, 1a.
(166) G. Vajda in *JJS* VI, p.221, suggests a parallel with Ibn Sina's *Perfect Man*. David Maimonides describes in his *Midraš Rabbi David*, I, pp.49 and 96, the *sahṣ al-kāmil*, who 'knows the mysteries of the law, has subdued his matter . . . receives the emanation of Reason's light, etc.'
(167) Liturgy for the Day of Atonement, S. Baer, *'Abōdat Yisrā'el* p.430.
(168) On the notion of *murāqaba*, see *Théologie*, pp.87, 115–6.
(169) *BT Ta'anit*, 2a. Cf. also *Sifri Deut.*, XI:13, *Yĕr. Bĕrākōt*, IV:1 *Guide*, III:51, Qāfiḥ, p.676, and the remarks of Z. Blumberg in *Zion*, LXXVIII, pp.135–145.
(170) Cf. *supra* note 147, p.127.
(171) Cf. *supra* note 33, p.119.
(172) Morning liturgy, *Siddūr Sa'adia Ga'ōn*, p.18.
(173) Cf. *supra* note 21.
(174) Cf. *Guide*, III:51, Qāfiḥ, p.678; *Guide*, II: 12, Qāfiḥ, p.304: 'Imagination is identical with the evil inclination.'
(175) *Textus receptus*: 'the bite of the fox.'
(176) Cf. Maimonides *Commentary on Abōt*, II:15, ed. Qāfiḥ, p.428. David Maimonides in his *Commentary on Abōt*, p.36, translates *lĕḥišāh* as 'bite of a serpent.'
(177) See II Kings V:26–7 and *Kifāya*, II, p.250.
(178) See Introduction, note 77, p.61.
(179) Cf. *Guide*, III:51, Qāfiḥ, p.679, and *Kifāya*, II, pp.386 and 394. One is tempted to draw a parallel with Sufi teachings on the *Ḥadīt* (Wensinck, *Handbook*, p.163) 'My eyes sleep but my heart is awake.' Cf. al-Ḫarrāz, *K. aṣ-Ṣidq*, ed. Arberry, Calcutta, 1932, p.73.
(180) A reference to the Messianic era, according to *BT Bĕrākōt*, 34b.

APPENDIX

A. INDEX OF SUFI TECHNICAL TERMS

B. INDEX OF PASSAGES QUOTED

C. LIST OF MSS CONSULTED

D. INDEX OF NAMES

BIBLIOGRAPHY

Abū Ṣāliḥ. *Churches and Monasteries of Egypt*, trans. B. Evetts, Oxford, 1895.
Altmann, A. 'Das Verhältnis Maiminis zur jüdischen Mystik', *MGWJ*, LXXX, 1936, 305–330.
—— 'The Delphic Maxim in Mediaeval Islam and Judaism', *Studies in Religious Philosophy and Mysticism*, London, 1969, 1–40.
—— 'the Ladder of Ascension', *ibid.*, 41–72.
—— 'Maimonides' Four Perfections', *Israel Oriental Studies*, II, 1972, 15–24.
—— and S.M. Stern. *Isaac Israeli*, Oxford, 1958.
Anon. *Risālat al-Asrār*, MS. *Bodl.*, Pococke 186.
Anon. Pietist. *Maqāla fi Derek̮ ha-Ḥasīdūt*, MS *Bodl.*, Huntingdon 382.
al-Anṣāri, Zayn ad-din. *Al-Futūḥāt al-Ilāhīyya*, ed. A.H. Harley, *JRSAS* Bengal, N.S., XX, 1924, 123-142.
Ashtor, E. *A History of the Jews in Egypt and Syria*, 3 vols., Jerusalem, 1944–71.
Asín Palacios, M. *The Mystical Philosophy of Ibn Masarra*, English edn., Leiden, 1978.
Assaf, S. *Texts and Studies*, Jerusalem, 1946.
Bacher, W. *Die Bibelexegese Moses Maimonides*, Budapest, 1896.
—— 'The Treatise on Eternal Bliss attributed to Moses Maimuni', *JQR*, IX, 1896, 270–289.
Badawi, A. *Aristoteles apud Arabes*, Cairo, 1948 (3rd. edn., Kuwait, 1977).
Baer, S. *Abōdat Yisra'ēl*, Rodelheim, 1868.
Bannerth, E. 'Dhikr et Khalwa d'après Ibn 'Ata Allah', *Mélanges de l'Institut Dominicain des Etudes Orientales*, XXII, 1974, 65–90.
Benaim, Y. *Malk̮ē Rabbānān*, Jerusalem, 1931.
Berger, M. *Islam in Egypt Today*, Cambridge, 1970.
Berliner, A. *Quellenschriften zur jüdischen Geschichte und Literatur*, Frankfurt-am-Main, 1896.
Blau, J. *A Grammar of Mediaeval Judaeo-Arabic*, Jerusalem, 1961.

Blumberg, H. 'Theories of Evil in Medieval Jewish Philosophy: Matter as a source of evil ', *HUCA*, XLIII, 1972, 149–168.
Blumberg, Z. 'Al-Farabi, Ibn Baǧǧa and Maimonides on the Regimen of the Solitary', *Sinai*, LXXVIII, 1975, 135–145.
Blumenthal, D. *The Commentary of R. Hoter ben Shelomo to the Thirteen Principles of Maimonides*, Leiden, 1974.
Brande, M. 'Maimonides' Attitude to the Midraš', in *Festschrift I. Kiev*, New York, 1971, 75–82.
Brann, M. 'Joseph Sambari's Nachrichten über das Geschlecht der Maimoniden', *MGWJ*, XLIV, 1900, 14–24.
—— 'Zur Genealogie der Maimoniden', *MGWJ*, XLIV, 1900, 138–140.
Burckhard, T. 'Die Symbolik des Spiegels in der islamischen Mystik', *Symbolon*, I, 1960, 12–16.
Cohen, G. 'The Soteriology of Abraham Maimuni', *PAAJR*, XXV, 1967, 75–98 and XXXVI, 1968, 33–356.
Corbin, H. *L'Archange Empourpré*, Paris, 1976.
—— *Trilogie Ismaélienne*, Paris, 1961.
Davidson, I. *A Thesaurus of Proverbs from Medieval Jewish Literature*, Jerusalem, 1957.
Efros, I. 'Saadia's General Ethical Theory and its Relation to Sufism', in *Seventy-Fifth Anniversary Volume of the Jewish Quarterly Review*, Philadelphia, 1967, 166–177.
—— 'Some Aspects of Yehudah Halevi's Mysticism', *PAAJR*, XI, 1941, 27–41.
Eppenstein, S. *Abraham Maimuni, sein Leben und seine Schriften*, Berlin, 1912–13.
—— 'Chapters 22 and 25 of Abraham ben Mošeh Maimonides' *Kitāb Kifāyat al-'Ābidin*', in *Festschrift I. Lewy*, Breslau, 1911, (Heb. sec.) 33–59.
Ezekiel, I.A. *Sarmad*, Punjab, 1966.
Fenton, P. 'Attitudes to Music in the Later Qabbalah', paper read at *Seventh World Congress for Jewish Studies*, Jerusalem, 1977.
—— 'A Jewish Sufi on Music', *Yuval* (IV, 1982).
—— 'Les Baqqašot d'Orient et d'Occident: un aperçu historique et descriptif', *REJ*, CXXXIV, 1976, 101–121.
—— 'Some Judaeo-Arabic Fragments of Rabbi Abraham he-Ḥasid, the Jewish Sufi', *JJS*, XXVI, pp. 47–72, 1981.
Fischel, W. 'Jews and Judaism in the Court of the Moghul Emperors', *PAAJR*, XVIII, 1949, 137–177.
Freimann, A. 'The Genealogy of the Maimonides Family' in *Alūmmāh*, Jerusalem, 1936, 1–29.
Gardet, L. 'Mystique naturelle et mystique surnaturelle en Islam', *RSR*, XXXVII, 1950, 321–365.
Gavison, A. *'Omer ha-Šikḥah*, Leghorn, 1748.
al-Ġazzālī, Abū Ḥāmid. *Ǧāmi' al-Ḥaqā'iq*, ed. Casas y Manrique, Upsala, 1936.

——*Iḥya' 'Ulūm ad-Dīn*, 4 vols., Beirut, 1967 (*Dar al-Ma'rifa*).
——*Kimiya as-Sa'ada*, Cairo, 1934.
—— *Kitāb al-Arba'īn*, Cairo, 1909.
—— *Al-Ma'ārig al-Qudsiyya*, Cairo, 1927.
—— *Rawḍat aṭ-Ṭālibin*, Cairo, n.d.

Goitein, S. D. 'Abraham Maimonides and his Pietist Circle', in *Jewish Medieval and Renaissance Studies*, ed. A. Altmann, Harvard University Press, 1967, 145–164.

—— 'Isra'īlīyyāt: the Sphere of Malik ibn Dinar', *Tarbiẓ*, VI, 1936, 89-101, 510-522.

—— 'A Jewish Addict to Sufism in the time of Nagid David II Maimonides', *JQR*, XLIV, 1953–4, 37–49.

—— *Jewish Education in Muslim Countries*, Jerusalem, 1962.

——'Islamic and Jewish Mysticism' in *Jews and Arabs*, New York, 1972, 148–154.

—— 'A Letter to Maimonides and New Sources regarding the Negidim of his Family', *Tarbiẓ*, XXXIV, 1965, 232–256.

—— *A Mediterranean Society: the Jewish Communities of the Arab World as Portrayed in the Documents of the Cairo Genizah*, University of California Press, 3 vols., 1967–78.

——'New Documents from the Cairo Genizah', in *Homenaje a Millas-Vallicrosa*, I, Barcelona, 1954, 707–720.

—— 'New Genizah Documents on Abraham Maimonides and his Pietist Circle', *Tarbiẓ*, XXXIII, 1964, 181–197.

—— 'The Renewal of the Controversy over Prayer for the Head of the Community at the time of Abraham Maimuni', in *Memorial I. Goldziher*, II, Jerusalem 1948, 49–54.

—— 'Review of A. Rosenblatt's Edition of Abraham Maimonides' *Highways to Perfection*', *KS*, XV, 1939, 442-444.

—— 'A Treatise in Defence of the Pietists by Abraham Maimonides', *JJS*, XVI, 1965, 105–114.

Goldziher, I. 'The Arabic Portion of the Cairo Genizah', *JQR*, XV, 1903, 526–528.

—— 'Das Prinzip der *takijja* im Islam', *ZDMG*, LX, 1906, 213–226.

—— *Die Richtungen der islamischen Koranauslegung*, Leiden, 1920.

—— 'Ibn Hud the Mohammadan Mystic and the Jews of Damascus', *JQR*, VI, 1893, 218–220.

—— *Kitāb Ma'āni an-Nafs*, Berlin, 1907.

—— 'Mélanges Judéo-Arabes: Le Amr ilahi chez Juda Halevi', *REJ*, L, 1905, 32–41.

—— 'Neuplatonische und gnostische Elemente im Hadith', *Zeitschrift für Assyrologie*, XXII, 1909, 317–344.

Habermann, A. 'The Chronological List Yemot Olam', *Tarbiẓ*, xx, 1950, 225–227.

Halkin, A.S. 'Classical and Arabic Material in Ibn Aknin's Hygiene of the Soul',

PAAJR, XIV, 1944, 25–147.
—— *Judaeo-Arabic Literature* in *EI*[2], vol. X, cols. 409–423.
—— and B. Cohen. *Maimonides' Epistle to Yemen*, New York, 1952.
al-Ḥarrāz. *Kitāb aṣ-Ṣidq*, ed. A.J. Arberry, Calcutta, 1932.
Heschel, A. 'Did Maimonides Believe he had Attained Prophecy?', in *Louis Ginzberg Jubilee Volume (Heb. sec.), New York, 1945, 159–188.*
Hirschfeld, H. 'The Arabic Portion of the Cairo Genizah at Cambridge', *JQR*, XV, 1902, 167–181.
—— 'A Hebreo-Sufic Poem', *JAOS*, XLIX, 1929, 168–173.
al-Huǧwiri. *Kašf al-Maḥǧub*, trans. R.A. Nicholson, London, 1911.
Ibn Abi Uṣaybi'a. *Uyun al-Aḫbār*, Leipzig-Cairo, 1884.
Ibn 'Aqnin. *Inkišaf al-Asrār*, ed. A.S. Halkin, Jerusalem, 1964.
—— *Sefer ha-Mūsar*, ed. W. Bacher, Berlin, 1910.
—— *Ṭibb an-Nufūs*, MS. *Bodl.*, Neubauer 1273.
Ibn 'Arabi. *Fuṣuṣ al-Ḥikam*, ed. 'Afifi, Cairo, 1946.
—— *al-Futūḥāt al-Makkiyya*, Cairo, 4 vols., 1329 A.H.
Ibn Ǧiqatilla, Joseph. 'Commentary on Maimonides' Guide' in Abarbanel's *Šĕ'ēlōt Šā'ūl*, part. II, f[os]19–31, Venice, 1574.
Ibn Ḫaldun. *al-Muqaddima*, Beirut, 1964.
Ibn Paqūda, Baḥya. *al-Hidāya ila Farā' iḍ al-Qulūb*, ed. A.S. Yahuda, Leiden, 1912.
Ibn Sina. *Kitāb al-Išārāt*, ed. S. Dunya, Cairo, 1947.
—— *Kitāb al-Išārāt*, trans. A.M. Goichon, Paris, 1951.
Jellinik, A. *Beitrage zur Geschichte der Kabbala*, Berlin, 1852.
al-Kāšānī. *Dictionary of the Technical Terms of the Sufis*, ed. A. Sprenger, Calcutta, 1845.
Katsch, A. 'From the Moscow Manuscript of David ha-Nagid's Midrash on Genesis', *JQR*, XLVIII, 1958, 140–160.
al-Kutubī. *Fawāt al-Wafayāt*, 2 vols., Cairo, 1951.
Landholt, Article *khalwa*, *EI*[2], vol. IV, 990–991.
Lane, E.W. *An Account of the Manners and Customs of the Modern Egyptians*, 3rd edn., London, 1842.
Lazarus-Yafeh, H. *Studies in al-Ghazzali*, Jerusalem, 1975.
Levi Della Vida, G. *Elenco dei manuscritti arabi islamica della Biblioteca Vaticana*, Rome, 1935.
ha-Lēvi, Yĕhūdāh. *Kitāb ar-Radd wad-Dalil fi ad-Din aḍ-Ḍalil* (*al-Kitāb al-Kazari*), ed. D. Baneth, Jerusalem, 1977.
Maimonides, Abraham. *Commentary on Genesis and Exodus*, ed. E. Wiesenberg, London, 1959.
—— *The High Ways to Perfection of Abraham Maimonides*, 2 vols., New York–Baltimore, 1927–1938. Vol 1, repr. New York, 1966, vol. 1–2, repr. New York–Jerusalem, 1970.

—— *Responsa*, ed. A. Freimann and S.D. Goitein, Jerusalem, 1937.
Maimonides, David. *Commentary on Tractate Abōt*, 1st edn., Alexandria, 1901.
—— *Midraš Rabbi Dawid ha-Nagid on Genesis and Exodus*, trans. A. Katsch, 2 vols., Jerusalem, 1964–68.
Maimonides, Moses. *Code of Law (Mišneh Tōrāh)*, edn. New York, 5 vols., 1963.
—— *Commentary on the Mišnah*, ed. and trans. Y. Qāfiḥ, 7 vols., Jerusalem, 1963–68.
——*Dalālat al-hā' irīn* (*Guide for the Perplexed*), ed. and trans. Y. Qāfih, 3 vols., Jerusalem, 1972.
—— *The Eight Chapters of Maimonides on Ethics*, trans. J. Gorfinkle, New York, 1912.
—— *Responsa*, ed. A. Freimann and J. Blau, 3 vols., Jerusalem, 1957-61.
—— *Ṯamāniya fuṣūl*, ed. M. Wolff, Leiden, 1903.
Pseudo-Maimonides. *De Beatitudine Capita Duo*, ed. H. Dawidowitz and D. Baneth, Jerusalem, 1939.
—— *Ma'ama' ha-yiḥūd*, ed. M. Steinschneider, Berlin, 1846.
—— *Musar na'eh*, in *Epistles*, ed. Lichtenberg, Leipzig, 1859, f[os] 38–40.
Mann, J. *The Jews in Egypt and in Palestine under the Fatimids*, Oxford, 1920.
—— *Texts and Studies in Jewish History and Literature*, 2 vols., Cincinnati-Philadelphia, 1931–35.
Margoliouth, R. *R. Abraham ben ha-Rambam*, Lwow, 1936.
Massignon, L. *Essai sur les Origines du Lexique Technique de la Mystique Musulmane*, Paris, 1922.
Maymūn ben Yōsef. *The Epistle of Consolation*, ed. and trans. L. Simmons, *JQR*, II, 1890, 62–101, Arabic text, 334–335.
Neubauer, A. 'Egyptian Fragments', *JQR*, VIII, 1895, 541–561.
—— *Mediaeval Jewish Chronicles*, Oxford, 1887, repr. Jerusalem, 1967.
Obadyah, D. (Ed.) *Fās wa-Ḥăkāmēha*, 2 vols., Jerusalem, 1979.
Prijs, L. *Die grammatikalische Terminologie des Abraham Ibn Esra*, Basel, 1950.
al-Qušayri, Abū l-Qasim. *ar-Risāla al-Qušayriyya*, ed. Maḥmūd and Šarif, 2 vols., Cairo, 1966.
Reines, A. 'Maimonides' Concepts of Providence', *HUCA*, XLIII, 1972, 169–206.
de Rietti, Moses. *Miqdaš me'aṭ*, ed. J. Goldenthal, Vienna, 1851.
Rosenthal, F. 'A Judaeo-Arabic Work under Sufic Influence', *HUCA*, XV, 1940, 433–484.
Rosin, D. 'Die Religionsphilosophie Abraham Ibn Esra's', *MGWJ*, XLII, 1898.
Rubin, V. 'Pre-existence of Light: Aspects of the Concept of Nur Muhammad', *Israel Oriental Series*, V, 1975, 62–119.
Safrai, S. 'The Teachings of Pietists in Mishnaic Literature', *JJS*, XVI, 1965, 15–33.
Sa'adya Ga'on. *Kitāb ǧamī' aṣ-Ṣalawat wat-Tasābīḥ* (*Siddūr Rab Sa'adyah Ga'on*), ed. I. Davidson, S. Assaf and Y. Joel, 4th edn., Jerusalem, 1978.
aš-Šahrastani. *al-Milal wan-Niḥal*, ed. A. Wakil, Cairo, 1968.

ha-Sarfaty, Vidal. *Imrē yōšer*, in *Midraš Rabbāh*, Warsaw, 1874.

Schimmel, A.M. *Mystical Dimensions of Islam*, Chapel Hill, 1975.

Scholem, G. 'From Philosopher to Cabbalist (A Legend of the Cabbalists on Maimonides)', *Tarbiẓ*, VI, 1935, 90–98.

—— *Kitbē yad be-Qabbālāh*, Jerusalem, 1930.

—— *Les Origines de la Kabbale*, Paris, 1966.

——Ša'arey ṣedeq: a Qabbalistic Treatise from the School of Abraham Abū l-'Āfiya', *KS*, I, 1925, 127–139.

—— *Sabbatay Ṣevi: the Mystical Messiah*, London, 1973.

Steinschneider, M. *Die Arabische Literatur der Juden*, Frankfurt-am-Main, 1902.

—— *Die Hebräische Übersetzungen des Mittelalters*, Berlin, 1893.

—— 'Zur Literatur der Maimoniden', *MGWJ*, XLV, 1901, 129–137.

Stern, S. M. 'A New Description by Judah al-Harizi of his Journey to Iraq', *Sefunot*, VIII, 1964, 145–156.

—— 'Some Unpublished Poems by al-Harizi', *JQR*, XLIX, 1958, 346-364.

Strotheman. Article *taḳiya*, *EI*[1], vol. IV, 628–629.

as-Suhrawardī, Abū Hafs. *'Awārif al-Ma'ārif*, printed as vol. 5 of al-Ġazzālī's *Iḥyā'*, Beirut, 1968.

at-Tirmiḏī. *Bayān al-Farq bayn aṣ-Ṣadr wal-Qalb*, ed. N. Heer, Cairo, 1958.

Trimingham, J. S. *The Sufi Orders in Islam*, London, 1973.

aṭ-Ṭusi, Abū Naṣr. *Kitāb al-Luma' fī al-Taṣawwuf*, ed. R.A. Nicholson, London, 1914.

Twersky, I. 'Some non-Halkhic Aspects of the Mishneh Torah', in *Jewish Medieval and Renaissance Studies*, ed. A. Altmann, Harvard University Press, 1967, 95-118.

Vajda, G. 'A propos de l'Averroïsme juif', *Sefarad*, 1952, 3–29.

—— *L'Amour de Dieu dans la Théologie juive du Moyen Age*, Paris, 1957.

—— 'Un chapitre de l'histoire du conflit entre la Kabbale et la Philosophie: Jacob ben Shalom Ashkenazi de Catalogne', *AHDLMA*, XXIII, 1956, 45–114.

—— 'Comment le philosophe juif Moïse de Narbonne comprenait-il les paroles extatiques des Soufis?', in *Actas del Primer Congreso de Estudios Arabes Islamicos*, Madrid, 1964, 129–135.

—— 'En marge du Commentaire sur la Cantique des Cantiques de Joseph Ibn Aqnin', *REJ*, IV, 1965, 185–199.

—— *Introduction à la Pensée Juive du Moyen Age*, Paris, 1948.

—— *Isaac Albalag, averroïste juif, traducteur et annotateur d'al-Ghazzali*, Paris, 1960.

—— *Juda ben Nissim Ibn Malka*, Paris, 1954.

—— 'The Mystical Doctrine of Rabbi Obadyah, Grandson of Moses Maimonides', *JJS*, VI, 1955, 213–225.

—— 'Mystique juive et mystique musulmane', *Les Nouveaux Cahiers*, II, 1966, 34–38.

——'Les observations critiques d'Isaac d'Acco sur les ouvrages de Juda ben Nissim', *REJ*, CXV, 1956, 25–71.
—— 'Un opuscule inexistant d'aš-Šadili', *Arabica*, VIII, 1961, 100.
—— 'La pensée religieuse de Maimonide, unité ou dualité?', *Cahiers de Civilisation Mediévale*, IX, 1966, 29–49.
—— 'La philosophie et la théologie de Joseph Ibn Çaddiq', *AHDLMA*, XVII, 1949, 93-181.
—— 'La théologie ascétique de Bahya Ibn Paqouda', *Cahiers de la Société Asiatique*, VII, Paris, 1947.
Vital, Ḥayyim. *Sefer ha-Ḥezyōnōt*, ed. A. Aešcoly, Jerusalem, 1954.
Wensinck, A.J. *A Handbook of Early Mohammadan Tradition*, Leiden, 1928.
—— Article *niyya*, *EI*[1], vol. III, 930–931.
—— 'On the Relation between Ghazzali's Cosmology and his Mysticism', *Med. Kong. Akad. Wetensch.*, Amsterdam, LXXV, no. 6.
Wieder, N. *Islamic Influence on the Jewish Worship*, London, 1948, and in *Melilah*, Manchester University Press, 1946, 37–120.
Wolff, J. *Researches and Missionary Labours among the Jews*, 2 vols., London, 1835.
Wolfson, H. 'The Classification of the Sciences in Mediaeval Jewish Philosophy', in *Hebrew Union College Jubilee Volume*, Cincinatti, 1925, 263–315.
al-Yāfi'ī. *Rawḍ ar-Rayāḥīn*, edn. Cairo, 1874.
Zĕkariāh b. Sulaymān. *Comm. in Cant. Cant.*, ed. Y. Qāfiḥ, in *Ḥameš Mĕgillōt*, Jerusalem, 1962.
Zohar, 3 vols., edn. Vilna, 1882.

ב27 אללהו ואלצ̇חך ואסתעמל אלצמת ולא תתכלם אלא ען צ̇רורה ולא / תאכל אלא ען פאקה ולא תנאם אלא ען גלבה וקלבך לאהג̇ בד̇לך אלמעני ופכרך ג̇איל פיה קאל פי ד̇לך אני ישנה ולבי ער וגו' וקאל דוד הקיצותי ועודי עמך פאג̇תהד פי חצול מא ארשדתך אליה פאן מא יג̇ברך מן כ̇ארג̇ שי מעשיך יקרבוך ומעשיך ירחקוך ואעלם אן אלמעני אלד̇י תתקדם אליה עט̇ים ויחתאג̇ תהיו ואסתעדאד וגם הכהנים הנגשים אל יי יתקדשו ואלפאידה אלחאצלה לך פי ד̇לך תהון עליך מא צעב מן אלתוטיאת וריאצ̇ת אלאכ̇לאק אם יתמהמה חכה לו כי בא יבא ולא יאחר צמח שמו ומתחתיו יצמח אשרי המחכה ויגיע עין לא ראתה אלהים זולתך יעשה למחכה לו

תמת אלמקאלה אלחוצ̇יה אלמנסובה לר' עבדיה בר אברהם החסיד ז'ל
ב' רבינו משה הגאון בר מימון זצ"ל

1 נוסח א15 : פאתרך אללהו 3 א15 כק' אלח' 6 א15 יחתאג̇ אסתעראץ̇ עט̇ים 6 אלתי בתתקדם 9 ומתחת 13 אלמקאלת אלחוצ̇יה

3 שיר ה:ב 4 תה' קלט:יח 5 עדויות ה:ז 6 שמ' כט:כב 8 חב' ב:ג 9 זכר' ו:יב / דני' יב:יב 10 ישׁ' סד:ג

תנביה

קד תכרר עליך אן אלעבאדה אנמא חקיקתהא אן תכון קלביה כקולה ולעבדו בכל לבבכם ובכל נפשכם פהי מקצוד אלשריעה ואד̇א אתג̇ה אליה אלשכ̇ץ יריד יכון בג̇מיע אג̇זא קלבה ומא אחד יפעל ד̇לך לא פי צלאה̈ ולא פי קראה̈ ולא ענד סמאע אלתורה בל אשתגלו באלעבאדה ען אלמעבוד ובאלעלם ען אלמעלום חתי אלמשהורין באלעלם אנמא קצדהם סמאע שרח פסוק או כלאם מסתחסן מת̇ל שער לבעץ̇ אלשערא יחסן בה צלאתה ובאלג̇מלה שי יעג̇ב אלחאצ̇רין פאד̇א כאן אלג̇מהור משתגלין בעול בית ובעול דרך ארץ וכ̇ואצהם משתגלין באלמשא ואלמתן ואלמעני אלכ̇ציץ באלנפס / 27א אלמסמי עבאדה ענד מן יכון עארף ויקף אלשכץ מנא ידעי פי צלאתה שובר אויבים ומכניע זדים שפוך חמתך על הגוים והו מנהם ויקול פי וקת אכר אשרי העם שה' אלהיו והו כ̇ארג̇ ענהם אד̇ לם יפהם מא יקול בל יוסיף על חטאתו פשע וצאר פעל מא יפעלה תקלידא ועאדה ג̇רת פקט ואנחרפו ען אלחק ואקתאדו באלכ̇יאלאת אלט̇אהרה אלתי הי יצר הרע חקיקה והיה כמחשך מעשיהם ות̇בת פיהם ורחוק מכליותיהם פאיאך תסלך מסאלכהם או תתמת̇ל בהם או תנקאד כ̇לף מא אנקאדו כ̇לפה בל אתבע אלאשכ̇אץ אלכ̇ואץ לא כ̇ואץ אלעואם והוי מתאבק בעפר רגליהם ואנט̇ר אלי יהושע ע'ה למא כ̇דם משה ושמואל למא כ̇דם עלי ואלישע למא כ̇דם אליהו ז'ל ואיאך אן תמשי מעהם עלי ג̇ריח לילא תעטב שנשיכתן נשיכת נחש ועקיצתן עקיצת עקרב פאנהם לא יקבלו רקיה ולא ידאו צ̇רבה ואעתבר בגחזי וכיף כ̇רג̇ מן קדאם אלישע ד̇לך אלכ̇רוג̇ אלצעב פאסתעמל אלד̇לה ואלכ̇שוע ואלכ̇צ̇וע בין ידיהם באלבאטן ואלט̇אהר ותכון מכפוף אלראס דאמע אלעין טאהר אלד̇יל צאים אלנהאר ולא תפרח במא יפרחו בה ולא תגתם למא יגתמו עליה ג̇מלה̈ ובאלג̇מלה לא תחזן לחזנהם ולא תסר לסרורהם אסתקבח

1 לפי נוסח הנכנס בטעות ב א15 : קד תכרר לך קולי אן אלעבאדה לא תכון אלא קלביה קאל 8 כאנה̈ 17 לאכ̇ואץ אך תוקן בגליון
21 רקאה אך השוה רמב"ם פ' אבות ב:טו

2 דב' יא:יג 11 תה' עט:ו 12 תה' קמה:טו 13 איוב לד:לז 15 ישי' כט:טו 16 יר' יב:ב 18 אבות א:ד 20 אבות ב:טו

ישפע פי ישני אדמת עפר והו אלד̇י יטלב אלרחמה עלי ישראל חתי יגאת̇ו מבין הגוים ובואסטתה יצל אלשכ̇ץ מנהם אלי בית קדש הקדשים כמא קאל אמרתי עמי הוא והוא יאמר יי אלהי אנט̇ר אלי הד̇א אלפצ̇ל מנה תעאלי אלד̇י רבט בנא וצלה אד̇א נחן חרצנא עליהא תעלק קדרתה תעאלי בנא מטפה סרוחה בדעה קלה ומעוטה פאד̇א חקק אלאנסאן נפסה יצח לה אן אתבעה יכון פי ג̇דאר רב אלעאלמין ויבקי בבקאה שד וסטך ואכ̇דם אלחק אלכ̇דמה אלצחיחה הד̇א אן כאן עבד חר ואן כאן עבד סו פית̇בת פיה ועבדת את אויביך וכו' תחת אשר לא עבדת את יי אלהיך ואנתבה זכור אל תשכח הוא יהיה עמך לא ירפך ולא יעזבך .

פצל

26א ד̇כרו עאס' מעני ראית אן אנבהך עליה וד̇לך אנהם קאלו אעתבר כל נץ ג̇א פיה רפעה̈ ג̇אנבה תע' ועלו מרתבתה תג̇ד בעד תואצ̇ע ואנכ̇פאץ̇ כמא ג̇אנא פי פסוק סולו לרוכב בערבות ביה שמו אבי יתומים ודיין אלמנות וכד̇לך מרום וקדוש אשכון ואת דכא ושפל רוח ואיצ̇א כי רם יי ושפל יראה המגביהי לשבת המשפילי לראות אמא קולה בעד מרום אשכון להחיות רוח שפלים לאג̇ל תכון אלנפס אליה ותתאנס בקרבה ובחצ̇רה̈ ג̇מאלה ולמא כאן אלאנסאן לא ימכנה אלדואם עלי אלחאלה אלרפיעה ולא בד מן אן יזול או ינחרף בחסב מאדתה פאנה אעתרף בכ̇טאה וזלתה בין ידיה צפח לה ק' תע' כי לא לעולם אריב ולא לנצח אקצוף ואלגרצ̇ בד̇לך כלה אן אלשכ̇ץ לא יג̇ב לה אלאקדאם עלי ד̇לך אלמעני אלא בעד קהר אכ̇לאקה וקתל שהואתה וצ̇עף תשוקאתה פאנה אן פעל ד̇לך וענדה תצ̇בט באלדניא מא יפלח ויביא עליו קללה ולא ברכה פאד̇א קטעת פכרתך מן מתאע אלדניא ואקבלת מתג̇ה אלי אללה תע בקלבך 26ב / ולא̈ תנקטע ען באבה פאנך (ת)תכ̇לץ מן שואיב אלדניא ואעראצ̇הא ואד̇א ת̇ארתך צ̇ראיר אלמאדה מת̇ל אכל ושרב פאסתחי ואכ̇ג̇ל מן ד̇לך פאן אלשכ̇ץ אלכאמל יבקי ענד פעל ד̇לך אבל וחפוי ראש מלא בושה וכלימה פיג̇ב עלי אלאנסאן אן קאם או קעד או משי (אן) לא יזאל קלבה מראקב לה תעאלי לעל יחרסה ד̇לך חתי יצל ללמקצוד והו אלד̇י ישפעה אד̇א אתג̇ה נחוה .

6 ג̇דאר ; השוה פרקים בהצלחה כח : בג̇ואר רב אלעאלמין 16 תאנסהם ותוקן בגליון ותאתנס

1 דני' יב:ב 3 זכרי' יג:ט 8 דב' כח:מח 9 דב' לא:ח
13 תה' סח:ה 14 ישׁ' נז:טו/ תה' קלח:ו 16 תה' קיג:ו 19 ישׁ' נז:טז 22 ברי' כז:יב 26 אסתר ו:יב

מא יסמי אלשכ̇ץ אוהב וחושק אלא אד̇א עלקת נפסה בד̇לך אלמעני לאן בתכראר ד̇לך תג̇ד מן יחצל לה שי מן ד̇לך יבקי האים ועלי קדר תעלקה בה יבקי הימאנה קאל דוד עאס' כאיל תערוג על אפיקי מים צמאה נפשי לאל חי ומן אג̇ל ד̇לך מא תרי אחד יתעלק בה יאוי אלא פי אלבראר' ואלקפאר חית̇ לא אנסאן ואלד̇י יפעלה הו אלצחיח לאן אלכרובים כת̇יר ג̇דא ו(הם) אלעקל כמא עלמת ולכת̇רה̇ גלבה̇ אלשג̇אעה פהם יקצדו אן יכ̇ף ענהם ת̇קל אלוג̇וד באסרה ות̇קל כלפתה וכד̇א פעל תעאלי מענא ענד מא אראד תכמילנא קטענא פי אלמדבר / ארבעים שנה 25א וכד̇א ועדנא ברפע אלגלות בג̇מלתהא לאן ברפע אלגלות יצח אלאתצאל ואלכמאל ואלאבות עאס' כאן אכת̇ר מקאמהם פי אלבריה קאל פי אברהם והוא יושב פתח האהל ופי יצחק ויצא יצחק לשוח בשדה ופי יעקב וישלח יעקב ויקרא לרחל וללאה השדה וקצה אליהו ז'ל ואלישע ע'ה וכלהם יקצדו הד̇א אלמעני וירמיהו ע'ה קאל מי יתנני במדבר מלון אורחים ואעזבה את עמי ומא כאנו פי אלבלד אלא לצ̇רורה וללאראדה אלאלאהיה או רסאלה אלי קום פאן אלאשכ̇אץ אלד̇י תברהן ענדהם קליל במרה ראיתי בני עליה והם מועטים כמו טפה מן הים והנשארים ימקו בעונם בארצות אויביכם לאנך לא תג̇ד פי כל עצר אלא ואחד בעד ואחד כמא תג̇ד פי עצר דור המבול נח ע'ה ומתושלח מן קבלה וחנוך ולמך ושם ועבר ואברהם ויצחק ויעקב וענדהם אנקטעת אלוצלה ומאת אלשפיע אלי אן ולד אג̇ל מולוד ואכרם מכ̇לוק משה רבינו ע'ה ואחיאה באראדה̇ אללה פקד צח אן מן לא לה שפיע יוצל בינה ובין מעשוקה פהו חשוב כמת פאד̇א ת̇בתת ענדך הד̇ה אלקאעדה רג̇עת תסתחי אן תד̇כר אלבארי ג̇ל ועז אלא אן כאן / קד חצל מי הוא זה ואיזה הוא אלד̇י תחתמל 25ב קואימה יקף בין ידי אללה בלא ואסטה ומא הד̇א אלא תג̇אסר עט̇ים פאלואג̇ב עלינא אן נכ̇ף ונקף ונחרץ פי אכ̇ד̇נא שפיע ותחצילנא איאה בלא פתור פאנה אלחארץ לנא פי דאר אלדניא אלמוצל לנא לדאר אלאכ̇רה לא תעתקד גיר ד̇לך ומע ד̇לך נקף ונדעו ונקול אתה יי לא תכלא רחמיך ממני לאן נחן מתכלין עלי מראחמה תעאלי והו אלד̇י

6 ואלעקל ונראה שהנוסח משובש כאן 17 באויביהם 20 ג̇ל
24 תג̇אסראן 28 תכלה

3 תה' מב:ב-ג 11 ברי' יח:א / שם כד:סג 12 שם כא:ד 13 ירמ' ט:א 16 סוכה מה: / ויק' כו:לט 23 אסתר ז:ה 27 תה' מ:יב

מעתקד פיה ובאלג̇מלה אסמע אלחק ממן קאלה לתסתעין בה עלי מא אנת
מחתאג̇ אליה פי טריקך ק' ע'ה איזהו חכם הלמד מכל אדם שנ' מכל
מלמדי השכלתי וכם פתחו ז'ל מן אלטרק וכם ג̇אהדו פי תנצ̇יפהא
ותנג̇ילהא מן לאלמעאת̇ר ומע הד̇א ולא מצאה היונה מנוח לכף רגלה
לולי יי שהיה לנו אלד̇י שם לנו שארית בארץ בהד̇ה אלשריעה אלתי
24א בינּנא כנא / קד תלפנא מת̇ל מא תלף ג̇ירנא מן אלמלל אלסאבקה ק'
תע' ואף גם זאת בהיותם בארץ אויביהם לא מאסתים וק' אם לא בריתי
יומם ולילה חקות שמים וארץ .

פצל

הד̇א אלפצל אלד̇י נאתי בה אלאן הו שבה
אלכ̇אתמה ורמת אני לא אצ̇עה פי הד̇ה אלמקאלה
לכן הי אחק בה לאן פיה גראיב פאג̇על באלך
מנה אעלם אן אלקוה אלנאטקה אלתי כ̇ץ אלאנסאן בהא ען בקיה̈
אלחיואן ליס הי ג̇סם ולא קוה̈ פי ג̇סם ואלאנסאן קיל פיה מן אג̇להא
בדמות אלהים ברא אותו ולד̇לך אד̇א חצל להא מעקול קוית בה אכת̇ר
ממא כאנת קבל אן יתצל להא פאלאנסאן אד̇א מאל בכליתה נחו אלעקל
האנת עליה אלאמור אלג̇סמאניה ולא יעוד יתאלם להא כמא כאן קבל
ולד̇לך כאן אדם לם ישער בכשף אלעורה למילה נחו אלעקל ומן אג̇ל
ד̇לך קד יבקי אלאנסאן איאם לם יטלב ג̇ד̇א לאשתגאל פכרתה בד̇לך
אלמעני ואסתגראקה פיה ולאג̇ל ד̇לך תרי מן קד חצל לה שי מן ד̇לך
יהון עליה אלעד̇אב פיה כמא קאל רצ̇ית הואני פי הואה באלצ̇ד מן
אלשכ̇ץ אלמאיל נחו אלג̇סם פאנה לא יצבר עלי מצאב בל ישתכי ויתקלק
24ב / מן ד̇לך אלאלם לאג̇ל אן נפסה פארגה פאד̇א אשתגלת אלנפס בד̇לך
אלשי פד̇לך אלאלם יכ̇ף עלי אלג̇סם לא יחס בה לאשתגאל אלנפס ענה
פאחרץ יא אבני עלי רפצ̇ אלאמור אלג̇סמאניה מא קדרת פאנה יכ̇ף עליך
ד̇לך אלקלק אלד̇י תג̇דה פי אול סלוכך וקד שבהו אלנפס ענד מא
תכ̇לצת מן שבכה̈ אלג̇סם מת̇ל פצ̇לת חריר אד̇א וקעת פי שוך כשושנה
בין החוחים כיף יכון פאן עלי קדר תעלקה באלדניא תכון מפארקתך
להא ומן אג̇ל ד̇לך קאלו עאס' הוי ממעט בעסק ועסוק בתורה יא אבני

4 האד̇ה   8 חוקת   18 אלערוה   20 באלצ̇ץ   28 הוי מעט עסק

2 אבות ד:א / תה' קיט:צט   4 ברי' ח:ט   5 תה' קכד:א   7 ויקי' כו:מד / ירי' לג:כה   14 ברי' ה:א   26 שיר ב:ב   28 אבות ד:יב

עד כי יבא שילה וצרנא נתכל עלי מן יצלי בנא ויסמענא ראשי דברים
פאן אתפק פהמנא מנה שי ואלא תרכנאה והד̇א צ̇ד מא קצד בנא /
23א וצארת אעמאלנא אלמצות אלשרעיה עאדה̈ ג̇רת וסנה̈ תקדמת כמא קרענא
תעאלי עלי יד אלנבי וקי' ותהי יראתם אותי מצות אנשים וקד עלמת
אן אעמאל אלמצות תוטיה ללאנסאן וריאצ̇ה לאכ̇לאקה חתי יקבל אלתורה
אלחקיקיה אלמקצודה בנא פאעמל עלי תחציל אלתוטיאת ונפי אלאכ̇לאק
אלמד̇מומה מנך לא ישבו בארצך פן יחטיאו אותך לי כי יהיה לך
למוקש ואנט̇ר אלי מא קאל בעדה ואל משה אמר עלה אל יי פאפהם הד̇א
אלתנביה אלד̇י אנבנא עליה גרץ̇ הד̇ה אלמקאלה .

תנביה

אריד אנבהך עלי תחציל אלמקרא וקראתהא קראת
משתאק טאלב ליס כמא יקרוהא האולאי אלנאס
אליום אלד̇י לא יעתברו מא יקרוה בל יתלו
פקט כאן אלגרץ̇ מנה הו אלתלאוה ולא איצ̇א אלקצד הו מערפה̈ כלמה
כ̇לף או כלמה ת̇קילה או כ̇פיפה או שרח לפט̇ה ישרחהא שכ̇ץ עלי מעני
ואכ̇ד̇ עלי מעני אכ̇ר גיר ד̇לך ליס הד̇א הו (אל)קצד בל אלקצד חפט̇הא
חתי אד̇א כ̇טר בבאלך מעני מא מן אלד̇י נבהתך עליה ווג̇דת פסוק
מטאבק ללמעני פאנך תאכ̇ד̇ מנה מעני מא ותתסלק מן מעני אלי אכ̇ר
23ב חתי תתצל אלי מטלובך ואל/חכמים עאס' נבהו עלי ד̇לך וקאלו פי
אלמדרש למה היו דברי תורה דומין עד שלא עמד שלמה לבאר שהיו
מימיה עמוקים וצוננים ולא היה אדם יכול לשתות מהם מה עשה פקח
אחד ספק חבל לחבל ומשיחה למשיחה ודלה ושתה כך היה שלמה ממשל
למשל ומדבר לדבר עד שעמד על סודיה של תורה וקאל שלמה מת̇ל ד̇לך
מים עמוקים עצה בלב איש ואיש תבונות ידלנה וקי' ישמע חכם ויוסף
לקח להבין משל ומליצה דברי חכמים וחידותם והכד̇א יטלב כל מן
יתקדם אלי עלם מא אול מא יחפט̇ הו אצולה ת̇ם ירג̇ע יעלם מא אלקצד
בה פאד̇א צח לה ד̇לך תקדם לבחת̇ עו גאיתה כד̇לך ינבגי אן תפעל פי
כלאם אלחכמים אד̇א ארדת אן תפהם אלגאזהם פתאמל כלאמהם תאמלאן
שאפי(אן) פאן לם תפהמה פכררה עלי שכ̇ץ חאד̇ק מאהר פי כלאמהם

28 תאמל אן שא פי אך תוקן בגליון

1 ברי' מט:י 4 ישי' כט:יג 7 שמי' כג:לג 8 שמי' ל:א 18 שהש"ר
רבה א:ח 22 משי' א:ה

פיה מא לא תעלמה ויכון מת̇אלך מת̇אל מן וג̇ד וג̇דה וכאן קבל ד̇לך
צ̇עיף אלחאל משהור באלפקר פי אכת̇ר אוקאתה כאן יתצדק מן אצחאבה
פלמא חצל לה מא חצל תכבר עלי אצחאבה וצאר ינעזל ענהם וינהרהם
באלקול ואלפעל פאכ̇דו אצחאבה יבחת̇ו ענה וען חאלה פלמא פהמו
ענה אנה קד וג̇ד שי ראפעו פיה ענד אלמלך פאסתאצל ג̇מלה̈ מאלה
ובקי פי חאל אצעב ממא כאן עליה אולא והו פקיר פינבגי למן פהם
שי ממא נבהנא עליה אן יצונה ולא יתט̇אהר בה מע אחד גיר אהלה
ולא יכ̇רג̇ ען אלצורה אלתי כאן עליהא מן קבל וינבסט מע אלנאס
ויחתמל מא ת̇קל מנהם ויהונה פי קלבה ויחרס נפסה איאך אן יקע
מעהם בכלאם ולא בתצריח ולא בתלויח בל יסייג̇ עלי כלאמה כמא אמר
אללה תעאלי ושמרתם את משמרתי ושרחו אלחכמים ז"ל עשו משמרת
למשמרתי ואסתעמל אלכתמאן כמא ק' אלחכמים פי / מת̇ל ד̇לך השבעתי ב22
אתכם בנות ירושלים פאד̇א / חצל לך מלכה פמא ידום הד̇א אלדול סוף ג
פתאום יבא אל היכלו האדון אשר אתם מבקשים ואד̇א לם יכן מא תריד
פארד מא יכון ולא יצעב עליך כונך ליס יתם לך אסתכמאל גד̇אך אמסך
בראס אלמאל אלד̇י מעך ובו תדבק ואתג̇ר פיה חסב קדרתך עד ישקיף
וירא יי משמים .

פצל

אעלם אן פי אלזמאן אלמתקדם כאנו אלפצ̇לא יג̇תהדון פי בניאן אלמדרשות ללטלבא ויטלקוא להם מאדה תקום בהם ותעינהם עלי אלאשתגאל באלתורה ועלם חצולהא וג̇זאיאתהא וגאיאתהא ומקאצדהא אלרפיעה אלתי הי אעלא מן אפהאם אלג̇מהור פאן ארי מן תלך אלחלבה קד צלח לד̇לך אלמעני אעטי טרף מנה בחסב תן לחכם ויחכם עוד ואולאיך כאנו יתסמון בני הנביאים פלמא תלפת עלומנא ואנקטעת טרק אנביאנא מן ביננא ואסתולת אלג̇אהליה עלינא בטול הד̇ה אלגלות אלתי נחן פיהא

1 ג אלי אן תע(למה) 14 א לם יכן מא תריד ריד מא יכון 16 תדבקי 23 ראי 26 ואסתולאת אלג̇אהליא אך אולי צ"ל אלמלל אלג̇אהליה ע"פ דלאלה̈ אלחאירין א:עא

11 ויק' יח:ל / יבמות כא. 12 שיר ב:ז 14 מלאכי ג:א 16 דב' י:כ / איכה ג:ב 23 מש' ט:ט

פצ̇ל

אעלם יא אבני אן אלעקל הו אלוצלה בינך
ובינה תע' וג̇דאה אלד̇י ימדה הו עלם אלאשיא
אלג̇יר מתג̇ירה ולא ימכנה ת̇באת ולא קואם אלא
6ג בהא וכמא אן אלג̇סם / ליס לה קואם אלא באלג̇ד̇א אלצחיח אלמנאסב
כד̇לך אלעקל ליס לה ת̇באת אלא באלעלום אלחקיקיה אלתי תבקא בבקאה
21ב ואמא מן יקרא עלום לא ידרי להא מעני / פאנהא לא ת̇באת להא ולא
מנפעה לא פי אלדניא ולא פי אלאכ̇רה אמא פי אלדניא פמא יסתלד̇
במעני ולא יוציא דבר מתוך דבר ואמא פי אלאכ̇רה פאנה תפנא בפנאה
פאנה ליס יחצל מנהא עלי מעני פנחן קד מן אללה עלינא בהד̇ה
אלשריעה אלכאמלה אלמכמלה אלתי באידינא אלתי תפיד קהר אלאכ̇לאק
וקוה אלעקל לאן אלעקל אלסאלם הו אלשרע אלכאמל ואלשרע אלאלהי הו
אלעקל אלסאלם ק' תע' פי מחכם תנזילה אתה הראית לדעת כי יי הוא
האלהים אין עוד וגו' פאד̇א פתח עלי אלשכ̇ץ כשיך̇ קוי מאהר פי פהם
אסראראהא חתי בויין לה שי מן ד̇לך בעד צחה̈ תג̇רבתה ואכ̇תבארה עלי
אלוג̇וה אלתי ד̇כרוהא עאס' אלתי מן ג̇מלתהא אן יכון צנוע ואינו
כועס ואינו משתכר ואינו מעמיד על מדותיו ודבורן בנחת עם הבריות
ועומד בחצי ימיו ובשרט אן יכון חכם ומבין מדעתו חיניד̇ מוסרין
לו ראשי פרקים פאנהא תנבהה עלי ג̇מלה̈ מעאני יסתכמל בהא ג̇רצ̇ה
ומקצדה לאן אלכל פיהא כמא וצפהא אלעארף בהא תורת ה' תמימה
משיבת נפש וגו' וקאלו ע'ה הפוך בה והפוך בה דכלא בה ובה תחזה
ומנה לא תזוז שאין לך מדה טובה יותר ממנה .

וציה̈

אעלם יא אבני אנך אד̇א תביין לך מעני מא מן
22א נפסך או מן ג̇ירך פלא תג̇על / לנפסך בה חט̇
ותסתהון במן הו דונך לילא תג̇לב עלי נפסך
אד̇יה ק' אלחכים סלאם אללה עליה משחית נפשו הוא יעשנה וקאל ולא
תעלה במעלות על מזבחי אשר לא תגלה וקד נבהתך אן הד̇א אלאמר לא
ישארכך פיה אחד ולא ימנעך אחד מנה פאן אבחת בשי מנה עמל עליך

7 א אלאכ̇רי 13 א פתח עלי אלשכ̇ץ בשי 19 א תורת..וגו' הושמט
23 ג תג̇לב לנפסך

12 דב' ד:לה 15 קד' עא. 17 חג' יג. 19 תה' יט:ח 20 אבות
ה:כה 25 מש' ו:לב / שמ' כ:כג

אבני אנא אוציך אד̇א רמת אלכ̇לוה וג̇לסת תתהיא ומר בכ̇אטרך שי מן אמור אלדניא אכ̇רג̇ה ואטרדה מן אלדאר וסכר אלבאב פי וג̇הה מכל משמר נצור לבך ותם שגלך וקוי אג̇תהאדך ולא יצעב עליך מפארקה̈ אלאמר אלד̇י כ̇טר פי באלך פי אלדניא פאן אלחאג̇ה אד̇א דעת אליה חצ̇רת לאן אמור אלוג̇וד מעקודה בבעצ̇הא בעץ̇ ולא יתעסר עליך שי מנהא פי וקת אלחאג̇ה פאן אלאמור אלצ̇רוריה תחצל באיסר סעי ומא סואהא פצ̇ול ואצרף פכרתך ענהא אנט̇ר אלי יעקב אבינו ע'ה מא טלב סוי לחם לאכול ובגד ללבוש כך היא דרכה של תורה פת במלח תאכל ועל הארץ תישן וחיי צער תחיה ובתורה אתה עמל פאן אלעלמא מא וצ̇עו לנא מא וצ̇עוה אלא לנטב בה נפוסנא וליסהלו עלינא צעובה̈ אלמראס פאן מא ירכב הד̇א אלטריק אלא מן לה אסתילא וקהר וסלטאן עלי הד̇ה אלמאדה אלמשבהה באלחיואן פארפק בהא לילא תתמרס בך כמא ג̇רא לבלעם וצ̇רבהא ועתב עליה אלמלאך למנאקרתה להא זה שלש פעמים 21א פאלחד̇ר תם אלחד̇ר מן אלמנאפרה כמא / נבהתך ואלחפט̇ ואלרעאיה בהא לילא יתב̇ת פיך כי עתה גם אותך הרגתי ואותה החייתי לאן קואדהא מסלם לך ואליך תשוקתו ואתה תמשול בו ואעלם אן אלטריק אלתי אנת סאלכהא פיהא אלהואם תטלב אלזאד כתיר ואלמא יכון מעך אכת̇ר אנט̇ר אלי אלאבות ע'ה מא כאן להם סעי וכד ומתג̇ר אלא פיה כמ' קאל וישב יצחק ויחפור את בארות המים אשר חפרו עבדי אביו בימי אברהם וכד̇לך ישראל פי אלמדבר מן שדה̈ עטשהם וילונו העם על משה לאמר מה נשתה וקי' ויצאו מים רבים ותשת העדה ובעירם והגר למא פנא אלמא מן החמת לולא וג̇דת אלמא מא עאש אלולד ויפקח אלהים את עיניה פאן עוולת עלי חפר ביר כמא פעל אבוך וג̇דך אפעל שתה מים מבורך ונוזלים מתוך בארך יפוצו מעינתיך חוצה .

1 ג ומר בבאלך   5 ג מעדוקה / יתעד̇ר   12 א אלמשאבה
13 ג למנאסרתה   15 א קואהא   19 ג בימי אביו

2 מש' ד:כג   8 בר' כח:כ / אבות ו:ד   13 במ' כב:לב
15 שם לג   16 בר' ד:ז   18 בר' כו:יח   20 שמ' טו:כד
21 במ' כ:יא   22 בר' כא:יט   23 מש' ה:טו

אלאמור ותמכנת מנהא וסאעדת מאדתך עלי ד̇לך אלאמר אחמד אללה
ואשכרה עלי תלך אלנעמה ולא תלתפת למא אלנאס עליה מן אלאקתנאע
פי צלאתהם מן אלכונה בפסוק שמע ופרשה ראשונה פקט פאן אלחק
יורי טריקה וארג̇ע אלי אתמאם אלגרץ̇ לא יכ̇דעך אלוג̇וד בג̇מאלה שקר
החן והבל היופי אשה יראת יי היא תתהלל פאד̇א צח לך אלמטלוב תנו
לה מפרי ידיה ויהללוה בשערים מעשיה וענד ד̇לך תקול הנה נא ידעתי
20א כי אשה יפת מראה את ויתבת פיך והרביתי אותך במאד מאד / ומלכים
ממך יצאו ואיצ̇א והקימותי את בריתי וגו' להיות לך לאלהים ולזרעך
אחריך אפהם ד̇לך .

פצל

אעלם יא אבני גראבה̈ הד̇ה אלאמור אלתי
ד̇כרנאהא עלי אלג̇סם ונפורה מנהא ואלאד̇האן
איצ̇א תנפר מנהא ולא תקבלהא באול כ̇אטר בחסב
אן אלטבע יאביהא ואלקוי תנפר מנהא ומא מת̇אל ד̇לך ענדי אלא מת̇ל
מן אכ̇ד̇ טפל צגיר חטה ענד מוֶדב יעלמה אלשריעה פצאר ד̇לך אלמודב
5ג יחכם עלי ד̇לך אלצגיר פי אכלה / ושרבה ונומה ויקצ̇תה וכלאמה אלי
אן נקלה מן אלצ̇ד אלי אלצ̇ד פתשכי אלצבי מן ד̇לך ותקלק לאן אפעאל
אלצבי כאנת פי אלאול מסלמה לה וענד אלמודב צאר מחכומא עליה
פלמא אשתד אלצבי וכבר עלם מקדאר מא פעלה מעה אלמודב ווקע אלג̇זא
בחסב אלנג̇אח כד̇לך חאל אלמאדה סוי מע אלעקל לאנהא כאנת קד
אעתאדת באשיא רבית עליהא פנקלהא מן ד̇לך צעב פאנקלהא עלי
אלתדריג̇ כפעל אלטביעה לילא תתלף פאן וקע נפור פי וקת מא פי אמר
מן אלאמור אלתי כאנת תמשי עליהא פד̇לך לאג̇ל אנחראפהא ענהא בסרעה̈
20ב פלד̇לך אמרתך אן תאכ̇ד̇ אל/אשיא עלי תדריג̇ פאנמא אלקצד בד̇לך תדביר
אלמאדה אלתי הי פי קאלבהא לילא תנחרף ויקע אלתעב פיבטל אלמקצוד
קי̇ אלחכים עאס' טוב אשר תאחוז בזה וגם מזה אל תנח ידך ואעלם יא

4 א תמאם בג̇מלה 12 א כ̇אטר הושמט 13 ג יאבאהא 14 ג אדכ̇לה
ענד 14 א מאדב 22 א פד̇לך הושמט 23 א תחרר אלאשיא 24 א
פי קאבלהא

4 משׁ' לא:ל 6 ברׁ' יב:יא 7 ברׁ' יז:ו-ז 25 קה' ז:יח

פצ̈ל

אעלם אן אלאשיא אלתי ד̇כרנאהא פי אמר אלמאדה
19א וד̇מהא ליס / מן אג̇להא פי ד̇אתהא בל מן אג̇ל
4ג מא יתולד ענהא לאן הד̇א אלרע אלבליעל מא ג̇א
אלי אלקריה אלא באלערץ̇ בגאות רשע ידלק עני ומע ד̇לך קד קאל
אלחכים אם רעב שנאך האכילהו לחם ואם צמא השקהו מים ואנא אוציך
אן תאכ̇ד̇ אלאשיא עלי תדריג̇ כמא אעלמתך פי אול הד̇ה אלמקאלה יתם
לך כל מא תקצדה .

וצ̈יה

אול מא ינבגי לך אן תקלל אלמעאשרה מע עואם
אלנאס ותכ̇ת̇ר אלאכ̇תלאט מע אהל אלפצ̇ל אלד̇י
פיהם רוח חתי תתעלם מנהם אלסירה אלפאצ̇לה
ואלאכ̇לאק אלג̇מילה ותבעד ענך אלאכ̇לאק אלד̇מימה קאל אלחכים הולך
את החכמים יחכם ורועה כסילים ירוע ותדרב נפסך עלי קלה̈ אלכלאם
אלא מא יכון נפעך פי אלדניא וסעאדתך פי אלאכ̇רה קאל אלחכים
ע'ה ברוב דברים לא יחדל פשע וקאלו עאס' כל המרבה דברים מביא
חטא וקאלו עאס' כל ימי גדלתי בין החכמים ולא מצאתי לגוף טוב
משתיקה ת̇ם תצלח גדאך מא אמכנך ותקלל מנה ג̇הדך חתי יציר לך מלכה
אן לא תסתעמל שי אלא מן וקת אלי וקת חתי תאיס מן אלפכרה פיה
19ב ותג̇אהד נפסך פי קלה̈ / אלנום קאל אלחכ'י שלמה ע'ה מעט שנות מעט
תנומות ותדרג̇ נפסך באן לא תרג̇ע לך פכרה אלא פיה תעאלי או פי מא
יקרבך מנה אלי אן תרג̇ע נפסך תקוי ותסאעדך עלי מא תעאניה ותקצדה
מן חצול ד̇לך אלמעני ת̇ם פי וקת צלואתך אצפי ניתך ועמר פכרתך פי
מא אנת תתלפט בה ואיאך ואלפכרה פי גיר מא אנת מנאשבה לילא יסרי
סם אלנחש פיך ואנת גאפל ומא יצח לך צלאה̈ ולא תקבל ומן הנא לזם
אלתהיו מן קבלהא ברחיצת ידים ורגלים חתי תסתיקץ̇ אלנפס ותנבסט
ואלזמו בתלאוה̈ מזמור קבלהא חתי החצל אלכונה ונהו ען אלצלאה פי
כ̇ראב ח̇דרא מן אשתגאל אלפכרה בגיר מא הו מנאשבה פאד̇א צחת לך הד̇ה

1 א פי אמור 3 א יתולד עליהא 6 א תסלך כל מא תקצד 10 א אלאכ̇לאק אלפאצ̇לה 12 א ותרבי 17 א אלוקת אלי אלוקת 20 א תרג̇ע תקוי 21 א אלמעני השמט 22 ג בתתלפט / א׳ יסרי השמט 23 א יצלח לך 26 א צחה̈

4 תה' י:ב 5 מש' כה:כא 11 מש' יג:כ 14 מש' י:יט אבות א:יז 18 מש' ז:י

אלמפסדין קסאוה קאל אלחכים ורחמי רשעים אכזרי כי הרוג תהרגנו ידך תהיה בו בראשונה להמיתו פאנך אן פעלת ד̇לך צלח חאל אהל אלמדינה ואנתצ̇מת אמורהם בתדביר אלמלך אלמאהל לתדבירהא ויתׄבת קול אלחכים פיהא אשריך ארץ שמלכך בן חורים ושריך בעת יאכלו ואנא אוציך אן לא תעדל ען הד̇א אלראי בוג̇ה כי הוא חייך ואורך ימיך וג̇מלהׄ אקול לך מא דאם אלמלך עלי הד̇א אלוצ̇ע תבנה ותכונן עיר סיחון ואן אכ̇תלף אלנט̇אם יקאל פי ד̇לך כי אש יצאה מחשבון ויתׄבת פיהא קו' אי לך ארץ שמלכך נער ושריך בבקר יאכלו ואן תצל נפאק יקאל פיהא ותבקע העיר וכל אנשי המלחמה יברחו ויצאו מן העיר לילה ונרג̇ע נתואיל ונקול חרבה עירנו ושמם מקדשנו וגלה יקרנו ונוטל כבוד מבית חיינו ואמרו כל הגוים על מה עשה יי ככה לארץ הזאת מה חרי האף הגדול הזה אלג̇ואב על אשר עזבו / את ברית יי אלהי ב18 אבותם פאפהם קדר מא ארשדתך אליה ואג̇הד פי כמאל נפסך ולא תפרט פי שי מן אקואתך ואקתצר עלי אלצ̇רורי פי בקאך פאן אלצ̇רורי אכתׄר בד̇להׄ מן אלגיר צ̇רורי כמא קד עלם פאן בעד וג̇וד אלכ̇בז ואלמא ואלהוי מא בקי ללאנסאן בעד ד̇לך ענת קאל אלחכים טוב מעט לצדיק ואיצ̇א טוב פת חרבה ושלוה בה ולא תתטלע למא אלנאס עליה מן אלאנהמאך פי אללד̇את אלבדניה ותקול יסעני מא יסעהם לאנך קד כ̇רג̇ת ענהם וען אחואלהם ופארקתהם בבאטנך פלא תריד אן תכון מתׄלהם ואעלם אן אברהם ע'ה אנמא סמי אוהב וחושק וירא וכד̇לך דוד ע'ה וג̇ירהמא אלא לתרכהם מא סואה ואנפראדהם במערפתה תע' ולד̇לך אוצא דוד שלמה ולדה וקאל ואתה שלמה בני דע את אלהי אביך ועבדהו בלב שלם וקאל אלנבי כי אם בזאת יתהלל המתהלל השכל וידע אותי פאיאך תזאל ען אלסכ̣ה במסלה נעלה דרך המלך נלך ומטלובך וקצדך אנכי ארבנו מידי תבקשנו לאנה תעאלי מגן הוא לכל החוסים בו ואפהם ד̇לך

1 א קאלו אלחכמים 3 א בתדביר חסר 4 א בן חורין ושריך בערב
10 א נתאול 14 א וג אוקאתך 14 א אכתׄר בד̇לה מן אלגיר
צ̇רורי הושמט 17 א ולא יטלע 18 א פרגת 19 א בכאטרך
20 א וגירהמא הושמט 24 א ען אלשבה 25 א ואפהם ד̇לך הושמט

1 מש' יב:י דב' יג:י 4 קה י:יז 5 דב' ל:כ 6 במ' כא:כז
8 קה' י:טז 10 יר' נב:ז 11 דב' כט:כג-ד 16 תה' לז:טז
17 מש' יז:א 22 דה"א כח:ט 23 יר' ט:כג 24 במ' כ:יט בר'
מג:ט 25 תה' יח:לא

אלמסכן אלחכם אלרש אלעני ואלאביון ואלחכם לה ואכ̇ד̇ אלחק מן כ̇צמאה ולד̇לך ונב אלנבי ישעיה ע'ה פי ד̇לך וקאל יתום לא ישפוטו וריב אלמנה לא יבוא אליהם אשארה̈ אליה וקי' אלנבי הגיד לך אדם מה טוב ומה יי דורש ממך כי אם עשות משפט וגו' פאנתבה מן נום אלגפלה ואצחא מן סכר אלג̇הל וחאסב נפסך ואנצ̇ף עקלך מן הואך
17ב וחכמה עלי הואך תחמד בהא אפעאלך ענד ד̇אך / ופיק מן סכרתך ואנג̇ו מן בחר ג̇האלתך ואעמל עלי מא ארשדתך תכ̇לץ נפסך מן אלהלאך ותסתריה ותסתקר פי מחלהא ושם ינוחו יגיעי כח ומן הנא אכ̇ד̇ פי אלארשאד לתדבירך למאדתך וכיף יכון תצרפך מע הד̇א אלשטן אלמלעון חתי ינטרד ענך וכיף תכון צורת אעתנאך באלעקל פי פצל בעד הד̇א .

פצל

אעלם יא אכ̇י אן אלאנסאן אד̇א עלם אן לה עדו קאצד הלאכה ודמארה מא יכפאה ד̇לך אלא ויקצד אן יאכ̇ד̇ זוג̇תה ויפעל בהא אלמכרוה בחצ̇רתה וישתת אולאדה כיף ינבגי אן יכון אחתראסה מנה פאנה ילזמה
3ג אן לא יגפל ענה ולא יגפל ען מקאומתה ולו ענד אכלה ושרבה / ונומה ויקצ̇תה ויג̇על פכרתה פיה לעל יקל ען פעל מא יקצד בה ולא יאמן לה סאעה̈ ואחדה לאנה אן ט̇פר בה לא ישאיר לו משתין בקיר ולא יהיה לו שריד ופליט ויבקיה עצור ועזוב כל הימים פאלצורה אלתי ינבגי לך אן תפעלהא אן תג̇לס אלעקל פי אלצדר על כסא ממלכתו ותאכ̇ד̇ אלנפס ותצירהא וזירא לה ותג̇על אלאעצ̇א אלראיסה אמרא קריבין מנה ואלאעצ̇א אלמראוסה כ̇דאם בין ידיה ותתרך כל עצ̇ו יתצרף פי מא
18א יוהלה ותחכם / אלעדו ותגלגלה בנחשתים ותדבר אתו משפטים ואפהם כיף תכ̇רג̇ מן דהאה וכ̇בת̇ה ולענתה לאנה רשע ערום צאחב חייל לאנה חסב חסאב אלפצ̇לא אד̇א וקע מעהם ערף כיף יכון כ̇לאצה מנהם. ותעלם כל דהאיה ידאפע בהא ען נפסה לא תחוס עינך עליו פאן אלרחמה עלי

1 א אלחכם..ואלאביון חסר 2 א לד̇לך יקול אלנבי 6 א מן פכרתך 7 א גהלאתך 12 א כמאדך 22 ג אהלא לה צ"ל ותגללה 23 א רשע חסר

2 ישי' א:כג 3 מיכה ו:ח 8 איוב ג:יז 17 מל' א טז:יא 18 ירי' מב:יז 19 דבי' יז:יח 22 ירי' לט:ה-ז 25 דבי' יג:ט

יובה אליה ולא יסמע לה כלאם אלא כמ' ק' פיה וחכמת המסכן בזויה
ודבריו אינם נשמעים ומא כפא ד̇לה ופקרה וגרבתה בינהם אלא וישנוה
וישנאו אותו ולא יכלו / דברו לשלום בל יטלבו הלאכה וקתלה ועתה ג2
לכו ונהרגהו וד̇לך כלה לקלה̇ נאצריה ואעואנה אלד̇י הם קואה
אלעקליה וסמי דל ועני ואביון ויצר הרע סמי מלך גדול לכתרת
מסאעדיה ומעאצ̇דיה והם קואה אלג̇סמאניה ולד̇לך אפתכ̇ר דוד משיח
אלהי יעקב עה' בקהרה וקתלה כמ' ק' והוא ירד והכה את הארי בתוך
הבור ביום שלג ואיצ̇א והוא הכה את שני אריאל מואב וקאלו אלחכמים
ז'ל איזהו גבור הכובש את יצרו שנ' ומושל ברוחו מלוכד עיר אלי
תרי פעלה מע אברהם אבינו עה' וקת אלעקידה כמא סטרו אלחכמים ז'ל
בא שטן אצל אבינו אברהם וגו' פאנט̇ר אלי פעל הד̇א אלרשע ותג̇אסרה
עלי אילן גדול מת̇ל ד̇לך אלסיד פכיף נחן אלד̇י לא נלתפת אליה ולא
נעבא בה אלא קד מכנא מן נפוסנא אכ̇לאקה אלמד̇מומה ותרכנאהא תפעל
פי / נפוסנא ותתחכם פיהא ונקף מע ד̇לך נטלב אלרחמה מן רבנא א17
ונקול סלח לנו אבינו ראה נא בענינו ונסינא קול אלנבי כי אם
עונותיכם היו מבדילים בינכם לבין אלהיכם ות̇בת פינא ויפתוהו
בפיהם יא קום אם כהתל באנוש תהתלו בו חתי קאל לנא עלי יד אלנבי
כי תבואו לראות פני מי בקש זאת מידכם רמוס חצרי וקאל גם כי
תרבו תפלה אינני שומע לא תוספו הביא מנחת שוא עולותיכם ספו על
זבחיכם ואכלו בשר כי לא דברתי את אבותיכם ולא צויתים על דברי
עולה וזבח כי אם את הדבר הזה צויתי אותם לאמר שמעו בקולי
והייתי לכם לאלהים למען ייטב לכם וקי' אחרי יי אלהיכם תלכו וקי'
ואהבת את יי אלהיך בכל לבבך וגו' כי כל לבבות דורש יי וקי'
אם תדרשנו ימצא לך וקי' פי מכאן דן דין עני ואביון היא הדעת
אותי נאם יי ישיר בד̇לך אלי מא תקדם ד̇כרה מן אלאעתני בד̇לך אלולד

4 ג לאג̇ל קלה̇ 6 ג דוד נעים זמירות 10 א מן וקת עד וגו' ש'
11 הושמט 25 ג אשאר אלעתנא

1 קה' ט:טז 3 ברי' לז:ד שם כ 5 קה' ט:יד 7 שמ' ב כג:כ
9 אבות ד:א משי' טז:לב 11 ברי' רבה נו:ה 15 ישי' נט:ב
16 תהי' עח:לו 17 איוב יג:ט ישי' א:יב-טו 20 ירי' ז:כא
23 דבי' יג:ה דבי' ו:ה דה' א כח:ט 25 ירי' כב:טז

והדר תעטרהו ביום ההוא יהיה יי צבאות לעטרת צבי ולצפירת תפארה לשאר עמו פאדׄא צח לך הדׄא אלבאב וארתפעת ענך גׄמיע אלמואנע פאנך לא תרגׄע תרי גיר אלנפוס ואלעקול ותתצור אלאנביא ואלאוליא פי צורה חסנה ותקוי פי דׄלך אלי אן תדרך מא פוק דׄלך אלדׄי לא יעבר ענה אלאנסאן בלסאן והדׄא יצח באלמלאזמה ואלתכראר פאנת אן צׄגׄרת או חלי ענדך שי מן אמור אלדניא וטמעת נפסך אן הדׄא אמר מוגׄוד אי וקת שית תהיית לה פקד אטמעתך / נפסך באלמחאל ומא ירגׄע מתׄאלך 16א אלא מתׄאל מן יקול אחטא ואשוב פאנך תעלם אן אלאנסאן לו אהל נפסה ואנקטע לדׄלך עמרה כלה אלי אן יציר שיךׄ כאן טאלב אלתזייד פיה לאן אלמקאם עטׄים מי ימלל גבורות יי ישמיע כל תהלתו ופי מתׄלה אם יתן איש את כל הון ביתו באהבה בוז יבוזו לו ואיצׄא קיל מי יתן לי אבר כיונה אעופה ואשובה נכספה וגם כלתה נפשי לחצרות יי כי טוב יום בחצריך מאלף בחרתי הסתופף בבית אלהי.

פצל

אעלם אן אלשי אלדׄי אלוח בה ואשיר פי כל מכאן ליס ימכן אלנטק בה ואלתעביר ענה לשדהׄ גמוצׄה ורקת מענאה ובעד גׄוהרה ולדׄלך אן ליס כל אנסאן מהיא לה ימכנה קבולה מן אול והלהׄ אלי אן ארתאצׄ פי מקדמאתה אלי תרי נצוץ כתב אלתנזיל וכתב אלנבוה כיף גׄאת באלעבארה ען הדׄא אלמעני באלאמתׄאל חתי ידרך וכדׄלך אלחכמים עאסי' מא תכלמו פיה אלא באלאלגאז ואלפלאספה באלאיגׄאז לאן הדׄה אלמעאני תלוח תׄם תכׄפי פאן עלי קדר אשתגאל אלאנסאן פיהא ולועה בהא יכון אדראכה להא ובעד הדׄה אלמקדמה ואנת תעלם אלמתׄל אלמצׄרוב פי ספר קהלת כקי' עיר קטנה ואנשים / בה מעט ובא אליה מלך גדול פאנה שבה 16ב מאדהׄ אלאנסאן בעיר קטנה ואנשים בה מעט ושבה יצר רע במלך גדול ואלאכׄלאק אלמדׄמומה הי אלמצודים ואלחרמים אלדׄי בנא עליה ושבה אלעקל אלמדבר להא בילד מסכן וחכם פכיף יכון חאלה פיהא שכׄץ לא

6 ג חטׄי 7 ג אן שית 9 א בדׄלך עמרה ולד 14 א בה חסר 16 ג דקהׄ 17 א אול והל 18 א גׄאבת אלעבארה 20 ג באלאיגׄאז א באלאלגאז 21 ג ולעה 24 ג וסמי יצר הרע 26 ג חילתה

1 תה' ח:ו ישי' כח:ה 8 יומא ח:ט 10 תה' קו:ב 11 שיר ח:י תה' נה:ז 12 שם פד ג-יא 24 קה' ט:יד 25 שם ז:כו 26 שם ט:טו

משתגל פי בית אביה בתכמיל נפסה כמא שהד אלכתאב ויעקב איש תם
יושב אהלים ולד̇לך אסתחק אלברכה דון עשו פלמא הרב מן עשו וג̇א
אלי לבן וכ̇רג̇ת רחל ותערף בהא ראי אלביר ועלם מקדאר אלתעב אלד̇י
ינאל אלשכ̇ץ קבל וצולה ללמא קאל והאבן גדולה על פי הבאר פכאנה
אשאר בד̇לך אלי אלמואנע אלתי תעיק אלאנסאן ען אלוצול אלי עץ
החיים עט̇ימה ת̇ם אנה אקאם תלך אלמדה מתאלם מן ד̇לך וקאל מתי אעשה
גם אנכי לביתי והכד̇א ינבגי אן תקיס נפסך עלי ג̇מיע אלפצ̇לא פאן
הד̇א הו ראיהם והו אלד̇י ינבגי אן יעמל עליה פי מת̇ל ד̇לך קאלת
אלתורה מי האיש אשר בנה בית חדש ולא חנכו יתאכ̇ר פי תחציל
אלחנוך אלד̇י הו כמאל אלצורה / אלמעטיה פקד קררת ענדך באן א15
אלגאיה אלמקצודה הי כמאלהא וקד אעלמתך אנך אן אכרמת אלד̇י כאן
בידך פי אלאול וחרסת נפסך מן ג̇מיע אלמהלכה לאכת̇ר אלכ̇לק
ואג̇תהדת פי ד̇האב אולאיך אלאויבים ואלשטנים מן אלקריה פאנהא
תעמר ותסכן וינפד̇ אמר אלסלטאן פיהא ואן אבקית אחד מן אולאיך
פיהא פהו סבב צ̇ררך והיה אשר תותירו מהם לשכים בעיניכם ולצנינים
בצדיכם לאן אד̇א כאנו אולאיך אלקום אלמבעודין ענהא עמרת ואסתקר
אלסלטאן פי קלעתה ונפד̇ ראיה פיהא ואנתשר אלעדל ואמנת אהלהא מן
אלעדו אלנאזל עליהא וכ̇אפו אלמלך וראקבוה ירא את / יי בני ומלך ג1
פדום עלי הד̇ה אלעקידה תרג̇ע מתצרפא פי אלעאלמין כרי' עקיבא עה'
ואמא אן אצ̇טרבת ומלת נחו אלכרובים פלחקת באלישע אחר או ברפיקה
אלד̇י הציץ ונפגע ...ומן אג̇ל ד̇לך חד̇רוא עאס' ען אלאשתגאל בהד̇ה ב15
אלאמור קבל אלתצ̇לע באלשריעה כמא ק' אין ראוי לטייל בפרדס אלא
מי שנתמלא כריסו לחם ובשר לאנהא תוטי אלאכ̇לאק לקבול הד̇ה אלמעאני
פאד̇א תמכנת פי ד̇לך לד̇ה לא תנקטע ולא תרג̇ע תצבר ענהא סאעה̈
ותבקי מחרוס מוקי בד̇לך אלמעני לאנה וקארך ותאג̇ך כמא ק' וכבוד

20 א ואן אטרבה̈ 21 א מביא כאן בטעות את א27-ב27 שורות 7 - 1 בקצת חלופים ונתוסף עליהן סימן של מחיקה 21 א חצ̇רוא 22 א קבל אלתט̇לע מן 23 א לקבול הד̇ה אלאכ̇לאק ולקבול הד̇ה אלמעאני 24 ג פאד̇א אג̇תהדת

1 ברי' כה:כז 4 ברי' כט:ב 6 ברי' ל:ל 9 דבי' כ:ה 15 במדי' לג:נה 18 משי' כד:כא 21 חגיגה יד: 22 יסודי התורה ד:יג

ענהא דקיקה מן שדה̈ אלאגתבאט וכל מא זדת פיה גבטא אזדת פיה עשקא ולא ירג̇ע יטיב לך לא אכל ולא שרב ולא קראר ובאלג̇מלה אנת אלראבח אם חכמת חכמת לך ואעלם אן אלשי אלד̇י וצלת אליה או קרבת מנה
14א מת̇אלה מת̇אל מן וג̇ד וג̇דה עט̇ימה / פאן הו רד באלה ענהא ועקל עליהא ועלם מקדאר מא חצל לה פאנה ילזמה אלשכר לה תעאלי דאים אלד̇י חצל לה ד̇לך בלא כלפה ובלא משקה ויצרפה פי כמאל נפסה ומן תהיג̇ רחמתה עליה ואמא אלג̇אהל פיט̇ן אן הד̇א אלשי אלעזיז יוג̇ד פי כל וקת ומא יעלם אן הד̇א אלד̇י וג̇דה ד̇לך אלשכ̇ץ הו עטיה מן אללה תע' אלד̇י אתצף באנה מוריש ומעשיר לאן ד̇לך תאבע לאסתחקאק ולא בד מן סהו כי אדם אין צדיק בארץ פצונה איהא אלטאלב פאנה מן אלאשיא אלעזיזה אלפאכ̇רה קשרם על גרגרותיך כתבם על לוח לבך יהיו לך לבדך ואין לזרים אתך פאצפי להא ואנקטע ען אלאשיא אלתי תשגלך ענהא ואנת בין אהלך ואקארבך ולא תט̇ן אן אלאנקטאע פי אלג̇באל ואלכהוף כמא יט̇נו אלמסאכין אן במג̇רד אנקטאעהם יחצלו עלי שי וליס כד̇לך ואצרף אלזמאן אלד̇י יפני פי אלמג̇אהדאת פי ד̇לך אלמעני אלד̇י ארשדתך אליה תנאל מטלובך ומן הנא אסמעך כלאם אלנאס פי הד̇ה אלטריק.

פצל

אעלם אן אלמחקקין מן אהל הד̇ה אלטריק כאנו יג̇תהדו פי כמאל אנפסהם קבל אלזואג̇ לעלמהם
14ב אן מא בעד חצול אלזוג̇ה ואלאולאד / פרג̇ה תאמה ואן כאן ת̇ם פרג̇ה פי תחציל שי פיכון קליל ובעד עשר עט̇ים אלי תרי אברהם עאס' לם יזוג̇ ולדה יצחק עה' אלא בעד כמאלה כמא צרח אלכתאב באן אליעזר למא אתא ברבקה אליה וג̇דה יתהיא פי אלצחרא ק' ויצא יצחק לשוח בשדה לפנות ערב וכאן לה מן אלעמר ארבעין סנה פי ד̇לך אלוקת והו וקת אסתחקאק ולם יפארקהא כמא קאל וישב יצחק עם באר לחי ראי לאנה תמכן מנה וכד̇לך יעקב עה' כאן

14 במג̇רה 23 וג̇דהו 25 יפארק

3 מש' ט:יב 9 שמ' א ב:ז 10 קה' ז:כ 11 מש' ג:ג שם ה:יז
24 בר' כד:סג 26 בר' כה:יא

יי ופי הד̇א אשארה אלי תטהיר אלקלב ותנצ̇יפה ונקאיתה ותעדילה מן שואיבה וחצ̇וצ̇ה ונקאיצה ואכ̇לאה ממא סואה תעאלי פאנה יטלע עלי אמור מפידה ג̇דא כאנת כ̇פייה ענה ויחצל לה מן ד̇לך מא לא יחצל לגירה פי אלזמאן אלטויל באלעלם אלגזיר קאל שלמה עאס' מכל משמר נצור לבך כי ממנו תוצאות חיים ואנת תריד ת̇תבת ותקלל אחתפאלך / באלאמור אלגיר צ̇רוריה זמאן טויל אלי אן תרג̇ע לא תתכלף ד̇לך בל יציר לך טבאע פאד̇א דמת עלי ד̇לך אלאג̇תהאד תצפי חיניד̇ אלקוה אלמתכ̇ילה ויט̇הר לך כל מא פי אללוח אלמחפוט̇ תרג̇ע תנטק באלמגיבאת לאשתגאל ד̇הנך בד̇לך אלמעני אלמקצוד ואחתרז בכל ג̇הדך מן פצ̇לה תבקי פי אלחוצ̇ ואיאך אן ינסרק שי מן אלוסכ̇ מע אלמא אלוארד פיה פאנה אן תבקי פיה שי פתרדה אלקוה אלמתכ̇ילה עליך פי חאל אלנום או אליקט̇ה וקת אלכ̇לוה פתט̇ן אנה אמר אתי מן כ̇ארג̇ והו מן ג̇מלה̈ מא יבקי פי אלחוצ̇ והו אלד̇י חד̇רוא מנה אלחכמים עאס' פי קולהם ארבעה נכנסו לפרדס אמ' להם ר' עקיבא כשאתם מגיעים אצל אבני שיש טהור ב13 אל תאמרו מים מים שכן כתוב / דובר שקרים לא יכון לנגד עיני פאסעא אבדא אלי אלאמיא אלגזירה אלג̇יידה אלתי תרוי אלאנסאן ואנתהי ען גירהא אלתי תזיד אלאנסאן עטש לילא ישתו התלמידים הבאים אחריכם וימותו ונמצא שם שמים מתחלל ותציר ממן קיל פיהם אותי עזבו מקור מים חיים לחצוב להם בארות בארות נשברים אשר לא יכילו המים פאעלם ד̇לך.

פצל

יא אבני אכרם אלשכ̇ץ אלד̇י יוצל בינך ובין באריך ג̇ל ועז פהו יתוסט לך באלכ̇ליר כי הוא המליץ בינותם ואחרץ בג̇מיע קואך עלי תחצילה פאן ליס הו אמר יג̇בר פאיתה פאן גפלת ענה ד̇הב וחם השמש ונמס התעיף עיניך בו ואיננו פלא תמל ולא תצ̇ג̇ר קאל דוד פי ד̇לך כי עליך הורגנו כל היום פאנך בעד וצולך להד̇ה אלדרג̇ה לא ימכנך תצבר

2 ב נקאיצה חסר 5 ב אחפאלך 6 צ̇רוריא 12 אליקט̇א 13 חצ̇רוא 19 בורות בורות

4 מש' ד:כג 13 חגיגה יד: 15 תה' קא:ז 17 אבות א:יא 19 יר' ב:יג 23 בר' מב:כג 24 שמ' טז:כא 25 מש' כג:ה תה' מד:כג

אבא באהל ביתי וכ̇לף מן אלד̇הב ואלפצ̇ה ואלנחאס ואלחדיד מא הו
מסטור פי מלכים לבניאן אלבית ליחל נורה תע' פיה והד̇ה נהאיה פי
אלמחבה בכל לבבך ובכל נפשך ובכל מאדך פתרג̇ע אי מעני כלפך בה
חביבך לא תתאכ̇ר ען קצ̇איה מן כת̇רה̇ אלמחבה כי עזה כמות אהבה ואד̇א
כ̇לות בנפסך בעד קהר אכ̇לאקך אנפתח לך באב תרי מנה אלעג̇איב וד̇לך
ענד בטלאן חואסך אלכ̇מס אלט̇אהרה תסתיקצ̇ אלבאטנה פיוריך נור / 5ב
באהר מן נור אלעקל ותדרך אצואת עט̇ימה מהולה מפזעה ידהש אלאנסאן
להא ברקים למטר עשה ויוצא רוח מאצרותיו ואפהם אן רוח אסם משתרך
וכד̇לך כל מא ג̇א מן אלאסתעארה פי אלמת̇ל ודלתי שמים פתח נפתחו
השמים פתחו שערים הו ללתנביה עלי הד̇א אלמעני ומן הנא / אכ̇תלפת 12ב
דרג̇את אלסאלכין פי הד̇א אלטריק לאנה בחסב תדביר אלשכ̇ץ נפסה פי
אכלה ושרבה ונומה ופכרה וג̇מיע תצרפאתה פי נפסה יכון תעבה וקת
תהיוה ק' שלמה עה' שומר פיו ולשונו שומר מצרות נפשו ואנט̇ר אלי
קולהם עה' אלדי הו דליל עלי מא תקדם ד̇כרה מן אכ̇תלאף דרג̇את
אלסאלכין פי הד̇א אלמקאם קאלו אברהם שהיה כחו יפה נדמו לו
בדמות אנשים לוט שהיה כחו רע נדמו לו בדמות מלאכים פקד ביינוא
עאלס' ג̇מיע אלתוטיאת אלמחתאג̇ אליהא פי סלוך הד̇א אלטריק ולא בד
מן תנביה אכ̇ר פי אלפצל אלד̇י בעד הד̇א אלפצל.

פצל 6א

אעלם אנך אן ארדת תפהם אלאלגאז אלתי פי
הד̇ה אלמקאלה פרד באלך אלי אלאמת̇לה אלתי
פיהא ואעזל פי ד̇הנך אן כל מנפד̇ אמר יסמי
מלאך אנזל אן בעץ̇ אלנאס ענדה חוץ̇ קדים מזמן אראד תנצ̇יפה מן
וסכ̇ה ואכדארה ופי ארשאדה וד̇לך נעמה מנה תע' עליה פיג̇ב אן יחרץ
אן לא יזיד ד̇לך אלחוץ̇ וסך̇ בל יעתני בתנצ̇יפה קליל קליל אלי אן
ינצ̇ף פאד̇א עלם ויתיקן אן לם יבק פיה שי מן אל/וסך̇ חיניד̇ ירד 13א
אליה ד̇לך אלמים אלחיים היוצאים מבית יי אלמקול פיה ומעין מבית

3 א פתתבע 5 א כ̇לית 7 א יד̇הב 8 לפני מלת פאפהם יש פצל חדש בכ"י ב 26 א יי-מבית יי חסר

3 דב' ו:ה 4 שיר ח:ו 8 יר' י:יג 9 תה' עח:כג יחז' א:א יש' כו:ב 13 מש' כא:כג 15 בר' רבה נ:ג 26 יואל ד:יח

פצל

הד̇א אלפצל אלד̇י נאתי בה אלאן הו אלקטב
אלד̇י ידור עליה גרץ̇ הד̇ה אלמקאלה והו
תוטיה למא יאתי בעדה פאג̇על ענאיתך פי פהמה
אעלם אן אלאנסאןהו צפוה̈ אלעאלם אלספלי לאנה אכ̇ר מרכב תרכב מנה
וסמי אלעאלם אלצג̇יר ד̇לך מן אג̇ל אלקוה̈ אלנאטקה אלתי ארתבטת בה
והי אלתי קאל ענהא אלנבי ותחסרהו מעט מאלהים וכבוד והדר תעטרהו
/ ומן אג̇להא לזמה אלאמר ואלנהי ואלג̇זא ואלעקאב והד̇ה אלקוה̈ להא 11ב
שרף עלי ג̇מיע אלקוי אלתאלפה לאן לכל עצ̇ו קוה̈ מא תכ̇צה והד̇ה
אלקוה אד̇א קארנתהא מאדה ג̇ידה אשת חיל פעלת באשראקהא עליה
עג̇איב ואד̇א קימהא ואעטאהא חקהא ולם יקטעהא ען פעלהא לאן
אלחכים מן אלנאס / אלד̇י יעטי כל ואחד מסתחקה כק' וצדיק יתן 4ב
ולא יחשוך ופעלהא הו אקתנא אלעלום ואלמעארף ואדראך אלעקל
ללבארי עז וג̇ל חסב טאקתהא פאד̇א תמכנת וארתפעת ענהא אלעואיק
ואלמואנע אלקאטעה פי אלעמל עלמת אלמג̇יבאת וליס מת̇ל אלקוה̈
אלמתכ̇ילה אלתי יפותהא מן אלד̇י תעלמה לאן פעל תלך אלקוה̣ צחיח
לא ריב פיה אד̇א אסתכ̇רג̇ מא פי קותהא ללפעל פאן אנ̣ת סאעדתהא נלת
ראחת אלדניא ואלאכ̇ר̣ה אמא אלדניא פירג̇ע כל מא הו מסתור ענך
ינכשף לך ואפהם אללגז פי קו' נפתחו השמים אלדי תקדם ד̇כרה פאד̇א
אנפתח לך הד̇א אלבאב מא תברח מלאזם אלדאר טול עמרך ואיאך
אלגפלה ען אעדאך אלד̇י מעך לילא תרג̇ע ממן קיל פיה ויגרש את
האדם פאנהם מא יצדקו בגפלה שרקו ויחרקו שן ותרג̇ע / תתעב פי 12א
כ̇רוג̇הם מן אלמכאן אפהם הד̇א אללגז פאנה ישפי גלילך פאנת אד̇א
לאזמת אלבאב אלד̇י הו עדן והו מעדן אלרחמה ושגל בה באלך תרג̇ע
אד̇א חצ̇רתך מצות עשה מא תתמאלך לשדה̈ שוקך לכת̇רת מא תחמוד יפיה
בלבבך ותקול הרבו עלי מאד מהר ומתן אולי אמצא חן בעיניו אלי
תרי שוק אלסיד דוד עאלס' פי בניאן בית המקדש מקום ליי וקי' אם

4 א לאנה חסר 5 ב אתצלת 9 א קארנהא מאדה תכ̇צהא 10 א קימהא
חסר 13 ב טאקתנא א אלעואיק חסר 15 ב אלתי יפותהא מן אלד̇י
חסר 19 ב אנפהם לך הד̇א אלמעני 24 א מא תתם לך 26 ב לבניאן
אלבית

6 תה' ח:ו 11 מש' כא:כו 18 יחז' א:א 20 בר' ג:כד 21 איכה
ב:טו 24 מש' ו:כה 25 בר' לד:יב 26 תה' קלב:ג

פצל

10ב אעלם יא אכ̇י אן נחן קד אנכשפנא מן אלקרב
אליה /תע' לקטענא אלוצלה אלתי ביננא ובינה
באשתגאלנא באלאמור אלגיר צ̇רוריה ואלתשבה
באלחיואנאת ואערצ̇נא ען אלנפס חתי צדית וצארת שבה אלמראה אלתי
לא תורי צ̇ו אלבתה לאנהא קד תג̇רמת בתרך אלאצלאח פאנא אשיר עליך
אן תטלב וג̇הה תעאלי פי וקת פרג̇תנא מן כלף מאדתנא ותסתרקד אלשטן
ותקום פי בהים אלליל תואג̇הה תעאלי באלתחנן ואלתצ̇רע ק' קומי
רוני בלילה לראש האשמורות שפכי כמים לבך נכח פני יי ואלמח
אלבאב אלד̇י לג̇ה̈ אלמקדש ופתחו שעריך תמיד יומם ולילה המזכירים
את יי אל דמי לכם פאנבאבנא הד̇א אלנץ עלי אלתוג̇ה אלדאים יומם
ולילה ואיאך אלגפלה כי כפשע ביני ובין המות ואפכר כיף יכון
לקאך לרבך בהד̇ה אלעקידה ואיצ̇א כאנו אלאנביא וכ̇לפאהם אלד̇י הם
אלחכמים עאלס' באטלאק ענד מא אשתגלו פי וקת מא בצ̇רורה̈ אלג̇סם
כיף אסלמו פי יד אלאעדא פכיף נחן אלד̇י לא עלם לנא ולא תהיו
ולא צפא ואד̇א ג̇את נפס אחדנא תצפו ותתקרב אלי אלמוצ̇ע אלמשאר
אליה בצדיקים יושבים ועטרותיהם בראשיהם ונהנין מזיו השכינה
איזו היא עטרותיהן אלו מעשיהם הטובים והנאין שעשו בעולם הזה
11א נצפנה להם לעולם שכלו / טוב וקצדת תנצ̇ם אליהם אי שי יקולו להא
גם מאת זה תצאי וידיך על ראשך אי כ̇גלה תכון באעט̇ם מן הד̇ה
בעודהא מן בינהם פיחק עליך יא אכ̇י אן תלאזם אלבאב כק' שלמה
עאלס' אשרי אדם שומע לי לשקוד על דלתותי יום יום ולא תגפל ען
נפסך וצנה פי קלבך ואיאך יסמעך סוי אלד̇י אנטות פי חקה ובל
וסאדך בדמעך ואנט̇ר כיף כאפית אלמחסן באלאסאה ורפצ̇ת אדב אלעקל
3ב ואלנפס אלד̇י הם רסל אללה ומלאיכתה אלד̇י אכ̇תצך בהם וג̇על / לך
פי קוי נפסך אד̇א תמכנת אן תתצל באלעקל חתי אד̇א אנצרפת מן הד̇א
אלעאלם כנת מטמאן אמן עלי נפסך ות̇בת פיך והלך לפניך צדקך
כבוד יי יאספך וזרח בחשך אורך.

3 צ̇רוריא 4 צדות 9 שערי 20 בעדהא 22 וציהו ובל צדאך 24 א
וג̇עלך פקוי 25 א תחצל 26 אמן עליהא

7 איכה ב:יט 9 ישי' ס:יא שם ו 11 שמ' א כ :ג 16 ברכות יז.
19 ירי' ב:לז 21 משלי ח:לד 26 ישי' נח:ח-י

אלכרם מן אלנפס ולאן תרג̇ע תפעל ד̇לך באלטבע פאנה אד̇א תמכן מן
אלשכ̇ץ כ̇לק מחמוד אנדפע ענה צ̇דה ואמא קולה כי תפגע כי תראה כל
אלמנה ויתום וגר לא תלחץ ומא שאבההם פד̇לך לתמכין כ̇לק אלרחמה מן
אלאנסאן אמא נהיה לא תלבש שעטנז לא תזרע כרמך כלאים לא יקרחה
קרחה בראשם ותגלחת פאת הראש והזקן פהו ללבעד ען אלתשבה באפעאל
עובד עז' ותת̇בית קאעדת אלתוחיד ולא יהיה לך אלהים אחרים לתת̇בית
קאעדת וג̇ודה תעאלי פי נפוסנא ונעלם אן אלשכ̇ץ מנא אד̇א כ̇טר בבאלה
ראי מא קבל אן ינטק בה פאנה תע' עאלם בה כמא ק' דוד עאלס' כי
אין מלה בלשוני הן יי ידעת כלה וקאל אני יי חוקר לב ובוחן
כליות תם יעלם אן חרכאתה כלהא וסכנאתה מעלומה ענדה תעאלי
מחפוט̇ה עליה כאנת כ̇ירא או שרא לאן אפעאלנא מכשופה בין ידיה
תעאלי ולד̇לך כאנו אלמאידין באלחק יתאפפון מן כשף רוסהם חשמה̈ מן
10א אלעקל פקד לזמהם אלתת̇בת פי וקת אטלאק ענאן אל/ג̇צ̇ב ואלשהוה פי
אי שי כאן מן אלנפס אלתי כ̇ץ בהא דון סאיר אלחיואן אלד̇י קיל פיה
1ב מן אג̇להא / אנה בדמות אלהים עשה אותו ות̇אניה מן אלעקל אלד̇י הו
מחאורה מלאחפה דאים אלד̇י קיל פיה כי בצלם אלהים עשה את האדם
ות̇אלת̇הא מן באריה ג̇ל ועז אלד̇י אן וקף אלאנסאן או קעד או אפכר
או נטק והו פי אעלא מכאן או אספלה הו בין ידיה תע' כק' אם יסתר
איש במסתרים ואני לא אראנו נאם יי פכיף יכון חאלה̈ אלשכ̇ץ והאולאי
אלת̇לאת̇ה מראקבין לה והו מתצרף בחצ̇רתהם ולד̇לך כאנו עאלס' ישאחחו
אלנאס פי משיהם בקומה זקופה משום מלא כל הארץ כבודו ק' אלנבי
ורמי הקומה גדועים פיג̇ב עלי אלאנסאן אד̇א אלג̇תה אלצ̇רורה אלי
אלתצרף פי אמר צ̇רורי מת̇ל אכל או שרב או מעאמלה̈ אלנאס ולחקתה
ג̇פלה פי ד̇לך ענהם חתי נסי אנה בחצ̇רתהם פליעתרף בכ̇טאה ויקול
חטאתי ליי אלהיכם ולכם ואן לם יעתרף פית̇בת פיה ק' הנני נשפט
אתך על אמרך לא חטאתי פאעתני באלעקל ואג̇על כסאו למעלה מכסא
המלכים אשר אתך.

2 צ̇צ̇ה 14 אולי צ"ל וחשמה̈ מן אלנפס 18 א נשק והו פי אלאעלא מכאן
22 א אלגאתה 23 א משאמלה ולחקתה

2 שמ' כג:ד-ה שם כב:כא 4 דב' כב:יא שם ט ויק' כא:ה 6 שמ' כ:ב
8 תה' קלט:ד 9 יר' יז:י 15 בר' ה:א 16 שם ט:ו 18 יר' כג:כד
21 יש' ו:ג 22 שם י:לג 25 שמ' י:טז יר' ב:לה 26 שם נב:לב

נאם והו עלי תלך אלצורה לא ירי אלא מא יזעג̇ה ויקלקה פלאג̇ל ד̇לך אחד̇רתנא אלשריעה אלטאהרה ואלמטהרה לנא מן ג̇מיע נג̇אסתנא אלט̇אהרה ואלבאטנה אמא אלט̇אהרה אלטהארה פי אלטבילה במי מקוה ללנדה ולבעל קרי וכד̇לך ג̇א אלאמר לאהרון ולבניו והו קולה תעאלי ורחצו ידיהם ורגליהם ולא ימותו והו מעני אלקידוש ועלה̇ ד̇לך אן אלאנסאן ענד מא ינגמס פי אלמא יתיקן פי נפסה אן קד יזאל ענהא מאנע אלי מעני יקארב אלתהיו ואלאתצאל בה תעאלי ואן כאן גיר מחתאג̇ אלי טבילה פיגסל ידיה ורגליה פתנבסט ענד ד̇לך אלחרארה אלגריזיה פתסתיקט̇ אלנפס באנתשארהא פי אלבדן וכד̇לך ג̇א איצ̇א אלנהי ען אלמסכר ענד ד̇כול אלמקדש לילא יחצל מאנע ען אלפכרה ויקע אלבדל והו קולה בעד ד̇לך ולהבדיל בין הקדש ובין החול ומן / 9א אג̇ל ד̇לך קאל קדושים יהיו לאלהיהם ואלאמר אלעאם לכאפה̇ ישראל קולה והתקדשתם והייתם קדושים ואמא אלטהארה אלבאטנה פהו אלנהי ען מאכלות אסורות אלמולדה ללעפן אלמפסדה ללבדן אלמבלדה ללד̇הן אלמקויה ללמאדה עלי אלאכ̇לאק אלמד̇מומה מת̇ל לחום אלכ̇ליל ואלכ̇נאזיר ולחם אלג̇מל וגירה והו קו' אל תשקצו את נפשותיכם ולא תטמאו בהם ונטמתם בם אל תקרא ונטמאתם אלא ונטמתם וכד̇לך נהאת אלשריעה ען אמור אכ̇ר לתקציר ד̇יל אלשהוה ולאן לא יכון אלאנסאן משאבה ללחיואן והי אלעריות בג̇מלתהא אלא מא כאן בכתובה וקדושין לאן ד̇לך ללאנסאן מן חית̇ הו חיואן וכד̇לך אמרת באלמילה מן ג̇הה̇ אלאלה אלתי יתם בהא פעל ד̇לך ואמא אלציצית ואלתפילין ואלמזוזה פאנהא סלמו לתנביה אלנפס וקת אלגפלה ען ד̇לך אלמעני אלמקצוד והו קו' פי אלציצית וראיתם אותו וזכרתם את כל מצות יי ופי אלתפילין והיה לך לאות על ידך ולזכרון וגו' אמא אלאמר בעמל מעקה ותגטיה̇ אלביר אד̇א פתחה אנסאן פי אלטריק פאן אלקצד בד̇לך חפט̇ אלנפס ואזאלה̇ אלמצ̇אר ואמא אלחלה / 9ב ואלתרומה ואלמעשרות ואללקט ואלשכחה ואלפאה ואלעוללות ואלצדקות ומא יג̇רי מג̇ראהא לתמכין כ̇לק

17 ונטמא אלא ונטמאטם 22 פאנה סלמא 24 ידכה 27 מג̇ראהמא

4 שמ' ל:כא 11 ויק' י:י כא:ו 13 שם יא:מד 16 שם מג 17 יומא לט. 23 במ' טו:לט 24 שמ' יג:ט 25 דב' כב:ח

חסד ולא בכ̇ל במא יוצלה אליהם פכאן יוצל לכל ש̇כ̇ץ̇ עלי קדר פהמה
תשבה באלעקל וימדו בעומר ולא העדיף המרבה והממעיט לא החסיר
איש לפי אכלו לקטו חתי וצלו וצלו למא וצלו אליה מן סמאע כ̇טאבה תע'
פעלמהם עאס' כיף יהד̇בון אכ̇לאקהם וכיף יסתעמלון אלתריאק אד̇א
לסעהם אלחנש לאג̇ל אן תלך אלארץ̇ כתירה̈ אלהואם קלילה̈ אלמא כמא
וצפת אלתורה נחש שרף ועקרב וצמאון אשר אין מים וכד̇לך למא עטשו
8א ישראל ואשתאקו ללמא פתשפע בין ידיה עאלס' ואג̇אבה הנני עומד/
לפניך שם על הצור פלמא כ̇רג̇ אלמא מאת אלדביב וכד̇א ועדנא פי
אלמסתקבל בקולה ומעין מבית יי יצא והשקה את נחל השטים אפהם
איהא אלנאט̇ר פי הד̇ה אלנצוץ מא אגרבהא והיה ביום ההוא יצאו מים
חיים מירושלים כי מימיו מן המקדש המה יוצאים.

פצל

אעלם אן אלאנסאן פיה אעצ̇א ראיסה ואעצ̇א
מראוסה ולכל עצ̇ו מנהם פעל מא יכ̇צה פיה אלי
מסאעדה̈ עצ̇ו אכ̇ר מת̇ל אלקלב ואלכבד וגירהמא
אמא אלדמאג פאן פיה ת̇לאת̇ קוי והם אלפכר ואלד̇כר ואלתכייל וקותין
אכ̇ר (!) והם אלוהם ואלחס אלמשתרך פהם מחג̇ובין ענה בט̇הור פעל
אלכ̇מס חואס אלט̇אהרה פי סטח אלג̇סם והם אלנט̇ר ואלסמע ואלשם
ואלד̇וק ואללמס פאד̇א בטל פעל אולאיך אלכ̇מס חואס אלמד̇כורה
ט̇הר פעל אולאיך וכ̇אצה̈ ענד אלנום פיחדת̇ ען ד̇לך אלמנאמאת
אלצאדקה אד̇א כאן ת̇ם צפא ואעלם אן כמא אד̇א תנאול אלאנסאן אגד̇יה
סו ודאם עלי אסתעמאלהם כיף יחדת̇ לה מן ד̇לך אמראץ̇ צעבה אלי
8ב אן יחיר אלטביב פי / עלאג̇ה ויאול ד̇לך אלי אן ילחקה אלג̇ד̇אם
ואלתנפ̇ך ואלאוראם אלחאדה חתי איצ̇א מא פי באטן אלדמאג מת̇ל
אלגשאוה פי אלעינין ואלטנין פי אלסמע וגיר ד̇לך וכד̇לך אד̇א גפל
אלאנסאן ען נפסה ותרך מרצ̇הא יתחכם באשתגאלה פי שגל אלדניא
לילה ונהארה פי ביעה ופי שראיה ופי מא ג̇רי לה ויג̇רי פאנה אד̇א

16 צ"ל אכ̇ריאן 26 אולי צ"ל יג̇רי מג̇ראהמא

2 שמ' טז:יח 6 דב' ח:טו 7 שמ' יז:ו 9 יואל ד:יח 10 זכ' יד:ח
11 יחז' סח:יב

לה אלשי אלד̇י הו מחבוב ענדך אולי תמצא חן בעיניו פאן בה תתסאעד
עלי ג̇מיע מטלובך ולא יזאל צאחבך אלי אן תפארק חיניד̇ יקוי ברפע
אלמאדה אלחאג̇בה לך ען אלאדראך

פצ̇ל

אעלם אן אלאנסאן ליס לה מאנע ען אלכמאל
7א כמא ליס לה מן ימנעה / ען אלמעאצי קאלת
אלתורה אלמטהרה הן האדם היה כאחד ממנו
לדעת טוב ורע וקאל ירמיה מפי עליון לא תצא הרעות והטוב ומן אג̇ל
הד̇א קאלו עאלס' בא ליטהר מסייעין אותו בא ליטמא פותחין לו פקד
תביין אן ליס ת̇ם ג̇בר עלי שי פיג̇ב ללאנסאן אן יקטע פכרתה מן כל
שי ויקץ̇ עקלה וישתגל בה מן חית̇ אנה אלוצלה בינה ובין כ̇אלקה
תעאלי פאד̇א אדאם פכרתה פיה וג̇דה קאל אלנבי דרשו יי בהמצאו
קראוהו בהיותו קרוב יעזוב רשע דרכו ואיש און מחשבותיו וישוב אל
יי וירחמהו ואל אלהינו כי ירבה לסלוח לאן מא בקי לה מאנע מן
חית̇ אנה שב אל יי פאן אלעאיק ען אדראכה אנמא הו כדור ג̇והרנא
והו אלמכנא בחשך ענן וערפל ישת חשך סתרו לאן אלבארי ג̇ל ת̇נאה מא
ענדה אלא אלנור אלמחץ̇ אלבאהר כק' והארץ האירה מכבודו פאד̇א חצל
מן אלשכ̇ץ ות̇בת ודאם ולם יצ̇ג̇ר אלי אן יצפא לה הד̇א אלבאב פאנה
ירי אמור כאנת מחג̇ובה ענה מסדודה ען גירה וקוות עזימת אלעקל
ואט̇הר מא פי אללוח פתרד עלי ד̇לך אלשכ̇ץ אמור אלאהיה לא יעלם עלי
7ב איה̈ ג̇הה̈ תחצל / פיבקי סאיר בצ̇יא עקלה מסתרשד ברשדה פאעתני
בנפסך וצון צורתהא פאן ליס להא ת̇באת פי אלנעים אלא בחצ̇ורה מעהא
ולד̇לך אוצא שלמה עאלס' קשרם על גרגרותיך כתבם על לוח לבך חיניד̇
תמצא חן ושכל טוב בעיני אלהים ואדם ותרג̇ע תג̇תד̇י אלד̇י כאנו אבאך
יג̇תד̇ו פי אלבריה כמק' לחם אבירים אכל איש וגו' וק' ודגן שמים
נתן למו ופי מת̇ל ד̇לך ק' נפתחו השמים וק' פתחו לי שערי צדק
ואיצ̇א זה השער ליי צדיקים יבאו בו פאן דור המדבר לם יצל אלי
דרג̈ה אלכמאל אלא בסבב אלאסתאד̇ אלמאהר אלד̇י בינהם וכונה מא ענדה

20 אמורא̈ אלאהיה מא יעלם עלי איי ג̇הה̈

7 ברי' ג:כב 8 איכה ג:לח 9 שבת קד. 12 ישי' נה:ו 15 דב' ד:יא
16 תה' יח:יב 17 יחז' מג:ב 23 מש' ג:ג 25 תה' עח:כה26 יחז' א:א
26 תה' קיח:יט

ת̇ם ד̇כר אלדוא מעט שנות מעט תנומות ובא מתהלך רישך ומחסריך כאיש
מגן תם תתנט̇ף מן מזכ̇רפאת אלדניא אלתי תחרץ עץ החיים כמק' אלנבי
רחצו הזכו הסירו רוע מעלליכם וגו' חינ̇יד̇ תצלח ללתקדם לעבאדתה
תעאלי וגם הכהנים הנגשים אל יי יתקדשו וגו' וקאל אלחכים שמור
6א רגליך כאשר תלך / אל בית האלהים ואעתבר באצילי ישראל למא
תהג̇מוא קבל כמאלהם כיף אסתחקו אלעד̇אב פינבגי לכל עאקל אנה לא
ירתקי לדרג̇ה הי אעלי מנה בל יעלם נפסה וידרג̇הא קלילא קלילא כמא
תפעל אלטביעה פאנהא תאכ̇ד̇ אלאשיא עלי תדריג̇ כקי' אלחכ' ז'ל אין
ראוי לטייל בפרדס אלא למי שנתמלא כריסו לחם ובשר וקי' תעאלי ולא
תעלה במעלות על מזבחי ישיר אלי אלמעני בעינה פאחרץ עלי נפסך
חתי אד̇א סלכת אלטרק אמנת אלכ̇וף כי המקום אשר אתה עומד עליו קדש
הוא פאפהמה .

פצל

אעלם יא איהא אלנאט̇ר פי הד̇ה אלמקאלה אן
אלאמר אלד̇י אשרנא אליה פי הד̇א אלמוצ̇ע לא
יחתמל באכת̇ר מן הד̇א פאלגאיה אנני אד̇א וג̇דת
נץ מא יכון מחתמל מעאני כת̇ירה פאני אפתח בה אלבאב ואתכל עלי
פהם אלשכ̇ץ אן כאן לה קריחה וענדה ד̇וק פהו יצל אלי אלמעני בנפסה
והו קולהם עאלס' אם היה חכם ומבין מדעתו מוסרין לו ראשי הפרקים

פצל

6ב אעלם אן אלבארי תעאלי אלפיץ̇ פאיץ̇ מנה דאים
עלי ג̇מיע מכ̇לוקאתה אולא עלי אלעקל בחסב
דרג̇את אלאשכ̇אץ ויתצל ד̇לך באלאפלאך אלי אן
ינתהי אלי אלד̇י בה אלענאיה פאן תלך אלענאיה תצחבה טאלמא עקלה
מפכר פי מכ̇לוקאתה תעאלי פאן גפל ענה אנצרף התעיף עיניך בו
ואיננו כי עשה יעשה לו כנפים כנשר יעוף השמים לאנה רג̇ע אלי
מעדנה ובקי ד̇לך אלשכץ נע ונד בארץ מא לה מן יחג̇בה והיה כל
מוצאו יהרגנו פאחרץ אנך תפעל רצ̇אה לעל יתאנס בך ותחצל בינך
ובינה מואנסה מנאסבה פיכון אבדא קצדך אתמאם גרצ̇ה ליסתכמל ואבד̇ל

1 ובא כמהלך ראשך ומחסורך 25 בשמים

2 ישי' א:טז 3 שמ' יט:כב 4 קה' ד:יז 9 שמ' כ:כג 11 שם ג: ה
18 חגיגה יג. 24 מש' כג:ה 26 ברי' ד:יד

אלחקיקה ופיה ק' דוד עאלס' אשרי אדם עוז לו בך מסלות בלבבם אשרי העם שה' אלהיו בלפט̇ אלפראד והו אלצחיח לאן הד̇א אלמעני הו אלצחיח ללאנסאן וחדה לא ישארכה פיה גירה ואמא אלמתחייר פהו 5א חשוב כמת פאנה לם יחצל לה אעתקאד צחיח / ית̇בת עליה והו אלד̇י ק' ענה אלחכים ומעקש דרכיו יודע ואמא אלד̇י יעתקד אלשי תקליד פכאנה מא כ̇לק ופיה ק' אלחכים איצ̇א טוב ממנו הנפל ובעד ד̇לך השומע ישמע והחדל יחדל

פצ̇ל

אעלם יא בני אן אלעלם באלמשא ואלמתן מע כת̇רה פואידה פי הד̇א אלעאלם וחפט̇ אלנפס ואלמאל מא לה מדכ̇ל פי הד̇א אלמעני לאן ד̇לך הו סיאסה̈ אלעאמה לאתפאק בעצ̇הם מע בעצ̇ ואנתט̇אם אחואלהם פי אג̇תמאעהם ואמא הד̇א אלעלם פאנה לך וחדך כק' אלחכים יהיו לך לבדך ואין לזרים אתך פאד̇א צח לך הד̇א אלעלם אמא מן נפסך או מן מנבה ינבהך עלי ד̇לך בעד אלריאצ̇ה פי עלם אלשריעה לאנה אלקטב אלדי ידור עליה ריאצ̇ה̈ אלאכ̇לאק לאנה אלסולם אלדי תצל בה אליה תאעלי כי לוית חן הם לראשך והכד̇א יעתקדון אלפלאספה אן אלריאצ̇יאת מתאכ̇מה ללטביעאת והי מתצלה באלאלאהיאת וענהא קיל כי אם בזאת 5ב יתהלל המתהלל השכל וידוע אותי וגו' פאד̇א תעלקת אמאלך / בה ינפך כ̇תמך מן אלטמע פי אלדניא ואגראצ̇הא ותרג̇ע אד̇א קיל לך ען שי אן יכון פיה אמר דניאי יכ̇צך תקול יתלה עולם באחרים לשגל באלך ענה וענה קיל אני לדודי ועלי תשוקתו ואעלם אד̇א ראם שכ̇ץ אלתקדם אלי אלחצ̇רה אלאלאהיה וג̇ב עליה אן יעלם אנה בריה קטנה אפלה שפלה מאדתה משארכה למאדה אלחיואן אלגיר נאטק פיריד אולא אן יתטהר מן אלאשיא אלתי הי שבה אלנדה והי פצ̇לאת אלקוי אלחיואניה מת̇ל פצ̇לה אכל ושרב אכת̇ר מן אלצ̇רורי ת̇ם בעד ד̇לך תנטבל מן אלזוהמה אלתי רמאהא אלנחש פי ג̇סמך אלד̇י גפלת ען מדאואתה באלתריאק אלמעד לך אלי אן קיל פי מת̇לך על שדה איש עצל עברתי ועל כרם אדם חסר לב פוצף כיף יכון עמראן הד̇א אלשדה פקאל בעדה ואחזה אנכי אשית לבי

11 אלסיאסה אלעאממא 16 אלריאצ̇את מתחאכמה

1 תה' פד:ו 2 שם קמד:טו 5 מש' י:ט 6 קה' ו:ג יחז' ג:כז 12 מש' ה:יז 15 מש' א:ט 17 יר' ט:כג 20 שיר ז:יא 27 מש כד:ל-לד

אלחקיקה לאן אלעקל הו אלוצלה בין אלבארי ובין מכ̇לוקאתה פכל מן
4א צרף המתה נחוה וג̇עלה / גאיתה חד̇א עיניה כקׄ דוד עאלסׄ שויתי יי
לנגדי תמיד כי מימיני בל אמוט פהו יוקיה מן אלאפאת באלפיץ̇
אלפאיץ̇ מנה כקׄ כי בי חשק ואפלטהו כמא תרא אלאמראה אלמרצ̇עה
ענדמא תפכר פי ולדהא ועלי אנה ליס חאצ̇ר ענדהא פאן אללבן ידר
מן ת̇דיהא ממא תהיג̇ רחמתהא עליה כרחם אב על בנים הכד̇א פעל אלעקל
אד̇א חצלת ת̇ם מנאסבה מא בינה ובין אשכ̇אץ אלנאס פאנה יציר מעה מא
יפארקה עמו אנכי בצרה וקׄ אל תירא כי אתך אני וקׄ כי תעבור
במים אתך אנכי אחרץ עלי הד̇א אלפן אלעזיז ואצרף גמלת זמאנך פיה
כקׄ אלחכׄ עאלסׄ אם יתן איש את כל הון ביתו באהבה בוז יבוזו לו

פצל

אעלם אנה אד̇א אתפק אלשכ̇ץ מנא אנתבאה והו
כ̇פיף אלצ̇הר וכאנת מאדתה איצ̇א מתאתיה לה
קאבלה מנג̇דבה פאן ד̇לך נעמה מן אללה תעאלי
עליה וחצל לה איצ̇א מע ד̇לך אלמואנע מרפועה ענה וכ̇אצה̈ אן כאן
שוקה לד̇לך אלמעני מתצל פאנה לא יקטעה ענה גרץ̇ מן אלאגראץ̇
4ב אלדניאיה כקׄ אלחכׄ פשטתי את כתנתי וגוׄ רחצתי את / רגלי פלא
יבק (!) לה תעלק סוי במעשוקה ולא תמסך סוי באד̇יאלה פקט כקׄ
אלחכים עאלסׄ דודי לי ואני לו אני לדודי ודודי לי והד̇א אלאמר
צעב ג̇דא והו אן יתעלק שכ̇ץ מנא כדר גלית̇ בג̇והר נייר בסיט   פי
גאית אלבסאטה כיף יכון חאלה אן ראם אלקרב מנה מרץ̇ ואן בעד
מנה תלף פמא בקי לה חילה סוי תגלית̇ אלוצלה אלתי בינה ובינה
ואלאעתראף באלעג̇ז כקׄ דוד יי לא גבה לבי ולא רמו עיני ולא הלכתי
בגדולות וקׄ למדני לעשות רצונך כי אתה אלהי וכוׄ וקׄ שלח אורך
ואמתך פמן חית̇ צעובה̈ אלאמר פי נפסה וגמוצ̇ה לא תצ̇עף המתך ותקול
אנא אסיר אלשהוה ואלגצ̇ב ואלג̇וע ואלעטש ואלחר ואלברד ואלכוף
ואלמרץ̇ פתפתר ניתך ען אלטלב בל קוי עזימתך ואנשט וג̇ד פי אלעמל
פאלד̇י ית̇בת עלי אלעמל פי ד̇לך אלמעני הו אלאנסאן   עלי

2 תהׄ טז:ח 4 שם צא:יד 6 שם קג:יג 8 שם צא:טו ישׄ מג:ה 9שם מג:ב 10 שיר ח:ז 17 שם ה:ה 19 שם ב:טז שם ו:ג 23 תהׄ קלא:ט
24 שם קמג:ג-ה

5 ירד

. . . .

3א תאג̇ך פי אלדניא ודלילך פי אלאכ̇רה כי יי יהיה לך לאור עולם וגו' בני אם יפתוך חטאים בחלאוה̈ אלסנה̈הם אל תבא פאנהם לא יסתקימו אלי אן ינאלו מנך אגראצ̇הם בני אל תלך בדרך אתם מנע רגלך מנתיבותם ואג̇על קצדך כמאל נפסך ואכ̇תר אלאג̇תהאד ולא תמל ולא תקלק ואד̇א ערץ̇ לך מאנע פי וקת מא לא תנקטע בל תת̇בת אלי אן יזול אלמאנע ק' אלח' עאלס' אם רוח המושל תעלה עליך מקומך אל תנח פאן חצל לך בעד מן יחג̇ב ענך אפ̇ה לאנך תחת הסתרת פנים פלו אנכשף לך אלמעני אנסתרת בסתר עליון בצל שדי תתלונן פאן אלפאידה אלחאצלה לך מן הד̇א אלפן אכ̇תר מן אלמג̇אהדה פי קהר אכ̇לאקך לאנך פי מקאם אלחצ̇ור ואלמשאהדה לאן אד̇א מכן אלאנסאן נפסה מן אלאכ̇לאק אלמחמודה אנטרדת מן בין ידיה אלאכ̇לאק אלמד̇מומה וארתפעת אלמואנע אלתי כאנת תעיקה ען חצול אלכמאל אלאנסאני אלתי ביין אלנבי אנהא עונות והו ק' כי אם עונותיכם היו מבדילים בינכם לבין אלהיכם פאד̇א צח לך הד̇א אלבאב ליס תעוד תתאלם למא אלנאס
3ב עליה מן אכל ושרב וכן ולבאס פוק אלצ̇רורי ותתכ̇לץ / מן זיף עט̇ים ותרג̇ע תתדבר באלעקל פתנג̇וא מן אלאתפאק ועוארץ̇ אלדניא אלד̇י תואעד בה תעאלי אלאשכ̇אץ אלמפסדין והו קולה ואנכי הסתר אסתיר פני על כל הרעה כי פנה אל אלהים אחרים וכד̇לך אשאר איצ̇א פי קולה ואותי השלכת אחרי גוך למן תרך אלנפס ואשתגל באלמאדה פאחד̇ר מן תסלט אלעדו עליך ואסתכ̇דאמה לך פי תרדיד אלפכרה פי אלכרובים אלחארצה לעץ החיים לילא ית̇בת פיה ועיני כסיל בקצה הארץ אפהם ד̇לך .

פצל

אעלם אן כל מא ג̇אנא פי כלאם אלאנביא עאלס' ואלפלאספה איצ̇א מן אלוציה באלעקל ואלאעתני בה ואטראח אללד̇את אלבדניה ואלקצד בה תמהיד אלטריק ללעקל חתי ידרך מן באריה מה ימכנה אדראכה אלי תרי כיף סמי יעקב אבינו עה' בישראל אשארה אלי תצרפה עאס' פי אלעאלמין כק' כי שרית עם אלהים ואם אנשים ותוכל וכ̇רג̇ ען חכם אלאתפאק וכד̇לך קאלו ז"ל אין מזל לישראל אלד̇י הם ישראל עלי

5 אתת̇בת 27 תצריפה

1 ישי' ס:כ 2 משי' א:י 3 שם טו 6 קהי' י:ד 8 תהי' צא:א
13 ישי' נט:ב 17 דבי' כא:יח 19 מלכי' א יד:ט 21 משי' יז:כד
28 ברי' לב: כט 29 שבת קנו.

אלמקאלה̈ אלחוצ̇יה̈

אלמנסובה̈

ללעארף אלכאמל מצופי המרכבה

רבינו עבדיה ב״ר אברהם החסיד ז״ל

בן רבינו משה הגאון ב״ר מימון זצ״ל

עני בתחקיקה ותעליקה ותרג̇מתה

לאול מרה̈ אלעבד אלממנון

יוסף ינון (פנטון)

אלפקיר אלי רחמה̈ רבה

מדינה̇ לנדן אלמחרוסה

סנה̈ לפני שׁמשׁ ינ̇ו̇ן שמו̇ לפ״ק